THE SOCIAL STRUCTURE
OF REVOLUTIONARY AMERICA

The
Social Structure
of Revolutionary
America

BY

JACKSON TURNER MAIN

PRINCETON UNIVERSITY PRESS
PRINCETON, NEW JERSEY
1965

For Gloria

THIS BOOK developed out of a conviction that an understanding of political history during the revolutionary era depends upon mastery of the underlying social structure. At the same time acquaintance with recent literature on the class structure of contemporary America suggested that similar techniques might profitably be applied to an earlier period. The present work is therefore preliminary both to a more general history of the revolutionary years and to an account of America's social development.

I had originally projected only a series of essays on the subject, which is a very extensive one; but I soon found myself with so much material that a full-length treatment, even though tentative, seemed justified. I have only sampled the vast number of inventories contained in probate records, and have examined only a small part of the unpublished manuscripts. On the other hand I have used most of the tax lists, almost all of the newspapers, and all—as far as I know—of the travel accounts, as well as the usual published materials. Therefore my research, though incomplete, has been considerably more than fragmentary.

I selected the period 1763–1788 for several reasons. Previous research had familiarized me with many of the sources. Moreover I was continuing work in the political history of those years, so that research could be conducted for both projects simultaneously. I had indeed originally planned to conclude this book with an essay on the relationship between class and the structure of power, but the subject proved much too large. I had also expected that the twenty-five-year period would be long enough to enable me to discuss social changes, and that I could at the same time examine the results of the Revolution. Both expectations were disappointed. Changes must be traced over a longer period, and the effects of the Revolution seem, on the whole, to have been less than I had expected. Further research is needed on both points. Indeed the need for more work in this whole field is so great that I have drawn attention, in an appendix, to the subjects which especially require investigation and to the sources which are available.

The book could not have been written without the help of a fellowship granted by the American Council of Learned Societies and a sabbatical leave from San Jose State College. A grant from the American Philosophical Society enabled me to strengthen the chapter on mobility. Merle Curti and S. Martin Lipset very kindly read the manuscript at an early stage and made valuable suggestions. My colleague Thomas Wendel saved me from many stylistic and other errors. I am also grateful for the invariable courtesy of librarians and archivists. The collections over which they preside are duly noticed in the text. I owe a particular obligation to the staff of the American Antiquarian Society, where for many happy months the basic research for this book was done. My greatest debt is acknowledged in the dedication.

J. T. M.

❦ TABLE OF CONTENTS ❦

THE SOCIAL STRUCTURE
OF REVOLUTIONARY AMERICA

Introduction

THE NATURE and importance of the class structure in early America have long been in dispute. On the one hand, major movements such as the revolts of Bacon and Leisler, Shaysites and Regulators, even the American Revolution have been interpreted as arising out of economic inequalities.[1] In opposition to this view, some historians have seen an "economic democracy" in which "the people were much of a piece."[2] Perhaps the primary reason for this disagreement lies in the basic assumptions held by the historians: the "school" of interpretation to which they belong. Those influenced by the Marxist view, writing primarily during the 1930's and 1940's, took for granted the existence of economic classes, the conflict between which was assumed to be vitally significant. Historians who have not subscribed to such a hypothesis have tended to emphasize the superior importance of factors other than class, and to minimize social distinctions and class conflicts. The latter attitude has been especially congenial to conservatives, many of whom have even denied that classes existed at all. Another reason for disagreement lies in the nature of the evidence, which is so conflicting that even historians who are resolutely objective may reach widely varying conclusions. Moreover, there has been so little systematic analysis of the evidence that interpretations have necessarily been based upon guesswork rather than fact. The resolution of these disputes therefore depends in part upon detailed research.

[1] For example, Curtis P. Nettels, *The Roots of American Civilization* (New York, 1963), 334–336, 348, 540–542, 660–663.

[2] Robert E. Brown, "Economic Democracy before the Constitution," *American Quarterly*, VII (1955), 257–274; Edmund S. Morgan, *The Birth of the Republic 1763–89* (Chicago, 1956), 7.

Such a resolution is desirable not merely because truth is always worth seeking. The evidence unearthed by such research would have obviously broad implications for our understanding of early American history and of later developments. Having with some certainty defined the class structure of early American society, historians would be in a better position to discover whether conflicts among classes actually developed and what, if any, effect such developments might have had on our political history. The historian might also assess with greater precision the relation between class and other aspects of culture such as education, religion, and the arts. If classes were absent, then of course historians can turn their entire attention to other factors. Historical interpretation of our revolutionary years should be considerably affected. For all these reasons, historians have been stressing the need for such research.[3]

Investigation into the eighteenth-century class structure is also essential for a general study of American social history. In recent years scholars have described in some detail our contemporary social structure. They have not, however, paid much attention to the differences between present-day society and that of the past. Most of these writers have not been interested in the historical process and have not tried to trace effects to their causes or to identify the directions in which society moved. When they have attempted to study the past they have been unable to do so satisfactorily because historians had failed to furnish the necessary background. Apart from a handful of limited studies, such as a few dealing with the ante-bellum South, there has been no systematic description of the social struc-

---

[3] For example, Richard B. Morris, "Class Struggle and the American Revolution," *The William and Mary Quarterly*, 3 series xix (1962), 26–27; Clarence L. Ver Steeg, *The Formative Years, 1607–1763* (New York, 1964), 130–131, 325.

ture during the nineteenth century, while as we have re-marked the very nature of colonial society is in dispute. The present work represents therefore a first step toward a history of American society.

In order to make this account as useful as possible for students both of recent history and of the revolutionary era, I have included a broad range of subjects. Basic is a description of the class structure. The dictionary definition of class as "a number or body of people with common characteristics" permits one to discover classes in almost any situation, and is obviously too broad to be very useful. Recently scholars have been emphasizing the distinction between economic and social classes. The first, of course, results from the unequal distribution of property. It is quite easily studied through objective data, and may exist whether or not people know it. The second depends upon public opinion. It is a prestige order, determined by how people rate others in their community. The factors which create social classes vary with the values of the community. If those values are exclusively pecuniary, then the economic and social orders are identical. If not, then there is no such exact coincidence, though there may still be a high correlation, which the student must determine. Scholars who have rebelled against economic determinism, and who consider class conflicts to be unimportant in America, have preferred to stress the prestige order, sometimes to the exclusion of economic classes. I will try to describe both types of class structure.

An important quality of any class structure is the opportunity it affords people to change their position within it. A totally rigid or "closed" society inhibits all movement, as is true of a caste system. The opposite "open" society by definition permits complete mobility. The relative degree of what has been called "vertical mobility" is important not only to the individual concerned but to the whole society: for example, conflicts between classes are related to mobility. Despite the importance in the American creed of equality of opportunity, the degree of social mobility has rarely been systematically examined aside from very recent studies of contemporary society. I will deal with two aspects of mobility in revolutionary America: the opportunity of men starting without property to become property owners, and the social origins of the wealthy "upper class."

Once the class structure has been established, its relationship to other characteristics of the culture can be investigated. The distribution of property and of income are obviously important determinants of class. The standard of living and consumption habits of the several classes and of groups within classes have been subjects for current analysis, and need to be delineated in early America. The correlation between the class structure and religion, education, art, and the like, can readily be discovered by anthropologists studying primitive, relatively stable societies, and with much less precision by sociologists using such techniques as the questionnaire and the interview; but the historian is handicapped both by the nature of his sources and because he must deal with the changes which take place in complex, advanced civilizations. Nevertheless I have essayed a preliminary chapter on the subject.

Despite the many books and articles which describe the society of early America, much research remains to be done. I hope that in the future scholars will extend their studies backward into the colonial period and forward through the nineteenth century, so that eventually someone can write a complete history of American society.

CHAPTER I

The Economic Class Structure
of the North

THE EXISTENCE of an economic class structure in revolutionary America may easily be ascertained through numerous tax lists and inventories of estates, but the interpretation of this data is not so simple. Far from revealing a society
which was everywhere uniform, the records show a great
diversity. Generalizations can indeed be made, but not until
full justice has been done to the variety of class structures
which characterized the new nation. Differences between
the northern and southern colonies, originating in geography and reinforced by slavery, are obvious. Each of these
sections contained smaller regions—New England, the
Chesapeake, the Carolina low country—while such factors
as the date of settlement, the pattern of property ownership
imposed by the colonizers, and subsequent development or
stagnation, created other sub-sections. Despite these local
variant societies, certain general features were of particular
significance because they occurred everywhere and resulted
in the existence of social structures common to all sections.
They permit the formulation of a synthesis.

One clearly identifiable type of society existed when an
area was first occupied. Although the pattern of settlement
was nowhere identical, ranging from the compact, pioneer
villages of New England to the extensive land holdings of
frontier New York, certain characteristics were always
apparent. These tended to be modified or to disappear as the
frontier stage ended. The social changes which then occurred depended upon a number of circumstances. If the
region possessed inferior soils, or if it was remote from

markets (as in the New England uplands), its economy produced little above subsistence. The primarily subsistence farm society also occurred when a scarcity of labor or of capital prevented the development of large-scale commercial agriculture, as was the case during much of the colonial period. However when the soil and transportation facilities were both good, and when capital and labor were relatively abundant, a commercial (or "plantation") farm society was created. A fourth type of social structure appeared with the rise of cities. Although every colony-state had its peculiar history, each possessed some variation of these four basic social structures: the frontier, subsistence farm, commercial farm, and urban.

The northern frontier was most commonly settled by the New England system, in which the people moved as a group and divided the land among themselves. Class distinctions were few. The rich stayed in the east, and although every frontier contained some poor men, the great majority of pioneers were property owners. The system of distributing land, at least in New England, often reinforced this relative equality, because during most of the colonial period every head of family had received a share. The proprietors of Wallingford, Connecticut gave to every "High rank man, or his hairs" 476 acres, to each "Middel Rank" family 357 acres, and to every man of "Loer Rank" 238 acres.[1] Evidently the proprietors thought in terms of a social hierarchy, but economically the effect of such a division was to create or reinforce the existence of a society in which small farmers formed the great majority. When shares of land were offered for sale, the prices were low enough to encourage settlement and could be paid over a period of time. For example, original shares in the town of Kent, Connecti-

[1] Joseph Perkins Beach, *History of Cheshire, Connecticut from 1694 to 1840* (Cheshire, 1912), 62.

cut, were offered for as little as £165 old tenor (which probably equalled about £50 sterling), and no payment had to be made for three years.[2]

When the pioneers settled individually instead of by groups, the outcome was not much different. Land prices charged by northern speculators were low enough so that poor men could become farmers almost at once. Speculative tracts in Worcester County, Massachusetts, were valued at 7s per acre before the war.[3] Elsewhere in New England wild land was worth from 3s per acre (Henry Knox's price for Maine land) on up to 12s an acre (Jacob Wendell's large tract in Berkshire County).[4] The better land, which was of course more valuable, could always be obtained on credit or even occasionally for nothing at all when a speculator was anxious to attract settlers.[5] Pioneers in New York paid James Duane £80 for one hundred acres—a considerable sum, but he allowed ten years in which to pay.[6] Newspapers advertised land for £30 to £75 the hundred (6s to 15s per acre) or at low rents with none at all for the first few

[2] Charles S. Grant, *Democracy in the Connecticut Frontier Town of Kent* (New York, 1961), 19.

[3] Probate Records, vols. 8–11, Worcester County Court House, Worcester, Mass. All figures are in currency unless otherwise indicated. The relationship between local money and sterling is discussed in the appendix. As a rule of thumb, sterling was equal to money minus one-fourth.

The value of revolutionary money in contemporary dollars depends upon the particular article, for inflation has proceeded unevenly. Roughly, the pound sterling equalled forty 1965 dollars in food and clothing, fifty dollars in shelter, and from ten to one hundred dollars in other items, the general average being about fifty dollars.

[4] Knox to James Jarvis, New York, Nov. 11, 1787, Knox papers, vol. XXI, no. 46, Mass. Hist. Soc.; Suffolk County Probate Records, Will Book 63, Suffolk County Court House, Boston, Mass.

[5] Jonathan Moulton's advertisement in *The New Hampshire Gazette, and General Advertiser* (Portsmouth), March 11, 1768.

[6] Duane to Christopher Yates, April 20, 1774, Duane Papers, N.Y. Hist. Soc.

years.[7] A traveller reported that land near the headwaters of the Susquehanna, in New York, sold for £20 to £40 the hundred (4s to 8s per acre) and that Wyoming Valley land cost only £5 sterling per hundred, which could be paid over a period of fifteen years without interest, plus a small quit rent amounting to an additional £6 for the period. In Pennsylvania the government sold tax-delinquent unimproved land at an average price of 14s per hundred.[8] Such land was probably inferior, not so much in quality as in location with respect to transportation. The farmer who hoped to prosper by the sale of his surplus crops or by the rising value of favorably situated land had to pay more. Land ten miles from the Mohawk was worth only 1½s per acre while that along the river sold for 5s or 10s. Still, this was a cheap price for valley soil.[9]

The pioneer therefore was able to obtain land easily. It is true that first-rate property required more cash than most settlers possessed, and that where speculators were permitted to engross large tracts the farmer had to pay the profit. Sporadic complaints indicate some dissatisfaction, but these were few enough to prove that the difficulty was not serious.[10] Thus hardworking settlers with little or no money could acquire land and survive even though they might not have a cash income for many years.[11]

[7] *The New York Mercury*, August 22, 1763, July 8, 1765; *The Hampshire Chronicle* (Springfield), Feb. 13, 1788.

[8] *The Pennsylvania Gazette*, June 20, 1771 (supplement); Richard Smith, *A Tour of Four Great Rivers,* ed. by Francis W. Halsey (New York, 1906), 49, 56.

[9] Patrick M'Robert, *A Tour through part of the North Provinces of America . . . 1774, & 1775* (Edinburgh, 1776, reprinted by Hist. Soc. Pa., pamphlet series 1, 1935), 36.

[10] Illustrations are, *The Cumberland Gazette* (Falmouth, Maine), June 8, 1786; *The Pennsylvania Packet* (Philadelphia), March 12, 1785; *The Providence Gazette; and Country Journal*, Feb. 8, 1783.

[11] *The Vermont Gazette* (Burlington), March 19, 1787; Harry J. Carman, ed., *Amercan Husbandry* (New York, 1939), 48, 90.

The typical frontier society therefore was one in which class distinctions were minimized. The wealthy speculator, if one was involved, usually remained at home, so that ordinarily no one of wealth was a resident. The class of landless poor was small. The great majority were landowners, most of whom were also poor because they were starting with little property and had not yet cleared much land nor had they acquired the farm tools and animals which would one day make them prosperous. Few artisans settled on the frontier except for those who practiced a trade to supplement their primary occupation of farming. There might be a storekeeper, a minister, and perhaps a doctor; and there were a number of landless laborers. All the rest were farmers.

The scattered but numerous tax records of New England towns make possible a more detailed description of the frontier class structure there. Ordinarily only polls, land, and certain farm animals were taxed, but narrow though the tax base was, it is possible to determine the distribution of land and to identify, in part, the occupations of the settlers.

Warren, New Hampshire, was a typical frontier community. Among thirty taxpayers in 1781 only one had over 500 acres. He and two other men, the "large property owners" of their town, formed the wealthiest 10 percent of the population. They owned about 30 percent of the taxable land and farm animals. This proportion, as will be seen presently, indicates a wide distribution of property. Seven heads of families (23 percent of the taxpayers) were landless, to which number may be added one person for whom a poll tax was paid, probably the son of the taxpayer. The rest of the men owned small farms. If, therefore, the word "small" is defined so as to include all farms of less than 500 acres—and this is a workable definition—73 percent of the community belonged to that class. Most New Hampshire towns, except those near the coast, conformed to this type.[12]

The colony did, however, contain some towns which developed as a result of speculative activity. Wolfeborough contained in 1774 fifty-three taxpayers, of whom five held much of the property owned by residents—over half of the livestock and improved land. At the other end of the social scale, about half of the residents did not own land. In this frontier community, property was concentrated in the hands of a few; and instead of the small landowners forming a majority, there existed a large number of landless men. The reason for this inequality lay in the presence of very large speculative holdings, especially the "Abbot-Wentworth" farm, which contained nearly 3,000 acres and on which were employed a number of landless men. Wolfeborough was not unique, but it was not typical.[13]

Towns of the Massachusetts frontier had a social structure like that of Warren. A good example is Ashfield, which was just emerging from the frontier stage in 1766. The tax lists of that year included no one who owned more than moderate property. The 10 percent who paid the largest tax held 36 percent of the taxable property, a low figure for the

[12] William Little, *History of Warren* . . . (Manchester, N.H., 1870), 551.

[13] Benjamin Franklin Parker, *History of Wolfeborough* (*New Hampshire*) . . . (Cambridge, 1901), 144–145, 242–251. Francestown, New Hampshire, levied its first tax in 1772. No one was a large property owner. Probably 30 percent of the men had not yet acquired land. The 10 percent who paid the largest tax held 17 percent of the taxable property. Even if polls are excluded, they probably had not much over one-fifth of the total. W. R. Cochrane and George K. Wood, *History of Francestown, N.H.* . . . (Nashua, N.H., 1895), 53. On the other hand, Sutton more nearly resembled Wolfeborough in that the wealthiest 10 percent owned 30 percent of the property, including polls. Yet here also there was no one of wealth and few who were poor. Mrs. Augusta H. Worthen, *The History of the Town of Sutton, N.H.* (Concord, 1890), 182.

colony. About 30 percent of the taxpayers did not have land. One of these was a doctor, who reported only a horse. The community also contained another doctor and three mill-owners but apparently no artisans.[14]

Highly informative are the town assessment lists taken in Massachusetts before the Revolution.[15] These record the annual worth of the real estate, technically the yearly rent. Supposedly the total value of the property was six times the rent, but judging from land prices given in probate records the assessors considerably undervalued the property. Unimproved and other types of relatively unproductive land were not taxed. In addition to land, the value of stock in trade and money at interest, tons of shipping, houses, shops, mills, stillhouses, warehouses, and the like, and certain farm animals, are included. The total worth of this property is not given, but the distribution of land can be analyzed and the occupations of the men can be deduced.

The Berkshire County towns of Sandisfield, Williamstown, and Tyringham were all recently settled in 1771. In the last, indeed, nearly half of the houses were called "log huts," and several of the farmers (identifiable because they owned oxen) had not yet taken title to their farms. About thirty percent of the men in these communities did not own land. Some may have been renting a tract, but this seems unlikely since few owned farm animals. They made up a class of agricultural laborers which probably consisted principally of pioneers' sons. The great majority of the residents were small farmers whose land was assessed at less than £10 annual value and usually at less than £4. Williamstown con-

[14] Frederick G. Howes, *History of the Town of Ashfield* (n.p., n.d.), 95–96.

[15] These are preserved on microfilm in the Mass. Archives, Boston. I have examined the lists for about two dozen towns in all parts of the colony.

tained four men who paid a tax on "factorage," which meant that they were selling goods as well as farming, but there were no professional men listed and no artisans except for one potash manufacturer and some mill owners who were primarily farmers. The property of the community was widely distributed, for there were no men of wealth.

Connecticut too had its frontier area. The town of Goshen was in 1741 just emerging from the pioneer stage. The village contained forty-nine taxpayers, who also paid the taxes for eight adult male polls not named in the tax list. This list does not indicate who held land, but if ownership of cows and oxen is any indication, forty of the men were landowners. Five paid a "faculty" tax, indicating that they had some non-farm means of income such as a mill, a store, a blacksmith's shop, or an inn. One of the landless men was among the five. All the rest—about 70 percent—of the men were apparently farmers, and since none owned more than thirteen cattle, obviously all were men of small property. The wealthiest five paid 22 percent of the tax, excluding the tax on polls.[16] By 1751 the town had doubled in population but had not changed its essential character. The tax list, which now included land, revealed a large proportion of landless—indeed about 30 percent. Of these some were artisans, others pastured their stock on land owned by relatives, and the rest, about one-sixth of the population, were farm laborers. A number of the landholders paid a small faculty tax. A lawyer, who also owned some land and a mill, was the town's largest property owner, but no one was rich. The 10 percent of the residents who paid the largest tax collectively held 28 percent of the taxable property other than polls.

[16] Goshen tax lists, Conn. State Lib. The wealthiest five men (i.e., the wealthiest 10 percent) paid 21 percent of the whole tax including that on polls.

New York had several frontier regions. That part of the state which adjoined New England became the frontier for settlers from Connecticut, Massachusetts, and New Hampshire, and its social structure resembled that already described. The region west of Albany, along the Mohawk, was settled by pioneers before the Revolution. The "German Camp" district of Albany (later Montgomery) County lay considerably west of the city. The tax lists of 1779, which recorded the value of the settlers' real and personal property, do not permit an analysis of the non-landholding population, for few of these seem to have been taxed; nor can the exact distribution of wealth be determined because the currency inflation of the war years distorted property values. For example, the median real property was no less than £250—or three times that of the rich Livingston manor. However, several characteristics of this frontier society are evident. Half of the taxpayers owned real estate worth between £200 and £400, near the median amount. There were few very small properties and even fewer large ones. Despite the inflated values, only 2 percent held as much as £500 in real property and none had more than £1,000. Finally, the 10 percent paying the largest tax accounted for only 19 percent of the real estate. German Camp's land was, therefore, equally distributed. There were few small farms, few large ones, but many of medium size.[17]

North of Albany similar communities were being founded. Even where a large estate existed, such as Philip Schuyler's in Saratoga district, the only difference in the class structure was a somewhat higher concentration of

[17] Tax list, N.Y. State Lib. See also the lists for Mohawk district, 1786, and for Caughnawago district, 1786. In all of these communities the wealthiest 10 percent, such as they were, had less than 30 percent of the assessed real property.

wealth. Most men had little taxable personal property and owned small farms which were worth, on the average, about £60—this seems to be a correct, not an inflated figure. Perhaps tax records other than those which have been preserved might reveal different types of society in New York, but the evidence strongly suggests that the New England pattern was repeated on the New York frontier.[18]

The characteristics of Pennsylvania's pioneer communities depended upon the nature of their settlement. The frontier county of Bedford experienced considerable land speculation. The tax records of 1783 show that in many townships non-residents held over half of the land. Such areas contained a relatively high percentage of men who did not have title to any soil. Some of these may have been tenants, for they possessed farm animals which required access to grazing land, but the majority, about one-third of the men, must have been farm laborers. In other respects the county resembled the New England frontier. There were no residents of wealth, and a large number of small farmers. Taxable property (land and livestock) was equally distributed.[19]

The 1781 tax lists for Washington County, on the other hand, reveal almost no speculative activity and a slightly smaller proportion of landless men. The wealthiest 10 percent of the county's residents owned 26 percent of the land. The average acreage of the western Pennsylvania farm was much higher than its New England equivalent, but the social structure was much the same.[20]

[18] See also 1779 tax lists for King's, Cambridge, and Hosick districts, N.Y. State Lib. I have used all the New York lists which have been preserved, as far as I know.

[19] *Pennsylvania Archives,* 3 series XXII (ed. by William Henry Egle, Harrisburg, 1897). Towns studied were Colerain, Dublin, Huntingdon, and Hopewell, pp. 211–217, 220–227.

[20] *ibid.,* XXII, 701–729.

The typical frontier society as revealed by these tax lists was characterized by economic equality. Charles Grant, in his fine study of Kent, Connecticut, concluded that this frontier town was democratic.[21] Land was cheap, property equally distributed, and classes scarcely existed. Towns of the Wolfeborough type, born of large speculative holdings, form exceptions to the rule. Such towns were, however, rare especially in New England, and equality was the normal characteristic of frontier society everywhere.

This equality did not exclude differences. The northern frontier community often contained all the elements of those complex societies which would ultimately develop. Here were the real or potential landed aristocrats—a Philip Schuyler of Saratoga, New York, William Butler of Warren, New Hampshire, with 620 acres, Colonel Henry Rust of Wolfeborough with 600. Here also were the creditors: John Mills of Kent was owed over £3,000 in 1760. Here were perhaps an innkeeper, a country storekeeper, a lawyer (Goshen by 1751), a doctor (Wolfeborough in 1774), or a minister. Here too were a scattering of artisans, especially millers, blacksmiths, and cordwainers (shoemakers). Many of these were farmers with a trade or artisans with a farm. Finally, every such society contained landless laborers and occasionally tenants. The generalized frontier society included a very few settlers who had a store or an inn, or practiced a profession, fewer than one in ten who followed a trade, one out of four or five who were laborers. The remaining 60 percent or more were farmers.

When the frontier stage of a northern community ended, farming continued to be its chief occupation, but society became more complex, more differentiated. Its growth and direction depended upon the nature of the land and the accessibility of markets: if the land was good and markets

[21] Grant, *Kent*, 170–171.

were close by, or if transportation to markets was cheap, commercial agriculture developed. Otherwise, the members of the community had to be largely, though of course never entirely, self-sufficient, which meant that most of them must be farmers. The availability of capital influenced a community's growth also, since a commercial farm required a large investment and higher operating costs, especially for labor. Even where both land and transportation were good, some time might elapse before capital could be accumulated. Meanwhile the farmer must supply most of his own needs.

The subsistence farm society was the most common type throughout New England and perhaps in the entire North. The social structure, like that of the frontier, remained simple. Great wealth could not be or had not yet been accumulated; therefore no wealthy class was present. Neither did the landless laborers increase in numbers, for land was not very valuable and therefore could be easily obtained; besides, those who wanted wealth did not remain in such an area but sought richer lands. Accordingly a majority of the residents continued to occupy a middle-class position and to remain small farmers. It was a frontier in arrested development.

Examples of this type of society are numerous. The town of Goshen, Connecticut, had passed from the frontier stage by 1771, yet it had developed only a small class of well-to-do residents and no one of real wealth lived there. In 1787 there was still no upper class. The richest 10 percent of the taxpayers had paid, in 1751, 23 percent of the tax. This proportion now increased slowly, reaching 27 percent by 1787 (compared with 36 percent in Milford, an urban center on the coast). Although total wealth increased, the per capita wealth was actually declining slightly. The proportion of men without land was about the same in 1787 as in 1751. Twenty-one men—11 percent—paid a "faculty" tax on the profits of a non-farm occupation. Most of the assessments were small, indicating that the taxpayer was an artisan or perhaps had a share of a mill. Three men paid the much larger tax typical of a shopkeeper or lawyer, and the presence of innkeepers and doctors is also suggested. However the town remained primarily agricultural, having changed little from frontier days.

Simsbury, Connecticut, was located near Goshen in the northwestern uplands. Its society in 1782 was very similar. No one was rich or even well-to-do: the estate with the highest assessed value (which determined the tax, and was based upon polls, oxen, cattle, horses, swine, improved land, houses, and faculties) was £116, owned by a man who had 94 acres and 19 farm animals. Only 21 percent of the men lacked land. A faculty tax was paid by less than 10 percent. The community contained one doctor, a minister, and probably a justice of the peace, but it seems to have lacked a shopkeeper. The wealthiest 10 percent of the taxpayers owned 20 percent of the taxable property, including polls.[22] In nearby Winchester the distribution of property was almost identical. Here the non-farm population included, out of 148 taxpayers, one storekeeper, who paid only a small tax; one doctor, also of average wealth; four men who had mills; two shoemakers; five tavernkeepers, one of whom was also a miller and farmer; and a blacksmith-farmer, the town's wealthiest citizen.[23]

[22] 37½ percent of the wealth was held by the top 20 percent. The top 10 percent owned 23 percent of the wealth, excluding polls. Tax list, Conn. State Lib.
[23] John Boyd, *Annals and Family Records of Winchester, Conn.* (Hartford, 1873), 158–160 (1783 assessment list).

The Massachusetts assessment lists for 1771 furnish further details. Harvard, in Worcester County, was a typical subsistence farm community, producing only a small surplus. There were two types of men who had no land: the taxpayer, whose name was given in the rolls and who paid his own poll tax even if he had no property, and the person whose poll tax was paid by someone else. Such an individual was not named and not listed separately but appears only as an additional poll for which the taxpayer was responsible. Since all men over sixteen years old paid the tax, most if not all of the dependents can be accounted for by assuming that they were under age, although a few may have been indentured servants (slaves were listed separately).[24] Harvard had few taxpayers without land (12 percent) nor were there many with just a few acres. On the other hand, no one had land evaluated at more than £25 annually. The proportion of men with medium-sized properties (£6 to £20) was exceptionally high. The annual value of the average family's land was about £5½. The 10 percent of Harvard's citizens who paid the largest tax owned 26½ percent of this taxable wealth, a proportion which emphasizes the economic equality in the town. Harvard's society was largely rural. There were no large shopkeepers, and the tax assessment list does not reveal a professional man, though a doctor lived there soon afterwards. One shopkeeper (a retired clergyman) had £180 in stock but not much other property; another had stock worth £100. Two other men, presumably artisans, owned smaller amounts. There was a tanner, a blacksmith, two mill owners, and one other man had some sort of shop. The soci-

---

[24] As a rule of thumb, one-fifth of the men over sixteen were less than twenty-one. Applying this to the tax lists, one finds that all but 3 percent of the unnamed polls are accounted for. The surplus, so to speak, existed in the western towns, where the proportion of young men was probably higher than usual.

ety was indeed almost indistinguishable from that of a frontier.[25]

Other towns in central and even many in eastern Massachusetts had similar characteristics. As a rule the proportion of landless men did not exceed 20 percent. Large property holders were absent; the typical resident was an independent small landowner. The richest 10 percent of the taxpayers held about one-third of the taxable wealth. There might be a prosperous storekeeper—one in Concord had a shop, potash works, and £300 in stock, while another (denominated "Esquire") owned a shop, £150 in stock, and £900 in money at interest—but most of those engaged in trade had only a few pounds worth of goods. About 10 percent of the men were artisans, including millers. Each town usually had one or more doctors, or men who called themselves doctors, and doubtless a minister who was not taxed. The overhelming majority were farmers owning or working land valued at £5 annually. The distance between top and bottom of the economic scale was relatively slight.

The most important and interesting materials for the study of social structure are the vast collections of probate records, especially the inventories of estates. In Massachusetts, these itemized not only the personal property, usually in meticulous detail, but also the real estate. The men who were appointed to evaluate the property did their work conscientiously and accurately. Some of these estates were sold at auction and the sum realized was always very close to the appraised value. A cross section of society appears in the records: rich and poor, "Esquires," "Gentlemen," and "yeomen," merchants, doctors, ministers, coopers, farmers, and laborers, though never, it seems, indentured servants. Examination of some five hundred inven-

[25] See Henry Stedman Nourse, *History of the Town of Harvard, Massachusetts. 1732–1893* (Harvard, 1894), 427.

tories in Worcester County during the years 1762–1770 and 1782–1788 illuminates further the social structure of subsistence farm communities.[26]

The Worcester records reveal a low proportion of men with little property. Only about one in ten had less than £50, and one in five owned less than £100. On the other hand, scarcely one in ten held as much as £1,000. In between was a great middle class of small property owners—70 percent of the men. As a rule, those at the bottom of the economic order had no land. Most of these were laborers, who comprised a small element in the population, certainly less than one-fifth.[27] About one-tenth of the men were artisans, most commonly blacksmiths, cordwainers, and housewrights, but there were also joiners, fullers, tanners, tailors, curriers, coopers, a surveyor, and a wheelwright. Millers invariably had sizable estates and were usually prosperous farmers rather than artisans. Of course many farmers had some other skill and quite often the necessary tools of a trade. Only three shopkeepers or traders appear on the records, though other men had some stock. There were innkeepers, seven doctors, six ministers, and a "clerk," together with other men who seem not to have been farmers but whose occupation is uncertain. The whole class of business and professional men together with the white-collar workers totalled about 10 percent of the population. Finally, nearly two-thirds of the estates belonged to farmers, who

[26] Probate Records, vols. 8–11, 18–21, Worcester County Court House, Worcester, Mass. In studying these and other probate records I omitted the revolutionary war years because of the uncertain value of money.

[27] Since the estates of indentured servants seem never to have been inventoried, their number must of course be added to the laboring class. Apparently there were few such in Worcester County, for the proportion of men who left estates of less than £50 in property corresponds closely with the ratio of landless as recorded in the tax lists.

left property ranging in value from a few pounds to the £9,631 fortune owned by Gardner Chandler, Esquire, of Worcester. Chandler and a handful of others formed a small elite which dominated their society, and which owned one-fourth of the property. The wealthiest 10 percent, which included roughly all those with estates over £1,000, had a little over 40 percent of the total wealth.[28]

Towns of the subsistence farm type were not limited to interior counties such as Worcester but were found within twenty miles of Boston. In Suffolk County, which included the city, a group of inland villages near Rhode Island were actually more extreme examples of the type than were the towns of Worcester County. Although the region had been settled for decades, the distance from Boston and Providence, together with the rough terrain and lack of navigable streams, made transportation costly. One observer remarked that he "never saw a Country so full of rocks & Stones." The amount of good soil was so limited that the farmers, though they seem to have eaten well, could not acquire large property, nor were merchants, artisans, or professional men attracted.[29]

The consequence was a society almost entirely rural. Probate records indicate that less than one-tenth of the men were artisans. There were few professional men, and fewer still in trade. A small class of landless laborers existed, but two-thirds of the men were farmers of whom a large majority had property worth less than £500. The inventories of nearly two hundred estates before and after the

[28] This is a higher figure than that revealed by tax records and probably indicates that the tax structure discriminated in favor of the rich.

[29] See Philip Padelford, ed., *Colonial Panorama 1775. Dr. Robert Honyman's Journal for March and April* (San Marino, California, 1939), 39–40; J. P. Brissot de Warville, *New Travels in the United States of America. Performed in 1788* (London, 1792), 145.

Revolution included no one who was well-to-do (more than £2,000) and only half a dozen who owned more than £1,000 worth of property. On the other hand fewer than one in five had less than £100. Further evidence for the equal distribution of property lies in the fact that the wealthiest 10 percent of the men held only one-fourth of the property—considerably below the figure for Worcester County.[30]

States south and west of New England had larger areas of fertile soil and better transportation facilities, so that commercial farming was more general. Indeed the distinction between commercial and subsistence agriculture was less significant than the contrasts resulting from different historical developments. In New York, the east bank of the Hudson always had been occupied by very large estates, whereas the west bank contained mostly small farms; and the most accurate dichotomy is perhaps between large- and small-farm societies. Yet most of the small landowners, by necessity, had to be primarily subsistence farmers. Many towns in Ulster and Orange County, or east of the Hudson back from the river, were indistinguishable from the New England communities. The tax lists for Cambridge, Hosick, and Claverack East districts, near the Massachusetts border, for Salem and North Castle in eastern Westchester County, and for Cornwall, Goshen, and Hannover west of the river all reveal societies which resemble the frontier in their equal distribution of property, the virtual absence of a wealthy class, and the large proportion of medium-sized farms.[31]

[30] These towns were Stoughton, Stoughtonham (now Sharon), Dover, Needham, Walpole, Medfield, Franklin, Bellingham, Wrentham, Foxborough, and Medway. They are situated in present-day Norfolk County. Suffolk County Probate Records, vols. 63–71, 81–87, Suffolk County Court House. I examined 500 inventories recorded before and after but not during the Revolution.

[31] Tax lists, N.Y. State Lib. See also Salem tax list for 1794 in *New York Historical and Biographical Record*, XLIII (1912), 8–11.

Similarly in Pennsylvania, Berks County conforms to the subsistence farm type of social structure. The tax lists do not encourage analysis of the distribution of property, but the occupational structure can be determined. About one-fourth of the men were laborers, most of whom owned no land. Artisans were increasing in number during the revolutionary era, but did not exceed 10 percent of the population, while a few innkeepers, shopkeepers, and professional men appeared. The great majority—nearly two-thirds—were farmers, almost all of whom held less than 500 acres, 100 acres being the most common amount.[32]

New Jersey's tax records for the years 1774–1788 demonstrate clearly the contrast between East and West Jersey. Unfortunately non-farm property was not taxed, so the commercial, manufacturing, and professional elements in the society cannot be analyzed. The distribution of land, however, reveals that the counties near New York (such as Bergen, Morris, Essex, and Monmouth) were occupied almost entirely by small farmers whereas the southwestern section (notably Burlington and Gloucester) contained many large estates. This sectional difference is the most important feature of the state's society. However, class structures which conform to the subsistence farm type can be identified in both areas. The town of Franklin in Bergen County included no one who held more than 400 acres, and only one person in ten was landless. The most prosperous 10 percent held less than 30 percent of the land, and only one-fourth of the value of all taxable property (which included some farm animals). Franklin is an extreme example. As a rule, New Jersey's small farm societies were not distinguished by quite such equality. About 30 percent of the

---

[32] *Pa. Arch.*, 3 series XVIII, 21–25, 48–53, 71–80. The towns of Bethel, Caernarvan, Heidelberg, Robeson, and Tulpehocken were selected as representative.

men were landless. Some of these were certainly artisans. One percent owned over 500 acres of land, and the rest were small farmers averaging about 80 acres each. The wealthiest 10 percent held about one-third of the land.[33]

The Delaware assessment lists, taken during the 1780's, are extremely valuable. According to the French traveller La Rochefoucault-Liancourt, these estimated the income of the citizens, except that poor people and bachelors always paid a small tax even though they owned no property. Such a tax on propertyless men, the equivalent of a poll tax, does not materially affect the accuracy of the records for a study of economic classes. Unfortunately the assessors did not indicate the occupations of the taxpayers, but the lists do furnish an excellent description of the distribution of property.[34]

Communities of the subsistence farm type were found through much of Delaware. All of Sussex County and most of Kent (except Dover hundred) were occupied mostly by small farms. In Sussex there were, in fact, only two taxpayers out of nearly 3,000 who had incomes estimated at more than £50. Probably the true incomes were much higher than that given by the assessors, but clearly the county con-

[33] Microfilm copies of tax lists in the New Jersey State Library. I analyzed the lists for nearly 40 towns in all parts of the state.

[34] I have used all of the lists in the Hall of Records, Dover, Delaware. See Duke de la Rochefoucault-Liancourt, *Travels Through the United States of North America* . . . (2 vols., London, 1799), ii, 269–270. The tax law before the Revolution had specified that no one, no matter how poor, should be rated under £8, and that single men without visible estates should be rated between £12 and £24. This requirement was no longer being followed by revolutionary times, and the tax acts of 1779, which defined the new procedure, were exceedingly vague. The assessors were simply instructed to rate everyone's estate, with due regard for the poor, and the best land, with improvements, to be rated at £3 per acre. *Laws of the Government of New-Castle, Kent and Sussex* (Philadelphia, 1752), 239 (27 Geo. ii); *Session Laws*, 1779, pp. 22, 48.

tained very few men of wealth. There were not even many large farmers, while on the other hand some 70 percent owned estates rated at less than £5 income. Presumably one-third to one-half of these were laborers. The median assessment was £3½. Such property as the people owned was evenly distributed, the wealthiest 10 percent possessing 34 percent of the income, a figure somewhat under that obtained from the Worcester County probate records but almost exactly the same as that recorded on the assessment lists of 1771 for Worcester County.

The characteristic feature of the northern subsistence farm towns, or of those resembling the type, was the presence of an exceptional proportion of small farmers, whose properties and geographical location prevented their producing any considerable cash crop. This fact required them to do most of their own work, so that their society contained a relatively small proportion of artisans and of laborers. Some of these communities contained a few men of considerable means, who used hired help, made purchases from artisans, and marketed a surplus; but many towns entirely lacked an upper class. Property was equally distributed, the typical resident owning about £100 worth of personal and over £300 worth of real property. It was a society which almost guaranteed a degree of comfort, but economic opportunities were slight. The path of wealth lay in the commercial farm area or in the city.[35]

[35] Of course within a predominantly subsistence area there were variations. A long-established rich farming community such as Lancaster in Worcester County produced an abnormal number of men with large property (the median wealth of estates probates was £600, and one-fifth had more than £1,000), while on the other hand Worcester, not far away, contained only half of the wealth per capita and produced, instead of well-to-do farmers, poor artisans. Other examples of these upland towns are found in the following sources: Frederick Kidder and Augustus A. Gould, *The History of New Ipswitch, from its first grant in MDCCXXXVI to the present time*

The commercial farm community, by definition, sold a much larger quantity of agricultural products than did the subsistence farmers. Good soil was of course a necessity, but most important was accessibility to market, either by being close enough to a major urban center so that goods could be carried easily (as was the case with towns near Boston, New York, and Philadelphia), or by being located on a navigable river or a good ocean harbor. In contrast to the subsistence farm villages, these towns had greater wealth, more rich men, a greater concentration of property in the possession of the wealthy, sometimes more artisans, professional men, and men engaged in commerce, a much higher proportion of large farmers, and fewer small ones. They also ordinarily contained more laborers. Examples are Groton, Connecticut; New Town and the Hudson River communities in New York; Waltham, Milton, and other

---

... (Boston, 1852), 70-73; "Early Records of the Town of Derryfield," Manchester Historic Society, *Collections*, VIII (1905), 117–118, 124–126, 153–154, 179–181, 210–212, 239–240, IX (1906), 54–58, 113–115, 162–164; Samuel T. Worcester, *History of the Town of Hollis, New Hampshire, From its First Settlement to the Year 1879* (Boston, 1879), 136–138; George Waldo Browne, *The History of Hillsborough, N.H. 1735–1921* (2 vols., Manchester, 1921–1922), I, 159–160; John F. Norton, *The History of Fitzwilliam, New Hampshire, from 1752 to 1887* (New York, 1888), 180–185; John B. Hill, *History of the Town of Mason, N.H. from the First Grant in 1749, to the year 1858* (Boston, 1858), 61; D. Hamilton Hurd, ed., *History of Merrimack and Belknap Counties New Hampshire* (Philadelphia, 1885), 276–277 (Bow), 478–481 (Loudon); Leonard A. Morrison, *The History of Windham in New Hampshire (Rockingham County). 1719–1883* (Boston, 1883), 72–73; George F. Daniels, *History of the Town of Oxford Massachusetts* (Oxford, Mass., 1892), 201–206; Richard LeBaron Bowen, *Early Rehoboth*, vol. IV (Rehoboth, 1950), 90–112; Beach, *Cheshire*, 140–143; *Proceedings of the Worcester Society of Antiquity, for the Year 1897* (Worcester, 1898), 375–388; Sylvester Judd, *History of Hadley* (Northampton, 1863), 423–424; Newtown, 1767, and Killingworth, 1788, Conn. State Lib.; Bethany, Conn., 1782, N.Y. Hist. Soc. (wrongly catalogued as Bethany, New York).

Suffolk County towns in Massachusetts; most of New Chester County in Delaware; Burlington County, New Jersey; and Chester County, Pennsylvania.

Groton, Connecticut, was an old town near New London on the Sound, which in 1783 contained over 500 taxpayers (including one identified as "the old Virgin"). The tax basis was primarily improved land, assessed at a low rate. The median assessed valuation was £33, and most residents held not far from that amount. There were however a number of men with estates valued at more than £100. The wealthiest 10 percent held 29 percent of the wealth, compared with about 22 percent in Connecticut's subsistence farm towns. Groton's society was more diversified than that of the inland communities. It had a lawyer, a physician who was also a shopkeeper, seven other shopkeepers (none of any size), fifteen tavernkeepers, nine blacksmiths, seven shoemakers, thirteen carpenters and joiners, as well as clothiers, tanners, tailors, and a goldsmith. The artisans formed about 8 percent of the population. There were also sixteen mills belonging to the substantial farmers.[36] A quarter of the men were rated at less than £20, which meant that they had almost no property since a poll was rated at £18. These formed the labor force for farmers and artisans. All told, the non-farm element totalled over one-third of the population. Most of the wealth, however, was owned by the large farmers.

Large farmers also dominated New Town, in Queens County, Long Island, one of the many communities which supplied New York City. The tax list of 1787 includes the value both of real and personal property. The average

[36] Seventeen men had rights in these mills. Their median assessed property was £52 compared with the general median of £33. They were all in the upper 25 percent of the population. Tax list, Conn. State Lib.

assessment was £470, three-quarters of which consisted of real estate. About one-fifth of New Town's residents had no land or houses. Some of these may have been artisans: the records do not indicate occupations. Other artisans and laborers were doubtless included among those who had only small amounts of real estate. A farmer would surely have owned at least £50 worth of land, to judge from probate and tax records. Therefore New Town contained an additional one-twelfth of the taxpayers who were not farmers. Together with the usual number of professional men, the non-farm part of the population probably comprised about three-eighths of the whole. There were of course a large number of small farmers, but the outstanding feature of the town was the presence of many well-to-do landholders, 17 percent of the residents owning more than £1,000 worth of property (compared with less than 10 percent in Worcester) and 34 percent having estates valued at more than £500. The 10 percent holding the most property had slightly over one third of the whole amount, a moderate concentration.[37]

More representative, or perhaps extreme, examples of the commercial farm type of society were the Hudson River districts such as Kinderhook, Livingston manor, Claverack West, and the Manor of Rensselaer (or "Ranselear"). The tax lists of 1779, as noted earlier, do not indicate occupations nor is it possible to discover for certain the proportion of landless men; moreover the currency used varied and was obviously inflated in certain cases. The characteristics which everywhere distinguished the class structure of the commercial farm society from that of the subsistence farm and frontier are, however, obvious. Large farmers were much more numerous. About one in seven of the men held real estate worth £500 or more, twice as many as in subsistence farm areas, and many times the number of large

[37] Tax list, N.Y. Hist. Soc.

owners on the frontier. Whereas the frontier almost never contained estates worth £1,000, they were common in the richer communities; and the proportion of taxable property held by the wealthiest 10 percent generally exceeded 40 percent, contrasted with 20 percent to 35 percent in the other New York districts.[38]

Additional detail concerning towns of this type is supplied by the Massachusetts 1771 assessment lists. Milton, Waltham, and Roxbury were commercial farm centers near Boston. About one-fourth of the taxpayers were landless, a fairly high percentage for that state, and one which suggests the presence of indentured servants and perhaps of tenants. There were, at the other end of the economic scale, an equal proportion who had land valued at £12 annually, which probably meant about £500 worth. Most of these were the substantial farmers characteristic of such a community. The median income from real estate of £7 was about twice that of Worcester County towns. The wealthiest 10 percent had about 46 percent of the real estate compared with less than 40 percent in Worcester. As usual, these towns had more artisans, shopkeepers, and professional men than did the subsistence farm societies, Milton in particular having several prosperous merchants and three doctors. Laborers comprised about one-fourth of the population. However farmers were of course the principal element.

The predominance of farmers is also shown by the probate records. Among the important commercial farm centers in Suffolk County were the towns near Boston such as Braintree, Cohasset, and Hull. About 60 percent of the estates inventoried during the years 1764–1771 and 1782–1788 were those of farmers, more than half of whom had substantial property worth over £500. Lawyers, doc-

[38] Tax lists, N.Y. State Lib.

tors, ministers, merchants, and the like made up about 8 percent of the population. The rest of the men were laborers and artisans, who were much more numerous than in subsistence farm towns. Among over 300 men whose estates were inventoried, thirteen left property in excess of £2,000, sixty-six more than £1,000, and 145 owned at least £500. The last included 46 percent of the men, as contrasted with about 30 percent in other Suffolk and Worcester County towns. The figure may be exaggerated, since the inventories do not reveal as many small estates as we know existed, but the error occurs in both areas, so that the comparison is just. The wealthiest 10 percent owned more than half of the property.

Delaware also had a commercial farm area which included most of New Castle (the northernmost county) and part of Kent. The inhabitants of this region owned properties two or three times as valuable as those in Sussex County, and there were far more large estates. Whereas in Sussex, almost no one was assessed for more than £50 income, in New Castle County 7 percent of the taxpayers reputedly received that amount, and in Redlion hundred (near the town of New Castle on the Delaware) one-eighth did so. St. George's hundred, immediately to the south, was almost as rich. The proportion owning what were probably substantial farms (£10 to £50) was over three times as high as in Sussex. It is evident that the vast majority in Sussex, the primarily subsistence farm area, were poor farmers and farm laborers; whereas in New Castle less than one-third fell into those categories.[39] Property was more concen-

[39] In Sussex, 69½ percent of the taxpayers were assessed for £4 income or less. In New Castle, 30 percent received 6 percent or less. La Rochefoucault-Liancourt, writing evidently of the latter county (for his remarks are not applicable to Sussex) set $20 or £6, as the sum assigned to poor people. *Travels*, II, 269–270. It is certain that the assessors had somewhat different standards from county to county.

trated in the hands of large property holders in New Castle than in Sussex, averaging 40 percent owned by the wealthiest 10 percent as against 33½ percent farther south.[40]

The tax lists of Burlington County, New Jersey, reveal a prosperous farm society in the Delaware valley. A very high proportion—considerably over half—of the men had no land, a fact which indicates the presence of many farm laborers. New Jersey farms were seldom large, but these southwestern communities had many more 500-acre estates than did the townships near New York. Especially striking is the concentration of real estate. Nearly half of the Burlington land was owned by 10 percent of the taxpayers. The same concentration existed in nearby Salem and Gloucester Counties.

Chester County, Pennsylvania, was a rich farming region in the southwestern corner of the state, adjacent to Philadelphia. The colony-state as a whole contained a higher proportion of landless men than did New England, and Chester in particular included a large percentage of such men, which varied from 40 percent in some townships to over half in others, averaging 47 percent in 1765. The explanation probably lies in the presence of indentured servants employed by the well-to-do farmers, sometimes identified in the tax lists as "inmates" as contrasted with "freemen." These "inmates" totalled about 10 percent of the adult men. Some towns, however, did not distinguish between "inmates" and "freemen," so that the true proportion of the

---

Thus at the bottom of the scale, New Castle assessors seem to have rated at £4 to £6 income, men who in Sussex would have been rated at £1 to £2. However, the contrasts are clear enough.

[40] New Castle hundred is here omitted because it was a business center. An error may exist in comparing the two counties if the property of the lower income groups was understated in Sussex, as seems probable. If so, then the true figure for the concentration of wealth in Sussex should be only about 26 percent.

former is probably nearer 15 percent. Some of those who lacked land were artisans, but there remains a laboring class which formed at least one-third of the population.[41]

The principal characteristics which distinguished commercial farm societies from the subsistence or small farm type are, first, the greater average wealth of the former; second, the presence of more large than small farmers (regardless of how these are defined), whereas in subsistence communities the reverse was true; third, a slightly larger proportion of laborers; fourth, a greater concentration of wealth in the hands of the large property holders; and finally, more artisans, shopkeepers, and professional men.[42] The last three characteristics existed to an even greater extent in the cities.

Cities during the revolutionary era may be divided into the lesser and the greater urban centers. With certain modifications in the former, they shared the same qualities. Both exhibited one fundamental feature: a wealthy class larger and richer than elsewhere in the North, controlling a greater proportion of the property. The wealth of this class

[41] Townships studied in Chester County were Haverford, Upper Darby, Lower Darby, Nether Providence, Middletown, Egmont, Upper Chichester, and Concord, all in the southeastern corner. *Pa. Arch.*, 3 series XI, XII. I am classifying the men who were related to a landowner as laborers. This procedure may be debatable, but surely a man of twenty-one, especially in those days, was no longer simply a dependent, nor can he be considered a landowner.

[42] See also for a good illustration of a commercial farm society, tax list in William S. Pattee, *A History of Old Braintree and Quincy* . . . (Quincy, 1872), 623–629. Lyme and Wethersfield, Connecticut, are other examples in New England. Tax lists, Conn. State Lib. The tax list of Rye, New Hampshire, can be compared with lists of other towns in the colony. Langdon B. Parsons, *History of the Town of Rye New Hampshire* (Concord, N.H., 1905), 142–143. Interesting for New Jersey are, Bergen County Historical Society, *Year Book* 11 (Paterson, 1915–1916), 40–49; *Cape May County Magazine of History and Genealogy*, I (1931) and II (1932).

was gained primarily from foreign trade, but in addition some large landholders made their homes in the city. Since many merchants invested in land, the townspeople not only possessed far more personal property than did the country folk but owned a substantial amount of real estate as well, including some sizable fortunes.

A variety of data demonstrate the higher concentration of property in these urban centers. The towns of York, Maine, and Charlestown, Massachusetts, both suffered heavy fire losses in 1775 which were reported in detail.[43] Nearly two hundred persons claimed damage in York. The twenty principal losers accounted for 43 percent of the total sum. None of these men was unusually rich, though three reported that they lost over £2,000. Charlestown's inhabitants claimed damage in excess of £100,000. The 10 percent who lost the largest amount owned 47½ percent of the total. Tax lists indicate the same concentration. In the trading center of Kittery, Maine, the 10 percent largest properties accounted for 45 percent of the total valuation, including polls.[44] The 1770 tax list for Portsmouth indicates that 5 percent of the taxpayers owned 34 percent of the taxable property, which means that 10 percent held nearly half.[45] According to the assessment list of 1771 for Waltham, Massachusetts, the 10 percent largest owners of real estate held 43½ per cent of the total value. In Newburyport they held 40 percent, while in Salem the proportion was no less than 60 percent. In Milford, Connecticut, it was only 36 percent, but the figure is high for that state, where 25 percent was average. In Albany, New York, the concentration

---

[43] Maine Hist. Soc., *Collections*, 2 ser. XIV (1910), 305–310; James F. Hunnewell, *A Century of Town Life: A History of Charlestown, Massachusetts, 1775–1887* (2 vols., Boston, 1888), II, 155–174.

[44] Maine Hist. Soc., *Collections*, 3 ser. II (1906), 205–220.

[45] Charles Warren Brewster, *Rambles about Portsmouth* (Portsmouth, 1869), I, 163n.

of real and personal property was 44 percent, about the same as that for the rich Hudson Valley districts. The top 10 percent of the town of New Castle, Delaware, received 49 percent of the income, the highest share in the state except Dover hundred. Even this great concentration of property is less than that in Boston, where, according to probate records, the richest 10 percent had 57 percent of the wealth; while in Philadelphia the same proportion paid over two-thirds of the tax.[46]

Further evidence for the existence of an exceptionally wealthy class may be drawn from other sources. The commercial farm centers had a higher proportion of men owning property valued between £1,000 and £2,000, but the cities contained a far larger percentage of residents who had fortunes of £2,000 and almost all of those owning £5,000. The towns of Dover and New Castle, Delaware, contained half of the men in the state who were assessed for incomes of over £200. On the Massachusetts assessment list, there were as many men in Salem and Medford whose real estate was rated at £25 annually as in the commercial farm towns of Milton and Waltham; and in addition the two small urban centers contained practically all of the well-to-do merchants. Among a dozen Connecticut towns, the only

---

[46] James A. Henretta, in an excellent article just published, estimates that the wealthiest 10 percent of Boston taxpayers as recorded on the 1771 assessment list, owned about 56 percent of the city's taxable wealth. This table seems to exclude the dependent labor force and the non-dependent, propertyless workers, which combined totalled 30 percent of the adult males. If so, then the wealthiest 10 percent of the men owned about 65 percent of the property. "Economic Development and Social Structure in Colonial Boston," *William and Mary Quarterly*, 3rd series XXII (1965), 82. Since the estates of indentured servants were not probated, the equivalent percentage derived from inventories is somewhat higher than that given in the text—say, 60 percent. Philadelphia figures are for Lower Delaware, Middle, Walnut, and Dock Wards, tax lists of 1769 and 1779, *Pa. Arch.*, XIV.

important urban center, Milford, had incomparably the largest number of men with taxable estates of £200: more, indeed, than all the others combined. The nearest rival, Wethersfield, was itself a smaller mercantile community on the Connecticut. Finally in Suffolk County, fourteen out of fifteen estates valued in probate for £5,000 belonged to Bostonians, who also owned forty-five out of sixty-seven evaluated at £2,000, or 72 percent of the large properties. Most of these men were merchants, but many of them had land, and several, such as Jeremiah Preble, who had £6,000 worth of land in Maine, were very large landowners.

The social structure of the major cities also included an exceptionally high proportion of men at the bottom of the economic scale. The lesser towns did not always have as many poor. New Castle contained rather fewer than did the surrounding areas, as did Milford, Connecticut, and Newburyport, Massachusetts. On the other hand Salem, York, and Medford included an above average proportion of men with little real estate. The town of Chester, Pennsylvania, contained in 1765 the remarkably high proportion of 61 percent landless men, about one-third of whom were "inmates." In general the more populous towns had the most poor people. New Hampshire probate records show that 30 percent of Portsmouth's inventories were valued at less than £100 total property as contrasted with 17 percent in the surrounding country.[47] Nearly 30 percent of the Boston estates were worth less than £50 and 40 percent were valued at less than £100, compared with 8 percent and 17 percent respectively in the nearby commercial farm towns. Urban society, therefore, tended to have relatively large upper and

[47] These figures are based on over 500 estates during the period 1750–1771. All figures lawful money, but subject to error because of the uncertain and fluctuating value of the colony's currency. *New Hampshire State Papers*, XXXIV–XXXIX.

lower classes, so that the middle group of property owners was proportionately smaller than in rural areas.

The occupations followed by the city dwellers were, of course, much more diverse than was the case in rural societies. Salem's tax assessment roll for 1771 listed thirty-six merchants and shipowners owning £200 worth of stock in trade, comprising one-eighth of the population. Richard Derby, the richest man in town, had £6,020 in stock, a still house, 5½ warehouses, a 5,300-foot wharf, and 415 tons of shipping, in addition to £160 annual value in real estate which was perhaps the equivalent of £6,000 worth. Another merchant had nearly as much land and stock and even more tonnage. In addition the town had thirty lesser shopkeepers and artisans with shops. The smaller center of Medford had a somewhat lesser proportion of merchants but even more shopowners. Nearly a third of Portsmouth's population were artisans. The probate records during the pre-revolutionary years indicate that perhaps an eighth of the men were merchants or shopkeepers ("traders" being the generic term there) and about a tenth were professional men. The town also had a large population of seamen (about one-fourth), and a lesser number of laborers who were landsmen. In contrast, the nearby commercial farm towns contained only a third as many artisans in proportion to their population, and far fewer traders. Similarly the artisans of Chester, Pennsylvania, comprised at least one-third of the population.

The two major sources for a study of Boston's society give much the same results. The tax assessor's book for 1780 lists over 1,300 persons. Of these, artisans accounted for 36 percent.[48] The same figure is derived from an examination

---

[48] *The Bostonian Society Publications*, IX (1912), 15–59. These are for wards 1–4, 7–9, and 12. Other ward lists are incomplete or do not give occupations. About one-fourth of the Philadelphians were iden-

of over 500 probated estates. The next largest class consisted of men in trade, including ship captains, traders, shopkeepers, and merchants. This group formed 26 percent according to the tax list and 29 percent in the probate records. Laborers are almost never identified as such, but they evidently comprised most of those whose occupations are not given and whose estates were small. Such poor men, together with the mariners, formed about one-quarter of the population in both tax and probate records. Since these records did not include indentured servants or slaves, the true figure is considerably higher. The assessment list of 1771 indicates that 39 percent of the population lacked property, but not all of these were laborers.[49] Many artisans, of course, were skilled workers rather than independent entrepreneurs. Professional men formed 3 or 4 percent of the population. Most of the rest evidently were tavernkeepers, pilots, farmers, or miscellaneous white-collar workers. Urban society was highly diversified and offered opportunities to many skills. The chances for advancement were good because the rapid economic growth constantly created new demands and new wealth.

The four types of social structure during the revolutionary era had distinctive characteristics. The feature most peculiar to the frontier—high mobility—will be discussed presently. Newly settled areas often had a higher proportion of people without land than did older areas. This oc-

---

tified as artisans by the 1769 tax lists. The true ratio may have been a little higher.

[49] See Henretta, "Colonial Boston," *Wm. and Mary Qtly.*, XXII (1965), 83, 85. The accuracy of probate records may be open to question. Some small estates were left by old men who had previously disposed of their property, and some belonged to young "Gentlemen," not laborers. However, these constitute a small minority of those who died poor. Although in any particular case the inventory may be misleading, in the aggregate the records convey a true picture.

curred most commonly in conjunction with land speculation, but was due also to the difficulty experienced by men
trying to get started. The class of poor people in Kent,
Connecticut (as defined by Charles Grant), was larger in
1740 than at any time during the next thirty years.[50]
Similarly in Goshen the proportion of landless men steadily
diminished between 1741 and 1787 as the poorer people
either moved on or secured land. As a rule, however, frontier communities had a high proportion of landowners from
the start. Few pioneers had large estates, and property was
equally distributed. The 10 percent of the men who owned
the largest farms held about one-third of the total wealth.

Land in subsistence farm areas was cheap, so that even if
many pioneers at first were landless, they soon acquired
farms, until only one in five were still without one. Since
the community produced little surplus, few men of wealth
were present. Instead, an even larger proportion of the men
were small farmers than on the frontier, and the concentration of property was about the same. Such a society was
almost entirely agricultural because most of the men had to
be as nearly self-sufficient as possible.[51]

Commercial farm societies contained far more propertyless men than did other rural communities. The proportion
was not high in New England because truly large-scale agri-

[50] Grant, *Kent*, 96.

[51] Probate records indicate that the wealthiest 10 percent in
Worchester County had 40 percent of the property, 35 percent in New
Hampshire outside of the commercial farm areas, and only 26 percent
in western Suffolk. Tax lists understate the degree of concentration
because the poll tax was usually levied and because certain sorts of
property owned by the richer people were not heavily taxed (such
as unoccupied land and income from trade). These records show that
in subsistence communities the wealthiest 10 percent held between
20 percent and 25 percent of the property in Connecticut, New
Hampshire, and Delaware, and about one-third in Massachusetts, New
York, and New Jersey.

culture did not develop there (though there are exceptions such as the Narragansett "plantations" in Rhode Island). Elsewhere in the North farm laborers and indentured servants were common and even a few slaves were used. This landless class made up nearly half of the male population in regions such as Chester County, Pennsylvania, and southwestern New Jersey. The farmers owned more property than did those on the frontier or in subsistence communities and some became rich. The wealthiest 10 percent paid between 30 percent and 45 percent of the taxes and owned nearly half of the property.

Urban society had an even greater proportion of rich men and an even higher concentration of property, probably exceeding 60 percent in both Boston and Philadelphia. There were also many poor people in the towns, including most of the slaves. Whereas in the country the great majority were farmers, city folk had many occupations so that urban society was diversified.

The general class structure of the North during the revolutionary era may best be analyzed through probate records. Of these, the Massachusetts series is particularly useful because real as well as personal property was evaluated. Everywhere there were people without land or houses. Such men almost always had little property of any sort and composed, generally, between one-fourth and one-fifth of the population in Massachusetts. When indentured servants are included it is a fair estimate that the class of poor people in the North comprised nearly one-third of the whole white population.[52]

[52] Another 10 percent or so had very little real property and were little better off financially than were the landless. In Massachusetts nearly one-fourth of the population left less than £100 (based on 1,500 probated estates). In New Hampshire the proportion was I think higher. New Jersey inventories include only personal property, so that comparisons are incomplete. However the number of poor people

At the top of the class structure were men with fortunes of £2,000 or more. These totalled at most 3 percent of the population in New Hampshire, 7 percent in Massachusetts, and perhaps 14 percent in New Jersey, the average for the northern states being about 10 percent. Substantial property owners with £500 to £2,000 made up probably 30 percent or so, and small property owners about the same proportion. The wealthiest 10 percent owned about half of the inventoried property in Massachusetts, 40 percent in New Hampshire, and 45 percent in New Jersey, the last figure being average for the North. This appears at first sight to represent a high degree of concentration, but according to recent studies the wealthiest 10 percent of families in the United States had 64 percent of the wealth in 1929 and 56 percent in 1956.[53] The outstanding feature of northern society was not its small wealthy class but the very large proportion of substantial middle-class property owners.

The middle-class character of northern society was also made clear by the occupations of its people. By far the largest number were engaged in agriculture as independent, though small farmers. Nearly 30 percent of New Jersey's men in pre-revolutionary probate records were denominated "husbandmen" or "yeomen," which almost always meant that they were farmers, and another 20 percent of the men were certainly farmers also. In New Hampshire half of the people were so identified and farmers probably made up 60 percent of the total number of men. Massachusetts assessment lists and probate records give a similar result, with the proportion rising to 70 percent outside the

there was almost identical with that in Massachusetts. *New Jersey Arch.*, XXXIII–XXXVI.

[53] Robert J. Lampman, *The Share of Top Wealth-Holders in National Wealth 1922–56* (Princeton, 1962), 215. He gives the figure for 1956. The proportion owned by the wealthy had been reduced by one-eighth since 1929, and I have made the estimate for that year accordingly.

urban area. Certainly farmers comprised fully half of the population.

Artisans were also an important element. They comprised over 20 percent of the men in Suffolk County, 10 percent in Worcester County, and the same elsewhere in New England. In New Jersey also they formed about one-tenth of the people, and this figure is probably a fair average for the North as a whole. About one-third of the men in New Jersey were laborers.[54] The proportion was a little higher in Pennsylvania and New York, somewhat lower in New England. Men engaged in commerce scarcely made up more than 2 or 3 percent of the population, professionals formed a similar proportion, and the rest followed a variety of occupations principally of the "white collar" type. Perhaps 20 percent of the people received their principal income from a non-farm property. Many laborers did so too, but it seems likely that 70 percent of the population depended directly on the soil. Society was diversified, yet still predominantly agricultural.

The reason why historians have disagreed concerning the northern class structure is obvious: their conclusions depended upon which set of facts they emphasized. Whoever studied the New England frontier, as did Grant, or the subsistence farm communities—even, in some areas, the commercial farm towns—naturally saw a democratic society. On the other hand the student who fixed his attention on the towns, or on most commercial farm areas, perceived obvious economic inequalities and a distinct class structure. The same contradictions appear in the South.

[54] I have added, to the data derived from probate records, an estimated 10 percent for indentured servants and 4 percent for slaves. Slaves comprised nearly one-eighth of the population in Pennsylvania and New York but not over 3 percent in New England, averaging 6 percent in the North generally. Stella H. Sutherland, *Population Distribution in Colonial America* (New York, 1936), 15–21, 23, 70, 98, 124–135, 220.

CHAPTER II

The Economic Class Structure
of the South

SOUTHERN SOCIETY differed from that of the North in a number of ways. The presence of far more Negro slaves increased the proportion of landless workers; the upper class was also much larger; and wealth was more concentrated in the hands of the well-to-do. The southern states were less similar to one another than were the northern. Whereas in the North, New England's society followed a uniform pattern which closely resembled that of the "Middle States," South Carolina's was entirely distinct from that of North Carolina, which in turn was quite different from the Chesapeake settlements. Finally, the sequence of frontier, subsistence farm, commercial farm, urban community, clearly discernible in the North, existed to the southward only in a modified way. During much of the colonial period subsistence farming had indeed been general. But by 1763 the very rapid westward advance, together with an excellent system of water transportation and the absence of a mountain barrier in much of the section, meant that southern frontier society could pass directly into the commercial farm stage without a long interval of subsistence agriculture. This transition was also made possible by the nature of the soil which encouraged large-scale agriculture just as the nature of much northern soil condemned many of its occupants to the level of subsistence. The commercial farm type of society therefore had come to predominate in all of the southern states except North Carolina. The city was, like the subsistence farm, considerably less important than in the North.

The southern frontier was settled in a way similar to that in the middle colonies, but large estates were more numerous. During most of the colonial period land prices were very low. By the revolutionary era the cost was rising, especially for desirable farms. Some of the better land cost 20s per acre or even more. However, credit was readily obtainable and farms could be rented at low cost; while tracts in certain areas still cost only 2s or 3s per acre. The general price level compared favorably with that in the North.[1]

The character of a southern frontier society depended upon the degree of land speculation which occurred. Virginia's "Northern Neck" (south of the Potomac and north of the Rappahannock) was from the beginning a vast speculative enterprise. As region after region was opened up, the great planters purchased large tracts which were developed with slave labor or rented to tenants. Only gradually did the tenants acquire property and become free farmers. In some counties not over 30 percent of the whites were freeholders, and a very small number of wealthy men— many of them absentees—held as much as 70 percent of the real property. Slaves were concentrated in like degree. The Northern Neck type of society occurred elsewhere, though without quite such inequalities. The upper James Valley in

[1] Newspaper advertisements are especially interesting. Examples are *The Maryland Journal, and Baltimore Advertiser*, April 6, 1784; *The Virginia Gazette* (Rind), Jan. 10, 1771; *The Virginia Journal and Alexandria Advertiser*, April 8, 1784. There is a good discussion of rising land values during the revolutionary era in Lewis Cecil Gray, *History of Agriculture in the Southern United States to 1860* (Washington, 1932), I, 404–405. Eastern lands were worth from £1 per acre up. For prices in South Carolina see the *Journal* of the House of Representatives, March 3, 1784. Interesting is Joseph Purcell to ?, August 16, 1786, Manigault Family Papers, Box 1, folder 14, South Caroliniana Library. The increase in rents after the Revolution is shown in the Bartlett Papers, vol. 4, Galloway-Marcoe-Maxie Collection, Library of Congress.

particular was easily accessible to the planters. Frontiers of
this nature were commercial developments from the start.[2]

More typical of the frontier was the settlement of Virginia's southern Shenandoah Valley, the Piedmont south of
the James, and most of the interior Carolinas. Lunenburg
County, Virginia, was just ceasing to be a frontier in 1764.[3]
A few large landowners had already arrived, but there were
no wealthy slaveowners. The richest 10 percent of the men
had about 40 percent of the land, a proportion somewhat
higher than that in the North but low for the South. Landless whites made up 35 percent of the white population. Of
these, about one-half were related to farmers and probably
could use the family land. Still, most of them were for the
time being dependent workers. The other landless men fell
into two equal categories. Some, apparently the heads of
families, paid their own taxes. These men sometimes owned
slaves and farm animals, in which case they perhaps rented
land. The rest had their taxes paid by someone else, and
presumably were servants or hired men living with the
farmers. Small landholders were the most numerous class.
Most of them had over 200 acres. Tax records do not usually identify the occupations of the men, but there existed
in Lunenburg County two schoolmasters, a blacksmith, and
nearly a dozen overseers. It seems likely that the non-farm
population was no more than 1 percent. Second in number
to the small farmers were the white farm laborers, who

[2] For a description of the Northern Neck development, see Fairfax
Harrison, *Virginia Land Grants* (Richmond, 1925). Material on
Virginia is drawn principally from research done for my articles,
"The Distribution of Property in Post-Revolutionary Virginia," *Miss.
Vy. Hist. Rev.,* XLI (1954-1955), 241-258, and "The One Hundred,"
Wm. and Mary Qtly., 3 series XI (1954), 354-384. See these for
citations.

[3] Tax lists in Landon C. Bell, ed., *Sunlight on the Southside: List
of Tithes, Lunenburg County, Virginia, 1748-1783* (Philadelphia, 1931).

made up perhaps 30 percent of the white society.[4] However their work was supplemented by that of over six hundred slaves, without whom the number of white workers might well have been larger. If the adult male slaves are included, the proportion of laborers rises to roughly 45 percent of the total population. There were few men of large property: only 6 percent of the men held a thousand acres or more.

By 1787 the frontier had reached Washington County, which included the southwestern corner of the present-day state of Virginia. No great planter was there yet, though one man did have 23 slaves. There were few other slave-owning whites; over four-fifths had none. The county contained, as did Virginia generally, a considerable number of landless men, most of them poor, some with no property.[5] These made up 30 percent of the white population. When slaves are added, the laboring class as a whole totals 36 percent of the men. An equal number were small farmers, and a few large landowners had arrived. The richest 10 percent had less than 40 percent of the taxable property.

The district of South Carolina called "Ninety-six" was also a frontier region during the revolutionary era, though by 1787, from which year a tax list survives, it was rapidly

[4] The estimate here that 30 percent of the whites were laborers is correct only if the landless men who were related to farmers are included. If they are not, then the percentage would drop to less than one-fifth.

[5] Here and throughout, I have divided the landless heads of families into two categories: those holding a fair amount of personal property, and those who had little. The first category includes the men who had a slave, or who owned no slaves but more than four horses and cattle. The choice is entirely arbitrary and is based upon the assumption that one could own a few such animals without renting land, but that ownership of more made land essential, being therefore evidence that they were tenants or at all events were not simply laborers. Presumably a person who had a slave was not a laborer either.

being filled with settlers. The unusual feature of its society was the virtual absence of a white lower class: only 6 per-cent of the men lacked land, and some of these were slave-owners. Even if adult male slaves are included in the social structure, the laboring class comprised only one-third of the population. A majority were small farmers holding 100 or 200 acres. Large planters, as was usual on the southern fron-tier, appeared early: 4 percent of the men had already ac-quired at least 1,000 acres. One of them held twenty-five slaves, but most slaveowners held only a few and more than half of the men had none. The richest 10 percent of the men had about 40 percent of the wealth.[6]

North Carolina also had a large frontier area in the revo-lutionary period. Typical were the counties of Surry in the northwest and Rutherford in the southwest.[7] Southerners had a disorderly way of settling without a land title, and in both counties one-third of the men paid no land tax. How-ever, many of these—probably one-third—were using some-one's land, and several had considerable property (one owned five slaves, four horses, and twenty-eight cattle), so that the true class of landless poor did not come to much over 20 percent. Some of the farmers were not much better off than the landless workers, but the typical westerner had a couple of hundred acres, three horses, and half a dozen cows. No one in either county had more than sixteen slaves and large landowners were rare, though a few (about 2 percent) of the men did have a thousand acres. All told, including slaves, about one-fourth of the men belonged to the class of dependent poor, and almost all of the rest were

[6] This tax list and others referred to subsequently are in the South Carolina Archives, Columbia, South Carolina.

[7] All of the extant North Carolina tax lists are available on microfilm. See William S. Jenkins and Lillian A. Hamrick, eds., *Guide to the Microfilm Collection of Early State Records* (Washington, 1950), 73-74.

free farmers. The wealthiest 10 percent had less than 40 percent of the land.

The class structure of the southern frontier, taken as a whole, possessed that same equality which distinguished most northern pioneer settlements. The proportion of landless whites was much higher in the South, but this seems to have been due not to greater poverty but to a different method of granting, or at all events of occupying, land; and to the greater quantity of vacant territory which squatters could use. The New Englander especially had available only a small amount of good soil, and though he might, like the southerner, let his livestock roam in the common woods, he would ordinarily obtain title to at least a small amount of mowing or pasture land. Conditions in New Jersey, Pennsylvania, and New York more nearly approached the circumstances of the southerner, who could use land without owning it. Many southerners of property held no real estate, but rented land. When from the total number of landless men are subtracted those who apparently had access to land, and those who were more than just landless workers, there remains the truly poor class of southern whites, only a shade more numerous than their northern equivalents. What swelled the proportion of laborers in the South was the presence of slaves. Even on the frontier they added another 8 percent, or thereabouts, to the total labor force. If these are included, one-third of the southern frontiersmen were landless workers. Most of the rest, as on the northern frontier, were small farmers. The western settlements in the South did have a class of large landowners almost entirely lacking in the North. Probably on the northern frontier the proportion of men owning £500 worth of personal property did not exceed one in twenty, whereas in southwestern Virginia, according to rather limited probate records, the ratio was one in ten, and in western South Carolina the number seems to have been even greater. These men had a larger share of the wealth than did their equivalents on the northern frontier—about 40 percent of the property. Pioneer society usually included very few artisans or professional men, and this seems to have been particularly true in the South.

Virginia contained few areas that can be termed subsistence farm regions. The soil was so fertile, the mountains so distant, the rivers so numerous and so navigable, that most farmers were able to produce a surplus and send it to market. Such subsistence farms as existed were located principally in the uplands between the rivers or in the west. The nature of surviving records makes the type difficult to analyze. Taxes were collected not through towns but by counties, and since the average Virginia county is large (one would reach from Boston to Worcester), both uplands and river lands are included in an indistinguishable mixture.

During much of the colonial period, subsistence farming had covered large sections of the colony, and Virginia's society had been characterized by a good deal of equality. However by the time of the Revolution slaves were present in large numbers almost everywhere, and large-scale "plantation" agriculture was becoming general. Even the Piedmont counties such as Orange and Fluvanna north of the James, and Charlotte, Prince Edward, and Halifax south of that river, had nearly four slaves per white taxpayer in 1787. Much of Princess Anne County, along the coast, was a subsistence farm region, but there were two slaves per white taxpayer in that county also. However slaves had by no means displaced white laborers. In the Virginia Piedmont, about half of the whites did not own land. Admittedly many of these were tenants or the sons of well-to-do farmers, owning slaves or other property which clearly raised them above the status of laborers. Still there remains a large number of whites with no land and little personal property, perhaps comprising one-fourth of the white male population. The whole labor force, including slaves, formed 40 percent of the total.

More like the northern subsistence farm type was Rockbridge County in the Shenandoah Valley. By the time of the Revolution the northern end of the Valley (Berkeley and Frederick Counties) had become a commercial area which was the scene of speculation on a grand scale and contained many large estates, but the southern part was the domain of small farmers. Half of the white men, curiously, did not own land, but many of these had several farm animals, and presumably rented farms, while a few are identified as artisans. Probably one out of four whites was a laborer. Slaves were not numerous, and the whole labor force totalled one-third of the men. There were fewer large estates than in the Piedmont. The wealthiest 10 percent owned a considerable proportion of the real property (about 45 percent). More artisans lived in Rockbridge than on the Southside, but even so, almost all of the people depended directly on the soil.

A series of probate records for a portion of Virginia's Southside before the Revolution add detail concerning this area.[8] About 40 percent of the men had less than £50 worth of personal property. Real estate is not included, but the inventories prove that almost all of these men were small farmers or farm laborers. Sixty percent owned less than £100. This figure is somewhat greater than that for Worcester County, Massachusetts, and reflects the small

[8] Halifax County Will Book O (1753–1772); Lunenburg County Will Book 2 (1762–1778), microfilm, Va. State Lib. The currency used in these Virginia inventories is the local money, equal in value to New England's "lawful money."

number of slaveowners in the Piedmont at that time. On the other hand, the existence of slavery accounts for the presence of more wealthy men than was the case farther north, 10 percent of the estates being evaluated at over £500. Thus both the upper and lower classes were larger in Virginia's Piedmont than in comparable northern communities, a difference which suggests that Piedmont agriculture was as much commercial as subsistence. Most of the men were farmers or farm laborers. One seems to have been a peddler, one a blacksmith, and one a shopkeeper. There was a joiner, a miller, and a "clerk." All told, the non-farm element did not exceed 6 or 7 percent of the people. The wealthiest 10 percent owned 44 percent of the property.

South Carolina also had an area occupied primarily by small farms which lay between the coastal rice and indigo plantations and the frontier. Here, as in Virginia's Piedmont, the slaveholders had penetrated quite early. By the time that the tax lists of 1786—the only ones which have survived—were being taken, the upcountry parish of Prince Frederick already contained four persons with over fifty slaves. The parish was divided, for tax purposes, into two sections. One (the tax list for which is incomplete) was entirely commercial, with nearly everyone owning slaves. There were 13 slaves and 640 acres per white taxpayer. The other section seems to have been more like the subsistence farm areas, containing 7 slaves and 400 acres per taxpayer. In the latter area, about half of the whites were not slave-owners. Many of these were landless, but this group included only one-fifth of the white men. Small farmers were the largest element in the society, those with less than 500 acres accounting for over 40 percent of the whites. Most striking however was the number of large landholders, who formed more than one-fourth of the population even in the less commercial section of the county and exceeded one-third generally. The non-farm element is identified by a tax on "faculty" which was levied on nineteen persons, or 18 percent of the people. One of these was a doctor, three were probably shopkeepers, and the rest were artisans.

Orangeburgh in 1787 seems to have been primarily a subsistence farm area. There were few slaves and only one large slaveholder. Most of the land was poor, and it must have been cheap, for all but 6 percent of the whites owned some. Nearly half of the farms were in the 100-acre class, and three-quarters were smaller than 500 acres. The laboring class was apparently tiny for since several of the landless whites had slaves, they could not have been wage workers, while there were only a few blacks; so that laborers, slave and free, could not have comprised more than one-sixth of the population. One out of twelve men were large landholders and all the rest, apparently, were small farmers—no one paid a faculty tax. These tax lists, together with probate records, indicate that in this part of South Carolina the wealthiest 10 percent owned a little over 40 percent of the property.

The section of the South which most closely resembled the northern subsistence farm area was the North Carolina back-country, including indeed much of the Tidewater, and extending west to the frontier. This vast area stretched for a hundred and fifty miles east and west and about the same distance north and south, overlapping into Virginia and South Carolina. Slaves were comparatively few, especially in the western parts.[9] About a quarter of the men did not have title to land, but half of these had personal property which probably raised them out of the laboring class. Land prices were low, and as a result farms were large. One-fifth

[9] There were generally about as many slaves as white taxpayers, which means that the ratio of adult white males to adult male slaves was about 5:1. Only one-fifth of the whites were slaveowners.

of the men owned 500 acres; the well-to-do planter had at least 1,000. Half of the men had farms of 100 to 500 acres, the median being about 250. Laborers, including slaves, comprised about 30 percent of the population, well-to-do landholders between 5 and 10 percent, and small farmers most of the rest. The wealthiest 10 percent held between 35 percent and 40 percent of the property. This part of the South, then, resembled its northern equivalent in having a small landless class, a low proportion of poor laborers, few rich men, a very large number of small farmers, and a relatively equal distribution of property.

The commercial farm society was the principal type of class structure in the South. As in the North, it was characterized by numerous landless workers, more large than small farmers, considerable wealth, and a concentration of property in the hands of the well-to-do. Much of Maryland, most of Virginia, eastern North Carolina, eastern South Carolina, and Georgia's coastal counties were commercial farm areas.

Virginia's Tidewater section was representative. It contained a high proportion of landless whites, averaging indeed about half of the men. Many of these—perhaps 15 percent or more of the whites—were probably tenants, often possessing considerable property, who of course were not farm laborers. Still, whites holding no land, no slaves, and few farm animals comprised at least 30 percent of the white men. Many of these were related to landowners and could make use of the family holdings, but there still remains a sizable number of landless workers. When adult male slaves are added, this class becomes enormous, reaching over four-fifths of the population in a rich county such as Middlesex and nearly two-thirds in the Tidewater generally. The number of large landowners varied greatly. In the easternmost counties, land had been divided and subdivided until estates of 1,000 acres were comparatively rare, but these increased in number farther west. Perhaps ownership of slaves is a better measure of wealth. If possession of twenty denoted a man of means, then about 6 percent of the men belonged to that class (the figure is 3 percent for the semi-subsistence farm region of the Piedmont). The rich upper class had a very large share of the wealth, owning 60 percent or more of the land and over half of all the property.

The probate records of Spotsylvania, Chesterfield, Essex, Richmond, and Westmoreland Counties prove the great wealth of the planter class, for 15 percent of the estates inventoried exceeded £1,000 in value (though these records exaggerate the number of large properties).[10] Only about one-fifth of the men had less than £50, but the tax records prove that there were really many more poor whites, so that obviously a higher proportion of the large estates than of the small were being evaluated. As in the North, indentured servants must be added to the lower class. Both probate records and tax lists demonstrate that the number of ordinary farmers in commercial farm areas was smaller than elsewhere in the South. Even if slaves are excluded, they formed less than 40 percent of the population (not counting tenants) compared with over half in the subsistence farm regions of the Carolinas and the North.

The probate records furnish some idea of the different occupations in eastern Virginia. The principal fact which emerges is the small number of men other than farmers. About one-fifth of the men whose estates were inventoried

---

[10] Spotsylvania Will Book D (1761–1772) and E (1772–1798); Chesterfield Will Book 3 (1744–1785) and 4 (1785–1800); Essex Will Book 13 (1775–1785) and 14 (1786–1792); Richmond Will Book 6 (1753–1767); Westmoreland Records and Inventories, no. 5 (1767–1776), microfilm, Va. State Lib.

lacked land, but of these many were workers on the land—perhaps indentured servants—and the proportion engaged in non-farming occupations seems not to have exceeded one-tenth. This estimate excludes skilled slaves, who often were trained as artisans. The overwhelming majority of whites were yeomen farmers. The relative ratio of small to large farmers depends upon the definition of these terms. If quantity of land alone is the criterion, then the Piedmont contained more large landowners than did the eastern counties, because farms were larger. However, real property was more valuable in the Tidewater. Probate records tell a somewhat different story. An inventory of £200 in personal property ordinarily meant that the individual had a total estate of over £500. If the large farmer is defined as one who was worth that sum, then in those counties identified above (which are typical) large farmers exceeded the small, whereas small landowners were more numerous farther west.

North Carolina also had a commercial farm society, though it was far less extensive than in the neighboring states. Hertford County in the northeast and Carteret on the central coast are representative. Like the state generally they contained, in 1779, a small landless class (30 percent of the whites) which included an even smaller class of white workers, comprising roughly one-fifth of the men. Since slaves were less numerous than in Virginia, the number of laborers, all told, was not much over 40 percent compared with 70 percent or so in eastern Virginia. The general structure of society resembled that of the Virginia Piedmont, being characterized by many more farmers than large landowners, but the concentration of wealth was greater in North Carolina.

Particularly interesting are the taxes levied in 1779 on cash, money at interest, and stock in trade. Records survive only from Hertford, Carteret, and Jones Counties, all of which lie in the commercial area. The total amount declared in the three counties was about £170,000, or roughly £130 per taxpayer: these were inflationary years. But the distribution of this form of wealth was most unequal. One-fourth of the people owned no cash, stock, or debts at all, and half had less than £15. A small number of the men held most of this property: 10 percent of the taxpayers held over three-fourths of it, and those holding £1,000 each had nearly half of the whole amount. If the concentration of this form of wealth was so great in these counties it is interesting to speculate what the situation was in other areas where an even greater proportion of real and personal property was held by the few.[11]

The commercial farm region of South Carolina resembled the Virginia rather than the North Carolina prototype, except that it had fewer landless whites, far more slaves, and incomparably more wealthy men. Tax records for St. Paul's and St. James' parishes (both rich rice plantation districts on the coast) for 1786 and 1787 show that about a third of the men lacked land. However most of these were slave-owners, so that only one-eighth at the most could have been propertyless laborers. So great was the number of slaves, however—nearly forty for each white man—that almost 90 percent of the adult males were laborers! Two of the whites were overseers, one is identified as a shoemaker, and there

[11] Distribution of money, etc., North Carolina, 1779:

	Under £1	£1–£10	£10–£50	£50–£100
Carteret	25%	15%	26%	9½%
Jones	26	18	28	7
Hertford	28	22	25	6½

	£100–£500	£500–£1,000	£1,000+
Carteret	17%	4%	3½%
Jones	16	3	2
Hertford	15	1½	2

was one doctor. None of these had land. Large farmers outnumbered the small by a ratio of two to one: in fact, one-third of the taxpayers had 1,000 acres and more than one-fourth had fifty slaves. The richest 10 percent had about half of the land and slaves.

The dominance of the well-to-do and wealthy in South Carolinia's eastern parishes is emphasized by the probate records. These records usually do not define the place of residence, but some of them do so, and many homes can be located by inference: it can be assumed, for example, that rice planters lived near the coast. The accuracy of this source is reduced because the poor people of the commercial farm areas were not represented in proper proportion. Still, even if the records are inaccurate, they reveal unmistakably a society of great wealth, which included relatively few poor whites. Only 3 percent of the estates were evaluated at less than £100 sterling (the true proportion as indicated by the tax lists is perhaps 12 percent). In contrast, 20 percent of the upcountry estates were worth less than that sum. Men of moderate property were also fewer in the east: one-third of the westerners and only one-sixth of the easterners died with £100 to £500 in personal property. On the other hand, five-eighths of the easterners left estates of £1,000—and this figure includes only personal property, not land. The percentages are inexact, but the inference to be drawn from them is obvious: the commercial farm areas contained a far greater proportion of wealthy men. The concentration of property too was much higher along the coast—at least half of the wealth was owned by the richest 10 percent. The probate records also demonstrate the predominantly rural nature of the society (excluding Charleston). Only some 10 percent of the men followed a non-farm occupation, and most of these lived in a few small towns. Here was the quintescence of the southern commercial farm society: a numerous laboring class, many extremely wealthy men, more large than small farmers, a high concentration of property, and a society almost entirely rural.[12]

The only major southern city was Charleston. Although it resembled Boston and other northern towns, it differed in two particulars: the presence of slaves furnished a much larger labor force; and the same slaves, considered as property, combined with the fact that some rich planters lived in the city, made Charleston far wealthier. Indeed whereas in Boston scarcely one-fifth of the men left personal estates exceeding £1,000, in Charleston nearly 30 percent did so. Of this property, more than one-fourth was in slaves. According to the probate records, even many artisans were slave-owners. There were fewer poor whites: only a fourth of the inventories were rated at less than £100 as contrasted with nearly 40 percent in Boston. It is probable that a larger proportion of the poor than of the other income groups died without inventories being taken, but the records do include some men who had no property at all, and there is no reason to suspect an error which would change the generalization.[13] The economic class structure, then, was top-heavy, if only the white population is considered, with far

[12] Inventory books in S.C. Archives. I used those from 1763 to 1768, when most of the inventories were being figured in currency having a depreciated value of about 7:1, and from 1783–1788, when most evaluations were made in sterling. Figures in the text are sterling. The currency used can best be determined by examining the price set upon an article the sterling value of which is known.

[13] Distribution of personal property, Charleston inventories:

Less than £100	26%
£100–£199	13
£200–£499	23
£500–£999	10
£1,000–£2,000	9
£2,000 and up	19

fewer poor than in Boston, and about the same proportion of medium-sized property owners. However if slaves are included, then the class of poor people was decidedly larger in Charleston. The concentration of wealth was about the same as that in Boston, the richest 10 percent owning five-eighths of the wealth.

The probate records furnish additional information concerning the occupational structure of the city. White laborers comprised about one-fifth of Charleston's population compared with one-fourth in Boston; but the contrast is deceptive, for when slaves are added the proportion of workers in the southern city jumps to 65 percent. The white artisan class was also somewhat smaller than in the North, but many of the blacks were skilled workers who in the North would be called artisans. Men in commerce comprised one-fourth of the total, the same as in Boston, while those in the professions and in miscellaneous occupations were somewhat more numerous in Charleston. Finally, Charleston furnished the residence for rich planters who added to the striking wealth of the city.

The southern social structure as a whole was characterized by great class distinctions, yet it varied enormously from place to place. The frontier was a region of equality. There were few slaves, and men of great wealth were uncommon except in certain areas. One-third or more of the white men did not own land, the proportion being considerably higher in Virginia but much lower in the Carolinas. However a few of these rented land, or owned considerable personal property, so that the class of landless workers included about one-fourth of the whites, the same percentage as in the North. Slaves raised the proportion of laborers to one-third, though relatively few pioneers enjoyed their help. Most of the population consisted of small farmers owning less than 500 acres. There were few tenants on the frontier, few artisans, and only an occasional trader or professional man. Both inventories and tax lists indicate the predominance of the middle class, for the majority of estates were those of small property owners. The southern frontier, however, did contain more men of wealth than the comparable northern communities. The concentration of property too was much greater in the South, where the richest 10 percent of the men owned about 40 percent of the wealth—less than this in North Carolina, but more elsewhere.

The subsistence farm type of society, strictly speaking, was rare in the South, but large areas, especially in North Carolina, were not truly commercial and resembled small farm communities in the North. The proportion of landless whites was less than on the frontier, probably because men found it essential to secure land titles; and perhaps also because there was not as much land speculation in the less desirable areas. In the Virginia Piedmont, half of the men did not own land. Many of the landless whites were tenants, who made up ten percent of the population, at a guess, or otherwise had access to land; so that the true landless white worker class totalled perhaps one-third of the population. The more typically "subsistence" region of North Carolina had a much smaller number of the landless. Slaves were more common than on the frontier, swelling the number of poor workers to 40 percent in Virginia and over 30 percent in the Carolinas. Wealthy men were more numerous than farther west, although those with £500 worth of personal property did not exceed 10 percent of the whole, and only about 3 percent owned 1,000 acres. The concentration of wealth was the same as on the frontier. Artisans, professional men, and others with non-agricultural occupations were almost as scarce as they were in the west and considerably less common than in the North. Small farmers with 100 to 500 acres made up about 35 percent of the white population in Virginia's semi-subsistence farm area, and 50 percent in the Carolinas.

The most important part of the South was the commercial farm sections. A majority of the people lived there, and it produced the most wealth. The landless class was especially numerous here, probably because all of the land worth having was already owned by someone, and was expensive, so that many people started as tenants or hired workers. Probably 40 percent of the white men did not have land: the number exceeded 50 percent in much of eastern Virginia (especially in the Northern Neck), though it was not over 30 percent farther south. The proportion of large landowners varied considerably, being highest in South Carolina where in some parishes half of the men held 500 acres, and lowest in the older Virginia counties, where the land had been divided and subdivided, so that the great planters formed only 5 or 6 percent of the population. The middle class of farmers was considerably smaller than in other regions. About one-third of the white men held 100 to 500 acres (more in North Carolina, fewer elsewhere). The wealthiest 10 percent owned more than half of the land.

Probate records for commercial farm counties reveal the same general situation. They emphasize the wealth which even the ordinary farmers had accumulated. Even those who lacked real estate often owned considerable amounts of personal property, and the truly poor class, with less than £50, did not exceed a fifth of Virginia's white population in these regions. This probably is average for the South, for if the proportion was much less in South Carolina it was decidedly higher in North Carolina. One-third of the men, other than those in North Carolina, owned less than £100. These were with few exceptions slaveless and most of them were probably landless as well. Another third, consisting of slave-owning farmers, left personal property valued at £100 to £500. This proportion was slightly smaller than in equivalent northern areas. Finally, the rest of the men, nearly a third of the total, owned personal estates in excess of £500. The remarkable wealth which this represented can be appreciated when we recall that in the commercial farm area surrounding Boston less than 10 percent left such a large amount. The richest 10 percent owned half of the property compared with a little over 40 percent in the North.

The most striking feature of this commercial society was the presence of Negro slaves in large numbers. Only 30 percent of the whites (possibly less) were laborers, nearly the same ratio as in the North, but Negroes brought the ratio up to 60 or 70 percent of the total population, white and black. Artisans, professionals, and the like totalled only about 6 percent of the whites. Negro artisans of course replaced the whites to a large extent. The great majority of the whites were farmers, equally divided between large and small.

Urban society was also affected by slave labor. Whereas in the North, cities characteristically contained a much more numerous class of poor workers than did the country, in the South the reverse was true. If Charleston is representative, the class of poor whites in southern towns was a good deal smaller than in the northern cities, though if slaves are included, the southern urban poor was a large element, comprising 65 percent of the total population. The number of artisans, professional men, merchants, and the like was about the same as in the northern cities. However the southern city dweller (at least in Charleston) was richer: more than one-fourth owned £1,000 worth of personal property compared with less than one-fifth possessing that amount in Boston. These men had an even greater share of urban wealth than the great planters did of rural property.

This discussion of these various southern class structures must be supplemented by some notice of each state taken separately, for the differences were considerable. South Carolina was, like the rest of the South, predominantly rural and slaveholding. The distribution of land is indicated by the quit rent roll of 1769, which included some 770 persons and, though obviously incomplete, seems to contain a fair cross section of the colony's population.[14] The rich did not escape payment: fourteen estates of more than 5,000 acres were listed. One-sixth of the plantations contained 1,000 acres, a proportion which is almost identical with that revealed by the tax records in six counties a couple of decades later. Indeed the two sets of records give similar results in every way. The planter class, if it be defined as including those who owned 500 acres, formed nearly 30 percent of the land-holding population, while 60 percent held between 100 and 500: even in the west the truly small farm was rare. The wealthiest 10 percent of the farmers according to both the quit rent roll and tax lists owned well over half of the land. This rich class also had considerably over half of the slaves and (according to probate records) nearly 60 percent of the personal property generally. South Carolina's white society consisted, then, of a poor class, landless and with little personal property, accounting for scarcely one-seventh of the white population. Artisans made up at most a tenth, merchants, shopkeepers, and the like, one-twelfth, professionals one out of twenty. Sixty percent of the whites were farmers and, if the probate records can be trusted, four-fifths of these held over £200 in personal

[14] South Carolina quit rents, 1768–1774, S.C. Archives. These rent rolls do not locate the properties taxed.

property. Certainly half owned 300 acres and nearly half (according to scattered tax records) held slaves. The rich were rich indeed, numerous, and economically dominant whether in the country or in Charleston. What particularly made South Carolina a land of inequality were the slaves, who formed, with the relatively small number of poor whites, a laboring class totalling nearly 60 percent of the adult male population.

South Carolina was not a typical southern colony-state, but incarnated and magnified certain southern characteristics. More nearly average was Virginia. The two resembled each other in several ways. Both had large landowners in numbers unknown to the northward: one-fifth of the farmers had 500 acres. The richest 10 percent of Virginians owned half of the land and (according to probate records) nearly that much of the personal property. However, in Virginia the class of landless whites was far greater than in South Carolina. Many of these were tenants, with personal property which places them in the middle class economically, but 30 percent seem to have been dependent workers, the sons of farmers, indentured servants, or hired help on the larger plantations.[15] In Virginia as in South Carolina negro slaves were an additional source of labor. When they are added, the laboring class becomes about half of the adult population.

Despite the important role played by the wealthy planters and the presence of numerous slaves and landless whites, the small farmers constituted a more significant element in Virginia's society than they did in South Carolina. In Virginia, about 30 percent of the whites held farms of between 100 and 500 acres, the average being 230 acres. These farmers

---

[15] In Lunenburg County, 1773, 24 percent of the men had their taxes paid by someone else. A few of those who paid their own tax were also probably hired workers.

were quite prosperous, usually owning personal property valued at over £100 and averaging about £250. Men other than farmers and planters comprised not over 5 or 6 percent of the white Virginians.

North Carolina was in some respects as much northern as southern. The landless laboring class in the North made up about a quarter of the population; in Virginia and South Carolina, including slaves, over half; in North Carolina, about a third. A landholding aristocracy was rare in the North, important in Virginia and South Carolina, present but less significant in North Carolina. There, the wealthiest 10 percent owned about 40 percent of the property, not quite as much as in the North, and far under the 50 to 60 percent in Virginia and South Carolina. The large middle class of small farmers in North Carolina, as in the North, constituted a majority of the white population, a fact underscored by the relatively democratic distribution of wealth. Thus North Carolina was not at all typical of the South, even though the large size of the plantations, the presence of slaves, and the almost exclusively rural character of the population, marked it as decisively southern.

Despite these significant local variations, the United States in the revolutionary era contained a general economic class structure which can be identified and described. There was a class of dependent laborers most of whom lived in the country. These men had no land and little personal property, usually less than £50 worth. About one in five whites belonged to this class, which therefore, as proletariats go, would have been extraordinarily small had it not been for the Negro slaves. These raised the proportion to over one-third of the adult men. A class of small independent property owners was the largest element in the population. Small farmers were the most numerous among this group. Negroes aside, they comprised perhaps 40 percent of the people. One out of ten whites was an artisan, and a scattering of other men—shopkeepers, inn-keepers, officials, some professional men and the like—also belonged to the middle class of small property owners, raising it to well over half of the white population. These people owned property worth anywhere from £50 to £500, averaging about £300 in real and £100 in personal estate. An intermediate, or upper middle class of substantial farmers, prosperous artisans, and professional men owned £500 to £1,000. Finally, some 10 percent of the whites at the top, consisting principally of large landholders and merchants, held, as a rule, £1,000 or more in personal property and the same amount in land. These men owned nearly half of the wealth of the country, including perhaps one-seventh of the country's people.

CHAPTER III

Income and Property

THE PROPERTY owned by revolutionary Americans ranged from zero to thousands of pounds, and although it is possible—indeed necessary—to divide the people into economic classes, stratifying them according to wealth, there really was no visible striation, no sharp gap separating the owner of £100 from him who had £200, nor was there a clustering around a given sum. The progression from class to class on the scale of wealth was not by steps, but by a ramp; it was a continuous and even flow. To progress might indeed require a significant change in status or occupation: from slave to free, landless laborer to farmer, apprentice to shop-owner, mariner to merchant. But in most occupations men could be found at nearly every level of wealth. There were farmers who owned a few pounds and those with thousands, penniless merchants and well-to-do artisans. Despite this variety, just as one can identify certain economic classes, generalizing from the tax and probate records, so it is possible to associate certain amounts of property with particular occupational groups: assign typical levels of wealth to farmer, doctor, blacksmith. So also the incomes of the people, various though they are, permit us to describe the earnings of laborer, lawyer, and planter.

Lowest on the economic scale was, of course, the slave. The slaves might have some very small amounts of personal property and even, though rarely, a little income. They occasionally received tips, and those who were skilled workers (such as barbers, waggoners, or shoemakers) may actually have expected some payment for services rendered to persons other than their masters.[1] They some-

---

[1] Louis B. Wright and Marion Tinling, eds., *Quebec to Carolina in*

times had gardens in which they worked on Sunday, and which furnished food for their own use and perhaps even for sale.[2] They seem to have been able to gamble, fight cocks, and even buy a drink—there are protests especially in Charleston concerning their behavior.[3] One northern house servant was given £40 and his freedom by a will, but we read that "Titus cares not, as he gets money apace, being one of the agents for some of the privateersmen, and wears cloth shoes, ruffled shirts, silk breeches and stockings, and dances minuets at Commencement; it is said he has made more profits as agent than Mr. Ansil Alcock or Dr. Whitaker by their agencies."[4] This was certainly an extraordinary, perhaps a unique, case. In general the evidence is rather that slaves had no property except what the master allowed, and as a rule no income.

Indentured servants were in the same position as slaves, temporarily. Like the slaves, they too were occasionally allowed a little property which might produce a small income, or at least make them more comfortable; but normally they earned no money during their term and probably owned no property.[5]

There is ample information concerning the wages of agricultural labor, but the facts differ from place to place,

---

1785–1786 . . . (San Marino, California, 1943), 258; Hunter Dickinson Farish, ed., *Journal and Letters of Philip Vickers Fithian, 1773–1774* (Williamsburg, 1943), 121, 128; diary of Francis Taylor, 1786–1795, May 30, 1788, University of N.C. Lib.

[2] For example, Fithian, *Journal*, 128; "Informations Concerning the Province of North Carolina etc. (1773)," N.C. *Hist. Rev.*, III (1926), 616 (this however was propaganda). The Maryland Senate in 1784 voted to allow slaves to earn money by working on holidays. *Journals*, Dec. 30.

[3] *The South Carolina Gazette*, August 27, 1772; Journals of the South Carolina House of Representatives, August 6, 1783.

[4] Fitch Edward Oliver, ed., *The Diary of William Pynchon of Salem* (Boston, 1890), 103.

[5] Abbot Emerson Smith, *Colonists in Bondage, White Servitude and Convict Labor in America, 1607–1776* (Chapel Hill, 1947), 291.

from time to time, with the type of work being done, and with the individual. The daily wage in New England before the Revolution averaged about 2s currency, or 1s 8d sterling per day, "not found"—that is, when the laborer was not given food or lodging. After the war wages rose to nearly 3s currency per day, or 2s 3d sterling. Two shillings sterling per day is, therefore, a general average for the period. The variation was considerable. One employer paid anywhere from 1/6 up to 3/ for general farm work before the Revolution and 2/4 to 3/6 after it.[6] Theoretically the average laborer, if he worked six days a week all year, might have earned £30 sterling before the Revolution and £45 after it. But actually this income was sporadic, not regular, for the worker was employed during the planting season or at harvest time or upon some other exceptional occasion. When he was hired by the month or year the wage was much lower because the work was steady and because he was usually "found": would receive board and room. For example, according to one source, daily wages in New England were 2s 7d, but if the man were hired by the month he received between 1/3 in the winter and 2/ during the summer. As a rule, "found" was considered to be worth about a shilling per day. The yearly wage averaged about £18 currency in New England, varying from £10 to £24, found.[7]

[6] Dr. Thomas Williams account book (Deerfield, Mass.), N.Y. Hist. Soc. The symbol "/" was a common and convenient substitute for "shilling." 1/6 therefore means one shilling sixpence. In this chapter the difficulties presented by the various values of money become very great. Where the currency used is not specified, it is that of the original source, presumably lawful money. I have translated into sterling, the common denominator, when this seemed necessary.

[7] Percy Wells Bidwell and John I. Falconer, *The History of Agriculture in the Northern United States, 1620–1860* (Washington, 1925), 118; Richard B. Morris, *Government and Labor in Early America* (New York, 1946), 128, n. 7; *The Connecticut Gazette* (New Haven),

Rural workers received about the same in the Middle Colonies, with the same wide variation. The least skilled laborers received as little as 1/6 per day, but better workers were paid 2/ to 3/ currency or even more, everything found, or another shilling not found. These wages were in local money which was worth less than in New England. Yearly earnings were anywhere from £12 to £15, found, to £27 sterling not found.[8] One Ulster County, New York, shopkeeper paid a neighbor £2 a month for general work, which would amount, in a year, to £24 currency or £13 sterling; and a Pennsylvania farmer hired a laborer for £30 per year (£18 sterling), washing included, "and he to make up for Lost Time or Sickness."[9] The ambitious young man could venture to the New York frontier and hire himself out to an innkeeper or miller for 55/ to £3 per month, thereby earning £33 to £36 currency annually.[10] Wages for unskilled labor seem to have been a little lower farther south, seldom exceeding 2s sterling per day, and varying from £14 to £18 per year. Western employers had higher labor costs, whereas in the older sections Negro competi-

Feb. 7, 1767 (optimistic); Joshua Barker Account Book 1761–1780, Oct. 14, 1762, March 9, 1780, Conn. Hist. Soc.; Ebenezer Dorr Account Book, 1772, Mass. Hist. Soc.

[8] Peter Kalm reported that £16 to £20 currency, found, was usual in Pennsylvania. Adolph B. Benson, ed., *Peter Kalm's Travels in North America* (New York, 1937), 204–205.

[9] Benjamin Snyder Account Book, vol. II, 1775, N.Y. Hist. Soc.; James Coultas Account Book, 1761–1762, The Joseph Downs Manuscript Library, The Henry Francis du Pont Winterthur Museum, Winterthur, Delaware (shelf list 61.64 and 61.65). This is the most informative single source for wages in Pennsylvania. The author of *American Husbandry* believed that "an able bodied man" would earn £10 to £16 sterling a year (p. 121). This was the equivalent of about £17 to £25 currency, presumably found. Interesting data is furnished by Arthur C. Bining, *Pennsylvania Iron Manufacturing in the Eighteenth Century* (Harrisburg, 1938), 119–124.

[10] Richard Smith, *A Tour*, 34.

tion kept wages down. Slaves could be hired for £10 a year and cost by the day 1/ or 1½/ before the war.[11]

As long as the worker remained healthy, single, and steadily employed, he could accumulate enough property to set himself up independently, for his wants above food and lodging were few. A good number, as will presently be seen, rose into the class of small farmers. Others did not; and their fate is shown by probate records.

Every series of inventories included men identified as "Labourers." With few exceptions they ranked at the bottom of the economic scale, owning property worth less than £50. Rarely indeed did they own land: for example, about one out of five "labourers" in Chester County, Pennsylvania had real estate. In addition to the men thus identified in the records, there were many others whose occupation is not given and who owned less than £50 or £100. Since artisans and farmers were usually designated as such, or are discovered by the nature of their possessions, most of the poor men who cannot be identified must have been laborers. For example, in New Jersey during the 1760's, 4 percent of the men, occupations unknown, died with less than £20 and another 6 percent had less than £50. Also of unknown occu-

---

[11] William Lenoir Papers, 1787, U. of N.C. Lib.; John C. Fitzpatrick, ed., *The Diaries of George Washington 1748–1799* (4 vols., Boston and New York, 1925), I, 338; Jones Family Papers, vol. 12 (1762), Lib. Cong.; *South Carolina Gazette and General Advertiser*, Nov. 4, 1783; Allen D. Chandler, comp., *The Colonial Records of the State of Georgia*, XIX, part 2 (Atlanta, 1911), 25–26. Wages rose after the war. *ibid.*, 258–259. White laborers' wages: Marion Tinling and Godfrey Davies, eds., *The Western Country in 1793 Reports on Kentucky and Virginia by Harry Toulmin* (San Marino, California, 1948), 39, 43, 50; Freeman H. Hart, *The Valley of Virginia in the American Revolution 1763–1789* (Chapel Hill, 1942), 20; Diary of Francis Taylor, 1786–1795, U. of N.C. Lib.; James Brooke Account Books, Md. Hist. Soc. Free Negroes in Maryland received £18 to £25 per year. The figure is presumably currency, equal to £11 to £15 sterling. James M. Wright, *The Free Negro in Maryland* (New York, 1921), 161.

pations were more than 6 percent of the men in Worcester County. Their estates were worth less than £50 and virtually all of them were landless. In Virginia, 9 percent of the men likewise were of unidentified vocations and were poor. The evidence indicates that about half of the laboring class (other than indentured servants and slaves) were worth less than £50 when they died. The rest did own more property, once in a while over £100, occasionally a little land. These men were moving up in the economic scale, and it may be remarked that when half of the free rural laborers are able to accumulate property, the economic class order is certainly fluid, and opportunities to rise are good.

Fewer urban workers saved as much. Wages were about the same as in the country (even women could earn £12 to £15 upon occasion) but there were two factors which hindered the city laborer from acquiring property: periodic unemployment, and the greater temptation to spend money, especially on clothes.[12] Therefore the urban center such as Boston contained a far higher proportion of poor workers than did the rural areas—indeed three times as many men there left less than £50, and the same was true of Charleston. Probably unemployment was the principal factor, for during many of the years before and after the Revolution when probate records were examined (1764–1771, 1782–1788) there was a depression. Nevertheless some city workers did acquire property.

Mariners resembled laborers in economic status. Their

[12] Account Book of Benjamin Clarke, Winterthur Museum shelf list 58.6; *New Hampshire Gazette,* Feb. 20, 1767; *Md. Hist. Mag.,* XXXVIII (1938), 186–187. Wages in general, see Richard B. Morris, "Labor and Mercantilism in the Revolutionary Era," in Richard B. Morris, ed., *The Era of the American Revolution* (New York, 1959), 92; McRobert, *Tour,* 9; *American Husbandry,* 137; Victor S. Clark, *History of Manufacturers in the United States 1607–1860* (Washington, 1916), 156; Smith, *Colonists in Bondage,* 27–28.

wages varied from £1.5 per month to £3.12, but £2.8 was usual. This was the equivalent of about 1/6 a day found, or 2/6 not found (lawful money).[13] If employment had been continuous, the yearly income would have exceeded that of city workers by 50 percent, but actually their work was sporadic. The majority of mariners accumulated no property. In Boston, nearly four out of five left no real estate when they died, and the same proportion owned less than £50 in total property.[14] Charleston mariners were little more fortunate. Portsmouth, New Hampshire, had many seamen who likewise were men of small property: their median holding was £20 to £25 sterling. The fortune-hunter did well to stay at home. Still, some did improve their economic status. One finds seamen with shops, land, and property worth some hundreds of pounds—there was one in Boston worth £800 before the war and another with the same amount after it. These men were referred to as mariners, though they apparently had retired from the sea and perhaps had acquired their means on shore. Those sailors who remained before the mast might advance in economic position if they became skilled. In 1785 the merchant Caleb Davis paid his seamen £2.8 per month, his mates £3.6, and his master £5. An occasional captain might make even more, venture goods, set up shop, and retire with a fortune in commerce.

The incomes earned by artisans and mechanics cannot be

---

[13] U.S. Department of Labor, Bureau of Labor Statistics, Bulletin 499, *History of Wages in the United States from Colonial Times to 1928* (Washington, 1929), 97; "The Commerce of Rhode Island," vol. 1, Mass. Hist. Soc., *Collections*, 7 series ix (1914), 117; Morris, *Government and Labor*, 238; Caleb Davis Papers, vols. 10–12, Mass. Hist. Soc. Wages in the South may have been lower. Arthur Middleton, *Tobacco Coast* (Newport News, 1953), 278.

[14] Over fifty mariners left inventoried estates during the years examined.

precisely determined, but their general economic status was favorable. Complaints of low wages were, indeed, heard particularly during times of depression.[15] Southern artisans objected to Negro competition; skilled craftsmen sometimes had difficulty collecting their wages; while employers lost by bad debts.[16] Some concluded that agriculture was more profitable or more congenial.[17] But the weight of evidence is that the pay was good and opportunities excellent. One observer wrote (with exaggeration) that the artisans could save money whereas government officials could not.[18] Even in the mid 1780's wages were high, yet master craftsmen could afford to pay them and still make enough to be accused of ruining the country by buying expensive clothes.[19] Certainly their income greatly exceeded that of ordinary laborers; whereas the latter seldom made much money, the artisans were generally prosperous.[20] One traveller wrote that he met a mason "who is now set down on good Estate and rides in his Chair every Day." [21] Wash-

[15] For example, "Probus," *N.Y. Journal*, Nov. 19, 1767, supplement.

[16] Carl Bridenbaugh, *The Colonial Craftsman* (New York, 1950), 153–154. Numerous account books testify to these losses.

[17] *The Norwich Packet; or, the Chronicle of Freedom*, Aug. 18, 1785. William Plumer's father, a master cordwainer, quit that business and became a farmer. William Plumer Papers, Autobiography, p. 4, N.H. Hist. Soc. See also *The Connecticut Courant* (Hartford), Oct. 30, 1786; "Brutus," in *The United States Chronicle, Political, Commercial, and Historical* (Providence), Sept. 21, 1786; Bridenbaugh, *Craftsman*, 31.

[18] *Address to the Freeholders of New Jersey, on the Subject of Public Salaries* (Philadelphia, 1763).

[19] *The New York Gazetteer and the Country Journal*, Sept. 23, 1785; Thomas Rutherford to Messrs. Ormston, Blair, & Ormston, Richmond, April 24, 1785, Thomas Rutherford Letter Book, Va. Hist. Soc.; *New Hampshire Gazette*, Feb. 3, 1786.

[20] Timothy Dwight, *Travels in New-England and New-York* (4 vols., New Haven, 1821), I, 194; *The Weekly Monitor* (Litchfield), Sept. 17, 1787.

[21] "Diary of John Harrower, 1773–1776," *Am. Hist. Rev.*, VI (1900–1901), 98.

ington paid his joiners, masons, millers, and coopers well, offering transportation, good food, washing, and lodging besides; yet working conditions were so favorable in Baltimore during the 1780's that he had trouble finding men.[22] Newspapers frequently carried advertisements offering high pay to artisans. Such proposals came most often from the country or small towns, where skilled workers were needed and special enticements necessary.[23]

The income of those artisans who worked for wages

[22] Tench Tilghman wrote to Washington from Baltimore, "Such is the demand for Carpenters and Masons, that the Master Builders in those Branches who are settled here, in order to intice the new comers to give them a preference, will agree to release a four years indented servant at the expiration of one year and an half. And as it is usual for the owners of Ships to permit the servants to chuse their own Masters, you may suppose few or none of such as you want, even go out of this Town, but upon such terms as I have mentioned. Indeed there is something so alluring in a Town to people of that Class, that they would generally prefer it, with some disadvantages, to the Country." July 15, 1784, Washington papers, vol. 230, no. 102, Lib. Cong. The following year Washington hired a cooper who was promised a "comfortable Dwelling House & Garden near the said Mill, plentifull keeping for one Cow, a sufficient quantity of Fire Wood, deliver'd in due Season at the door, during the said term of two Years,—six hundred weight of good Pork, or equivalent in Beef & Pork, as the said Davenport may prefer, . . . to raise Poultry for his own Family use, . . ." and $200 in silver or gold for the two years. *ibid.*, vol. 233, no. 4. See also vol. 233, no. 2 and Washington's *Diaries*, 366; III, 137.

[23] Probably the first-rate workmen remained in the cities (McRobert, *Tour*, 9), while others not so skilled could obtain high wages by moving where a labor shortage existed. Weavers, fullers, blacksmiths, coopers, and joiners were especially in demand in the country. Examples are, *New Hampshire Gazette*, Jan. 16, 1787; *The Essex Gazette* (Salem), April 25, 1769; *The Maryland Journal, and Baltimore Advertiser*, Sept. 16, 1777; *The New York Journal, and the General Advertiser* (Poughkeepsie), Nov. 2, Dec. 1, 1778, Apr. 5, 1779; *Pa. Gazette*, Oct. 24, 1765, Jan. 3, 1771; *Virginia Gazette and American Advertiser* (Richmond), May 11, 1782 ("extraordinary encouragement" to one able to supervise a rope walk in North Carolina); Litchfield *Monitor*, March 15, 1785, Jan. 14, 1786.

varied greatly. On the average they earned two or three
times as much as did ordinary laborers. The wages of
carpenters were typical. The common carpenter earned as
little as 2/6 or 3/ per day. Housewrights received more,
averaging 3/ to 4/ sterling, while shipwrights made as much
as 4/6 sterling in Connecticut and 6/ or even higher in
South Carolina. Weavers and tailors were usually paid by
the piece rather than by the day. Their wages were slightly
below those of carpenters. Masons and smiths often earned
more. Therefore if a carpenter, for example, worked for
300 days he might receive anywhere from £45 to £90
sterling, not found, or £30 to £60, found. But such full
employment was unusual. Scattered sources indicate that
most artisans could expect from £25 to £30 sterling found
or £40 to £45 not found, though poor ones were paid as
little as £20 not found and first-rate men received as much as
£50 sterling found.[24] One master housewright actually

[24] See for South Carolina, Richard Walsh, *Charleston's Sons of
Liberty: A Study of the Artisans, 1763–1789* (Columbia, S.C., 1959),
143–145; [James Glen], *A Description of South Carolina . . .* (London,
1761), prices written in the margin of page 80 of the copy in the South
Caroliniana Library, Columbia, S.C. The managers of a "China Manu-
factory" attracted skilled workers from England by offering them one
and a half guineas a week for five years, which meant £82 sterling
per year; while a journeyman printer commanded as much as £100
currency (£60 sterling) "found," in Philadelphia. *The Pennsylvania
Journal; and Weekly Advertiser*, Nov. 11, 1772; *Pa. Gazette*, Apr. 27,
1785. The foremen of distilleries were paid at least £40 to £50 sterling.
Boston Evening Post, Aug. 8, 1763. For other examples see *The New
York Journal or, The General Advertiser* (New York), April 2, 1786,
supplement; *The New York Gazette; and the Weekly Mercury*, Jan.
29, 1770; *Pa. Journal*, Jan. 25, 1770; *Maryland Gazette*, Dec. 13,
1787; *The Columbian Herald, or the Independent Courier of South-
Carolina*, Nov. 20, 23, 1786; Morris, "Labor and Mercantilism," 97;
Bureau of Labor Statistics, *Bulletin* 499, p. 53; Conn. Hist. Soc., *Col-
lections*, xx (1923), 204; Nina Moore Tiffany and Susan I. Lesley,
Letters of James Murray Loyalist (Boston, 1901), 81; James Hill to
Washington, York County, May 14, 1772, in Stanislaus Murray Ham-

obtained a job in Charleston, S.C., for $50 (£15) per month, with "Suitable Victuals and Lodging." [25] The ordinary laborer, by contrast, averaged only £15 sterling found per year.

The foregoing figures apply to skilled workers hiring themselves out rather than to those artisans who had their own businesses, employed labor, and earned a profit not by wages but through the sale of finished products. Such entrepreneurs had a better chance of making a substantial income. One general estimate assumed that the "profits of the labour" of men engaged in agriculture or manufacturing was £30 annually.[26] Unfortunately almost no precise information is available concerning these profits. The great majority of the small manufacturers probably earned little more than the skilled wage workers, averaging perhaps £50 sterling. However the towns contained some large establishments which were much more profitable. Testimony was produced that the Boston distillery owned by a Loyalist was worth upwards of £500 a year; a Marblehead ropewalk also was reputed to return £500, and a printer supposedly made £300. These particular figures may be exaggerated, but such incomes are not improbable.[27] The evidence of tax lists and inventories demonstrate that those artisans who owned sizable businesses earned enough to acquire large estates. How-

ilton, ed., *Letters to Washington and Accompanying Papers* (5 vols., Boston, 1889–1901), IV, 128–129, Aug. 30, 1772, IV, 147; *Diaries of Washington*, I, 178n, 282, 399. All figures sterling unless otherwise indicated.

[25] Caleb Davis papers, vol. XII, March 1, 1785, Mass. Hist. Soc.

[26] *The Country Journal, and the Poughkeepsie Advertiser*, Sept. 16, 1788.

[27] Hugh Edward Egerton, ed., *The Royal Commission on the Losses and Services of American Loyalists 1783 to 1785* (Oxford, 1915), 229, 70, 312. These figures are sterling. I think that they are probably accurate.

ever the great majority not only of the journeymen but of the masters received incomes that were adequate but no more.

The inventories of some 800 artisans in five colonies and states prove that on the average they accumulated more property than did mariners, fishermen, soldiers, and common laborers, but less than farmers, professional men, or men in trade. Whereas the median personal estate of all men was £150 currency, that of the artisans was about £110. Farmers had almost twice as much property; merchants and shopkeepers four times as much. Tax lists confirm that in all parts of the country, whether rural or urban, most artisans had considerably less wealth than did farmers. Moreover as was to be expected they accumulated an even smaller proportion of real estate, for many of them did not own land but only rented a house. Although most artisans left moderate estates there were great variations. Some were found in every economic class. The less skilled or less fortunate owned very little property while others died rich. Carpenters, for example, ordinarily could expect to acquire an estate of £100 or £200 in personal property (hardly a fortune), but one out of five would not even leave £50 worth, while one in ten or so amassed £500—there are even carpenters whose personal estates exceeded £1,000.[28]

The economic prospects of an artisan depended, to some

[28] The following table presents the assessed value for tax purposes of estates in Philadelphia, 1769, Lower Delaware, Walnut, and Middle Wards.

	General	Artisans	Merchants
no tax	47%	44%	12%
£1–9	14½	23	27
£10–19	10	11	9
£20–49	11	9	15
£50–99	8	7	12
£100+	9½	5½	24

extent, upon his particular trade. Tailors are proverbially poor, and were so in fact. In the major cities such as Boston, where they sold expensive clothes to the rich and had a fairly reliable market, they fell only slightly below the average in wealth, but in the country they fared badly. Throughout the colonies, thirty-two of them left median estates of only £70, and they were always near the bottom of the tax lists.

Housewrights were just as poor in personal property but as might be expected they usually furnished themselves with dwellings, often of considerable value, so that their total wealth was about average. Cordwainers (shoemakers) were uniformly poor. Nearly half of them did not own their homes, whereas three-fourths of all artisans were homeowners. Coopers and masons seldom achieved even average estates, though there were exceptions, especially among the masons. Those artisans practiced trades which did not require expensive equipment, so that the person who had little capital could easily enter the field; nor were the finished products costly, so that profits were minimal. Probably housewrights and masons were especially vulnerable to depressions when construction declined.

Blacksmiths owned an average amount of property. Few of them were poor, for their work was essential in the country as well as in the city: there were more blacksmiths than any other sort of artisan. In rural areas they did not acquire wealth, but since their products were necessary the farmers paid them well, not as a rule in money but in kind and labor. A few smiths were well-to-do. In New Jersey and Pennsylvania the blacksmith might become an iron-master and, still calling himself "blacksmith," might leave over £1,000 in personal property. Even in rural Worcester County one was worth £900 and earned the title "gentleman." However many such men probably obtained their capital from agriculture or trade and entered the iron business as capitalists rather than as artisans.[29]

The property of shipwrights varied greatly. Some of them were nothing more than rather poorly paid hired workers, but others were independent artisans owning shipyards, who employed other laborers. Such men were more prosperous though none became wealthy. "Carpenters" were more often identified specifically as shipwrights, housewrights, and the like, the term itself being commonly used in New Jersey and South Carolina but rarely in New England. Their property was of average value. Weavers belonged to the same category, seldom becoming well-to-do.

The artisans hitherto discussed usually had small incomes and acquired less property than the average man. According to the Suffolk probate records, about one in five died without any real estate. Their total wealth, real and personal, was ordinarily not over £230 compared with a general mean of £325. Of more than one hundred men who followed these trades, only five left estates of £1,000.

However artisans did exist who achieved a much greater degree of success. These men were almost invariably engaged in a business requiring considerable capital—men whose financial resources were necessarily large, and many of whom might more properly be called manufacturers than artisans. Distillers, tanners, and ropemakers are the most numerous examples. Goldsmiths and sugar refiners also were

[29] Pennsylvania founders (the most highly paid iron workers) earned £12 per month for eight or nine months and a daily wage for odd jobs the rest of the year. Probably their annual income was between £120 and £150. This figure is apparently currency and is equivalent to £72 to £100 sterling. Managers received £70 to £120, again presumably currency. The income was a good one but did not permit the acquisition of substantial property. Bining, *Pennsylvania Iron Manufacturing*, 119–120.

usually well-to-do. The personal property owned by such men averaged about £300—two and a half times the usual amount left by artisans, and twice the average for Americans generally. Their total property, to judge from twenty-eight Bostonians, ordinarily exceeded £500, and one-third had estates of £2,000. A Dorchester tanner left £3,186 lawful money, including £1,484 worth of real estate and notes due to him of £1,238. Isaac Gridley, Esq., owned a ropewalk in Boston with assets of £2,810 and liabilities of £534. Andrew Henshaw, distiller, also an Esquire, died in Boston with £2,694 worth of property; while Zachariah Johonnot, Esquire, distiller, owned real estate in the city valued at nearly £4,000 and Edward Carnes, ropemaker, left almost as much. The inventory of Capt. William Downes Cheever, Boston sugar baker, totalled £5,756, including stock worth £2,243, £263 in other personal property, and real estate estimated at £3,250.[30] These men still referred to themselves as artisans, but they had risen far above the usual artisan class and were entering the ranks of the economic elite.

The economic status of millers was comparable to that of the prosperous artisans. The probate records, as far as they have been examined, do not reveal a poor one. Usually they had £100 or £200 in personal property and often they had very substantial fortunes. Millers and millwrights were everywhere in demand and were certain of a steady income.[31] They were nearly always able to acquire land, sometimes obtaining it as part of the mill right. Millers received a percentage of the grain which they ground, so that they were certain of their pay; they were also assured of steady employment. So essential and profitable were mills that well-to-do farmers often built them. Robert Carter's

---

[30] Caleb Davis Papers, vol. 14a, Feb. 1788, Mass. Hist. Soc.
[31] Brissot de Warville, *New Travels,* 188.

cost £1,450 (Virginia currency) and was calculated to grind 25,000 bushels of wheat a year.[32] Therefore either millers became large landowners or large landowners became millers. Saw mills were just as necessary and probably as profitable as corn or grist mills. Mill owners ranked high among the propertied men of most communities. Thus in Goshen, Connecticut, where the median amount assessed for tax purposes in 1783 was £33, the millers declared £146, £110, £109, £98 (an "Esquire"), £97, £75, £62, £56, £55, and £50. Probably most of these men were primarily farmers, but the distinction is one of degree.

The artisans and mechanics clearly did not comprise a uniform economic class. Some received no more than a living wage, and suffered from occasional unemployment. Such men acquired very little property and remained dependent wage-workers. On the other hand a few owned large business organizations, commanded considerable capital, hired workers, became well-to-do, and achieved social recognition. Despite these divergences, generalization is possible: the great majority belonged to the middle income groups, owning personal property of £100 or so and real estate worth twice that amount. As a whole they ranked below the farmers in their economic status, but belonged to the same general class of small property holders. Within urban society they were clearly distinguished from the laborers and mariners below them, while above them were the merchants and professional men.

The income and wealth of men engaged in commerce was similarly diverse. In roughly ascending scale, these were the peddlers, traders, shopkeepers, and merchants; or, in a different sequence, seamen, captains, and merchants. Innkeepers may also be considered in the same category, while

[32] Fithian, *Journal and Letters*, 91.

many artisans were also retailers who might even become wealthy merchants.

At the bottom of the mercantile economic order were the peddlers. Peddling was with few exceptions a business for young men, mostly of New England origin.[33] There were a lot of them: in 1772 the Treasurer of New York sold licenses to twenty-two and stated that many were trading contrary to law.[34] The evidence concerning the profits which they made is conflicting. Settled storekeepers complained that their business was injured by the intruders, and before the Revolution laws were passed licensing or even prohibiting "hawkers, pedlars, and petty chapmen." [35] During the war they were accused of profiteering and even of making fortunes: one man was reputed to have started with a hogshead of rum and ended with £5,000.[36] In the 1780's Vermonters asserted that they were responsible for the money shortage by selling their unnecessary trifles for cash.[37] But when we confront the individual peddler we find him a poor man. Men who were unfitted for farming by ill health or the loss of a limb took to the road, and often were ruined by the trade. Usually they travelled only until they found an opportunity to settle down, or were married and perforce rooted.[38] Among the eighteen peddlers who

[33] Richardson Wright, *Hawkers & Walkers in Early America* (Philadelphia, 1927), 21–22, 27.

[34] *New York Gazette and Mercury*, June 18, 1772.

[35] J. H. Trumbull and Charles Hoadly, eds., *The Public Records of the Colony of Connecticut . . .* (15 vols., Hartford, 1850–1890), XII, 356, XIII, 364–365. Restrictive legislation was also enacted in Virginia, New Jersey, Maryland, Delaware, and Pennsylvania. Massachusetts joined these states after the war.

[36] *The Independent Chronicle* (Boston), Dec. 23, 1779; *The Connecticut Journal* (New Haven), Nov. 12, 1777.

[37] *Vermont Gazette*, March 6, 1784.

[38] *Pub. Rec. Conn.*, XIII, 64, 227; Marquis de Chastellux, *Travels in North-America, in the Years 1780, 1781, and 1782* (2 vols., London, 1807), I, 342–344; Wright, *Hawkers*, 21–22.

took out licenses in New York, only four had a cart, six had one horse, and eight were on foot.[39] When they died, their inventories revealed them to be at the very bottom of the economic scale: in South Carolina one had nothing but a horse, book debts, and dry goods worth in all £180 currency (£26 sterling), while another left goods worth £229.5, one horse, a saddle and bridle valued at £60.2.6, £28.2 in wearing apparel, and £56.6.2 in cash—a total of about £53½ sterling.

From peddler to country or city shopkeeper was a large step up. The distinctions between merchant, trader, and shopkeeper were sometimes vague in the minds of contemporaries and are therefore unclear today. A writer in the *New Jersey Gazette* began an article, "The merchant, or rather the shopkeeper (for alas! alas! it is devoutly to be wished that we had a competent number of the first denomination, before we are ground into atoms by Philadelphia and New York). . . ."[40] From this it seems that there was a difference, and that the distinction was one of function, not of location, since merchants could exist in New Jersey as well as elsewhere. What was this function? According to a Huntington County, New Jersey, grand jury, the shopkeeper was a retailer,[41] so that the difference was between the retailer and the wholesaler. There are other instances in which the terms merchant, shopkeeper, and trader were used as though they were dissimilar.[42] Yet merchants could become retailers and often did so without ceasing to be called merchants. One newspaper correspondent called himself "A Retail Merchant," and referred to

[39] *New York Gazette and Mercury*, June 8, 1772.
[40] May 24, 1784.
[41] Donald L. Kemmerer, *Path to Freedom: The Struggle for Self-Government in Colonial New Jersey 1703–1776* (Princeton, 1940), 281.
[42] Fithian, *Journal and Letters*, 39; *New Hampshire Gazette*, Oct. 20, 1787.

wholesale merchants who became retail merchants.[43] Others
used the words trader and merchant, or trader and shopkeeper, interchangeably, and sometimes the term trader
or merchant became generic.[44]

Under these circumstances any definition must be arbitrary. However, we may define as merchant one who imported and who characteristically sold at wholesale, though
he did sometimes retail goods to local customers.[45] This
definition agrees with that of Johnson's *Dictionary*, which
stated that a merchant was "one who trafficks to remote
countries" whereas a shopkeeper was "a trader who sells in
a shop; not a merchant who only deals by wholesale."
Trader was the generic term. At a much later date Noah
Webster, while acknowledging that in popular usage the
merchant was any trader buying or selling goods, believed
that he was properly a wholesaler engaged in foreign trade.
The importers were usually men of large property,[46] so
that the term "merchant" therefore carried with it an
assumption of wealth and merit and was clung to even in
misfortune or perhaps appropriated by parvenus who really
had no right to it. The shopkeeper at times equalled the
merchant in riches, but typically he was a small retailer who
only occasionally sold goods at wholesale. Merchants, by
the nature of their business, lived in those towns which had
an overseas trade, and it is a practical confirmation of our
definition that they are never found inland. Shopkeepers
might live anywhere. Merchants were engaged primarily in
commerce, secondarily in occupations connected with commerce (shipbuilding, banking, insurance) or resulting from
their accumulation of capital (speculation in land); shop-

[43] *New Haven Gazette*, May 26, 1785.
[44] *New York Journal*, Aug. 9, 1787; *Cumberland Gazette* (Portland),
Feb. 23, 1787.
[45] For example, *New Hampshire Gazette*, Oct. 29, 1775.
[46] *Norwich Packet*, March 11, 1784.

keepers often were artisans who began by selling their own manufactured products and who were apt to be mentioned in conjunction with "tradesmen." Indeed the two terms were sometimes used synonymously. Finally, the "trader," though at times referred to as anyone engaged in trade, was more often a country storekeeper, usually in towns some distance from the coast, and was frequently mobile.[47]

The income received by men in commerce is hard to determine. Account books are of little help, for they contain principally the payments made or debts owed by customers rather than the profits and losses of the firm. Probably country shopkeepers earned slightly more than the average farmer, while the great city merchant might command thousands of pounds. At one extreme was a storekeeper in the Shenandoah Valley who was paid £15 to £24 a year plus "keep." Some Virginia factors earned only £35 to £60, but the Virginian Thomas Jett offered to serve as a factor for £200, all expenses paid, while Peter Colt, a Hartford shopkeeper, received £500 lawful money annually, clear of personal expense, for superintending a counting house.[48] These men were employees rather than independent entrepreneurs, who presumably earned higher incomes at greater risk. John Norton, the Virginia merchant, received about £400 annually as his share of the company's profits. Loyalist merchants claimed losses ranging from £200 to £1,500 sterling annually.[49] Probably the average

[47] E.g., *New Hampshire Gazette*, Dec. 16, 1786. Probate records furnish many examples.

[48] Hart, *Valley of Virginia*, 20; Robert E. and B. Katherine Brown, *Virginia 1705–1786: Democracy or Aristocracy?* (East Lansing, 1964), 24; *Wm. and Mary Qtly.*, 1 series XVII (1908–1909), 23; Wadsworth and Carter to Peter Colt, Williamsburg, Dec. 30, 1781, Jeremiah Wadsworth Papers, Conn. Hist. Soc.

[49] Frances Norton Mason, ed., *John Norton & Sons Merchants of London and Virginia* (Richmond, 1937), 129; *Loyalist Claims*, 184, 288, 358, 380.

income of the established merchant was well over £500 sterling, while shopkeepers earned less than half of that sum.

The country "traders" and the "shopkeepers," whatever the difference between them might have been, accumulated equal amounts of property. At a time when the usual personal estate was worth £150, they owned nearly £300 and, according to Suffolk County probate records, about £800 in property of all sorts. Although a majority had wealth above the average, they did not constitute a single propertied class, for as many left estates of less than £100 as died with £500. Still, they clearly exceeded the artisans in wealth. Whereas very nearly half of the artisans owned less than £100, only some 20 percent of the shopkeepers left so little. The artisan in search of profits did well to open a store. The country shopkeepers as a rule had less property than did those in the city, but were usually more prosperous than their farmer neighbours. The Massachusetts assessment lists show that men who owned stock in trade consistently had more than an average amount of land. In Milford, Connecticut, the wealthiest taxpayer and largest landowner was a merchant. In Groton, where the median assessment was £33, the "shopkeepers or traders" had £129, £122, £104, £95, £70, £59, £51, and £50. The poor shopkeeper was certainly not unknown, but the typical trader was a man of substantial property.

Merchants similarly ranged from poor to rich. There were numerous instances of bankruptcy,[50] and some left no property whatever when they died, still clinging to the prestigeful name of their occupation. But these were decidedly exceptions: out of 151 probated estates in various

---

[50] For example, *Pub. Rec. Conn.*, XIV, 28–29, 34, 106, 110, 180, 224; *The Newport Mercury*, May 23, 1774 for one who lost £1,071 sterling in five years.

parts of the country, only fourteen were valued at less than
£100 in personal property, while 27 percent were worth
more than £2,000 and 43 percent left £1,000. A considerable majority owned £500. Naturally their total property
was worth even more. In Boston, although a few merchants
acquired no land, most of them owned over £400 in real
estate and more than a fourth held £1,000 worth. Merchants
of that city ordinarily left at least £1,000 in total real and
personal property, the median being £1,500. Forty percent
were worth £2,000 and one out of eight had an estate of
£5,000. In all sections of the country commerce offered the
best opportunity for success, and merchants stood at the
very top of the economic class structure.

One way to enter the ranks of the merchants, though it
was seldom successfully followed, was to become a ship's
captain, venture something on the voyages or save the commission from selling the merchants' goods, retire, and enter
into business. Every seaport had its ex-ship's captain turned
shopkeeper, or even plain mariners who turned to trade.
However the ships' captains were not as prosperous as one
might suppose from their title and responsibilities. Their
salaries were not remarkable: the most experienced master
might receive £8 per month, but £4 was more common.[51]
Most of them saved little. Out of over fifty inventories,
twenty-eight were valued at less than £100, so that as a
group the captains were scarcely better off than were the
artisans. Moreover most of the rest—80 percent of the total
—left less than £200. These figures are a little misleading,
for some men who were called merchants had once been
captains; but it is evident that very few seamen were on
their way up. Exceptions can be found. A Boston captain
with shop goods and the thirty-second part of a ship died

[51] Caleb Davis Papers, vol. 10–12, Mass. Hist. Soc.; Middleton, *Tobacco Coast*, 279.

worth £810. Another left an estate of £2,171, mostly in real property. Still another had an £1,196 estate including a brigantine. Similarly a Charleston, South Carolina, captain owned £837 in personal property including eleven slaves. More representative was the Bostonian who left £413.10 Old Tenor (about £60), part of which was 596 gallons of rum. One may suppose that he died happy, though poor.

The merchants paid their clerks no better than they did their captains. The wage varied from £40 to over £50 which, if not found, was little better than the earnings of artisans. However the job of clerk was probably a temporary one for the aspiring young merchant. He was often the son of another merchant serving an apprenticeship rather than a permanent employee.

Innkeepers too were engaged in commerce and some-times sold products other than liquor and food. The prices charged were often regulated by the government, but the hostlers seem to have done well, receiving much and giving little, according to most travellers. Anyone who owned a tavern necessarily had a certain amount of property, and their position in the community, judged by their economic status, was somewhat above average. They certainly earned more money than did most artisans, and more than ships' captains too. Their median personal property was about £180, and they were found at every level of wealth except the highest. Most owned at best a couple of hundred pounds, but in pre-war South Carolina an innkeeper died with ten slaves, £2,722 currency in personal property (which brought £2,638.14.10 at sale) and £3,471 in debts receivable—the total being £6,193 currency, or nearly £900 sterling. The situation in Groton, Connecticut, was typical except for the numbers of men involved. Here, when the general median assessment was £33, all but one out of fifteen innkeepers were rated at a larger amount. Tavern owners of

Chester County, Pennsylvania, had considerably more property than the average. One, indeed, owned 500 acres and became an Esquire. Thus the innkeeper might be a man of some economic importance in the community: there were, in fact, many professional men who made less money.

Schoolteachers in particular were poorly paid unless they were located in a major city or taught in a college. Low salaries were characteristic even of New England, where learning was supposed to be worthy of reward. According to a newspaper article, many Connecticut schools before the Revolution paid as little as 40s to 50s per month, because the "vulgar" believed that men of learning were not entitled to any better pay than that of a common laborer.[52] The writer's hope that salaries would be doubled was not fulfilled, for a decade later another Connecticut correspondent remarked that in many places 40s per month was still the salary and, he added, the people received a proportionately poor education.[53] Country towns paid anywhere from £20 to £75, the lowest salaries being in the subsistence farm towns and perhaps found. Teachers with minimum incomes might be allowed to charge tuition fees. The existence of "Dame Schools," which paid even poorer wages, depressed incomes. The schoolmaster in Epping, New Hampshire, received as little as $5 to $8 per month (£1.10 to £2.8) plus board.[54] Larger or more prosperous towns and cities in New England paid much more. Teachers at the secondary

[52] "Observer, Number VII," *The New London Gazette*, March 19, 1773.

[53] "Hortensilis," *The New Haven Gazette*, Jan. 20, 1785.

[54] Bureau Labor Stats., *Bulletin* 499, pp. 131–133; various salaries in Clifford K. Shipton, *Biographical Sketches of Those Who Attended Harvard College* . . . (vols. VI–XII of *Sibley's Harvard Graduates*, Cambridge and Boston, 1933–1962); Walter Herbert Small, *Early New England Schools* (Boston, 1914), 122–161; Lynn W. Turner, *William Plumer of New Hampshire 1759–1850* (Chapel Hill, 1962), 3.

or "grammar" schools were almost always young college graduates who received, on the average, £40.[55] Masters in pre-revolutionary Boston earned £100 plus certain other income (including private tutoring) which brought the total to perhaps £180. After the war they were paid, as a rule, about £200 plus a house. Bostonians felt that this was too high, and in 1785 salaries were reduced to below £200.[56] Ushers in the same schools earned only half as much, but their income was still above the average for teachers generally.[57]

Farther south the earnings also varied. The lowest salaries were paid to the young men, especially those who accepted positions in rural areas. Georgia schoolmasters earned as little as £23, while those in the Shenandoah Valley never received over £18 a year—and much of that was paid in kind. Similarly Luther Martin was paid £20 currency in a Maryland school. Probably these teachers were "found." [58] Devereaux Jarrett's school in western Virginia scarcely supported him, and he was hired for some years at £15.[59] As in New England, the prosperous commercial farm areas could pay higher salaries even at the elementary levels. The

[55] Clifford K. Shipton, "Secondary Education in the Puritan Colonies," *New England Quarterly*, VII (1934), 653–654.

[56] "A Friend to the Town," *The Massachusetts Centinel*, March 11, 1786.

[57] Sidney Kaplan, "The Reduction of Teachers' Salaries in Post-Revolutionary Boston," *New England Quarterly*, XXI (1948), 373–379; Robert Francis Seybolt, *The Public Schoolmasters of Colonial Boston* (Cambridge, 1939), 22–25, and *The Public Schools of Colonial Boston* (Cambridge, 1935), 80–81.

[58] Robert L. McCaul, "Education in Georgia During the Period of Royal Government 1752–1776," *Georgia Historical Quarterly*, XL (1956), 103–112, 248–259; Hart, *Valley of Virginia*, 29; Willard S. Elsbree, *The American Teacher* (New York, 1939), 88–89.

[59] Douglass Adair, ed., "The Autobiography of the Reverend Devereaux Jarratt, 1732–1763," *Wm. and Mary Qtly.*, 3 series IX (1952), 363–376.

master of a school in Dorchester County, Maryland, received £20 currency "together with the Benefit arising from the Scholars," which meant perhaps £35 sterling all told; and he had besides the use of a plantation with a large brick house. Towns could offer even better positions. A New York schoolmaster taught thirty poor children for £60 (probably currency) and the use of a house and garden; he was also allowed to instruct other children and keep school in the evening.[60]

Academies—private schools at the secondary level—paid much higher salaries, especially to trained men. Ushers, who were usually young men just beginning their careers, received less than the masters, yet they could earn £30 sterling plus another £20 or more from fees, while the master was paid as much as £250. The man who knew Latin might expect 50 percent more than the teacher who knew only English.[61] A typical academy in Fredericksburg, Virginia, offered £100 a year plus £35 for board to its professor of humanities and £75 plus board to the professor of mathe-

---

[60] *Pa. Gazette*, Aug. 30, 1764; Hugh Hastings, ed., *Ecclesiastical Records. State of New York*, VI (Albany, 1905), 4,260–4,261.

[61] Thomas Woody, *Early Quaker Education in Pennsylvania* (New York, 1920), 211, 243; *Pa. Journal*, March 9, 1774; "John Penn's Journal," *Pa. Mag. Hist. Biog.*, III (1879), 288; *The Pennsylvania Packet, and Daily Advertiser*, April 4, 1774; *Va. Gazette* (Alexandria), May 4, 1786; *Rivington's New York Gazetteer . . .* , June 1, 1775; William Webb Kemp, *The Support of Schools in Colonial New York by the Society for the Propagation of the Gospel in Foreign Parts* (New York, 1913), 56, 101–106; Edgar W. Knight, ed., *Documentary History of Education in the South before 1860* (5 vols., Chapel Hill, 1949–1953), I, 92, 95, 127, 171. Robert Middlekauff finds that New England grammar-school teachers made enough to support them quite easily if they were young and unmarried. However the pay was so low that teaching was seldom a career, and the young men quickly entered business or a profession. *Ancients and Axioms: Secondary Education in Eighteenth-Century New England* (New Haven, 1963), 23, 175, 178, 180.

matics. In addition they collected one guinea and one-half guinea per scholar, respectively, as entrance fee.[62] The best income was made by directors of academies, who collected tuition fees and hired tutors. If the school attracted enough students the headmaster might boast, as did one in Philadelphia, that he "had sufficient to support me in easy circumstances." Perhaps this was the immigrant of whom Benjamin Rush wrote, "He will have his choice of two or three public schools each of which will be worth not less than £150.0.0 sterling a year to him."[63] The majority of teachers, however, earned just enough to sustain them—if that. Philip Freneau, the poet and future newspaper editor, quit his Maryland school in part because he received only £40, and the Newbern schoolmaster who was paid £60 sterling counted himself exceptionally fortunate.[64]

Wealthy southern landowners often hired college graduates to teach their children. These positions paid well, since the tutor lived at the planter's expense and could save almost the entire salary. Philip Fithian was promised £60 currency (£35 sterling) and actually was paid £40 sterling to teach Colonel Robert Carter's children, with all accommodations, use of the library, and a servant. This was a little above the average income for tutors, which was probably about £30 sterling.[65]

[62] The guinea was worth 21 shillings sterling. *The Virginia Herald, and Fredericksburg Advertiser,* June 19, 1788.

[63] Andrew Brown to Jaspar Yeates, Philadelphia, Sept. 3, 1783, Jaspar Yeates Papers, Correspondence, 1781–1788, Hist. Soc. Pa.; Rush to William Cullen, Philadelphia, Sept. 16, 1783, L. H. Butterfield, ed., *Letters of Benjamin Rush. Volume I: 1761–1792* (Princeton, 1951), 311.

[64] Philip Freneau to James Madison, Somerset County in Maryland, Nov. 22, 1772, William T. Hutchinson and William M. E. Rachal, eds., *The Papers of James Madison,* i (Chicago, 1962), 77; *Col. Rec. N.C.,* vii, 98.

[65] Fithian, *Journal and Letters,* 8; Brown, *Virginia,* 27; R. H. Lee to Arthur Lee, Chantilly, April 5, 1770, James Curtis Ballagh, ed.,

Professors in colleges naturally received more than did other teachers. Harvard paid £100 in 1764—but even this was scarcely more than the clerk of the House earned, and one-eighth the salary of a Superior Court Judge. In 1766 Yale paid its President £150, its Professor of Divinity £113.6.8 (both with houses), and its tutors £65 and £57. Professors at the College of Philadelphia received about £180 sterling after the war. Those at the College of New Jersey earned less, those in St. John's College, Annapolis, somewhat more.[66] Tutors or assistants received a third or a fourth as much as professors. These salaries permitted one to save, but were far less than the sums earned in other professions. In general the humble schoolmaster survived; the more fortunate maintained themselves in decency; but none accumulated wealth.

Probate records and tax lists prove that the average schoolmaster left less property than did most artisans— indeed the poor teacher joined the poor tailor at the bottom of the economic scale among those who had some skill. Most teachers left less than £100 in personal property, the median being £75. Few had over £200 and only a handful of college trained men, mostly professors, acquired moderate estates of £500. There were many like John Miles, schoolmaster of Lunenburg, Virginia, who had no land, or slaves, or horses, or cattle in 1765, and moved west to Montgomery

The Letters of Richard Henry Lee (2 vols., New York, 1911, 1914), I, 44; *The Virginia Gazette* (Purdie), July 4, 1777; Jones Family papers, box 17, Lib. Cong.; *Va. Gazette* (Dixon and Hunter), Dec. 26, 1777; Thomas Bolling Diary, June, 1793, Va. Hist. Soc.

[66] *Pub. Rec. Conn.*, XII, 513; Johann David Schoepf, *Travels in the Confederation* (trans. and ed. by Alfred J. Morrison, 2 vols., Philadelphia, 1911), I, 74; Andrew Burnaby, *Travels through the Middle Settlements in North America, in the years 1759 and 1760 . . .* (ed. by Rufus Rockwell Wilson, New York, 1904), 104; J. Hall Pleasants, ed., *Archives of Maryland*, LVIII (Baltimore, 1941), 310; *Md. Hist. Mag.*, XXIX (1934), 305.

County, where after the Revolution he still had no land, slaves, horses, or cattle; or James Rigby of Upper Chichester, Pennsylvania, a landless teacher who turned up in three other townships between 1765 and 1780, finally settling down with seven acres. For most men, teaching was not a career but a poorly paid temporary job.

Ministers were much better rewarded. Although clergymen sometimes were obliged to turn farmer or merchant to support themselves, their income ordinarily was sufficient to maintain them in the profession, while the greater respect in which they were held also made their calling more attractive than that of the teacher. In New England there was a great range of salaries. Small country towns paid as little as £40 currency, but of course this included a house, some land, often firewood, and fees. Larger towns paid over £100. A Boston minister received, in 1767, a base salary of £1,040 Old Tenor (about £150 lawful), £390 additional pay, nearly £200 in wood, £64 in marriage fees, and £126 worth of presents, or a total of about £260 currency. The Anglican minister at the same time was receiving not quite £200 sterling.[67] Incomes such as these were not unheard of elsewhere in New England, but the average was more nearly £70, plus other benefits which raised the total to perhaps £100. Beginning ministers expected their low initial salary to be sweetened by a "settlement" of a hundred pounds or more.[68] Salaries in the middle states varied greatly. A New Jersey minister received only £52.10, but Samuel Seabury (the future bishop) earned £128 sterling in addition to about £80 from a school, while Jacob Duche's income was

[67] A. Eliot [?] diary in a copy of Nathaniel Ames, *An Astronomical Diary*, 1767, catalogued under Samuel West, Mass. Hist. Soc.; Anne Rowe Cunningham, ed., *Letters and Diary of John Rowe Boston Merchant 1759-1762, 1764-1779* (Boston, 1903), 159.

[68] Data gathered principally from Shipton's *Harvard Graduates;* see also *Loyalist Claims*, 121, 154-155, 191, 223.

at least £300 sterling.[69] The average income probably exceeded that of the New Englander.

Southern clergymen usually earned much more. In 1769, Maryland's Anglican ministers were paid, on the average, £300 sterling. Virginia's clergy received 16,000 pounds of tobacco, which usually amounted to £160 or £200, together with 200 or 300 acres and a house which combined might be worth another £35 or so.[70] North Carolina was a poorer colony, but prior to the Revolution she could count on help from the Society for the Propagation of the Gospel in Foreign Parts. Ministers received £133.6.8 proclamation money (£100 sterling) with a glebe of 300 acres or £20 cash. They also charged 20s for a marriage by license, 5s for marriage by banns, 40s for a funeral, and fees for administering the sacraments (such as 15s for a baptism).[71] Charleston clergymen earned as much as £300 to £400; the Savannah church paid about the same, and even in Augusta a minister was given £75 by the Society. Although country districts paid less than did the towns, even in the rural South the clergy received twice the income of a New England minister.[72]

Ministers did not always obtain what they had been promised, and the annals of many a church testify to a prolonged struggle with the congregation over back salaries. The Connecticut legislature, for example, found that the Canaan minister was in debt to nearly the whole value of his estate, and ordered the town to pay him four years' back

[69] Burnaby, *Travels*, 48–50; *Loyalist Claims*, 357, 199, 204.

[70] Burnaby, *Travels*, 84; *Loyalist Claims*, 35, 268.

[71] *Col. Rec. N.C.*, XXIII, 660; *N.C. Hist. Rev.*, II (1925), 235, XXXII (1955), 5.

[72] Charles Woodmason, *The Carolina Backcountry on the Eve of the Revolution* (ed. by Richard J. Hooker, Chapel Hill, 1953), 70–76; C. G. Chamberlayne, *St. Paul's Parish*, 407; Knight, *Doc. Hist. Ed.*, I, 126–127; Hart, *Valley of Virginia*, 40–41.

salary of £80 a year. Jefferson was informed that because of the clergy's low incomes, "Fontaine has been almost starved; Andrews has quitted his Gown, he says, to avoid starving." [73] But most ministers were able to accumulate property above the general average. An Anglican clergyman in North Carolina complained that he had only two slaves while other ministers owned twenty.[74] In Dover, Delaware, the minister collected donations from two or three churches other than his own. With this money, a diarist wrote, "added to his Salaries & the Lucrative perquisites of Marriages Births & Burials he has already acquired a pretty & will I believe in time amass a Large Fortune." One Presbyterian minister in New York earned over £950 a year, so that "he lives in elegant style, and entertains company as genteely as the first gentlemen in the city." [75] Over fifty ministers throughout the country left personal estates averaging about £250—three times as much as the property of schoolmasters, and at least 50 percent above the general average. Yale's clerical graduates, according to the data supplied by the college's historians, left somewhat more.[76] Harvard-trained ministers did just as well, accumulating as a rule £600 worth of property, real and personal.

[73] *Pub. Rec. Conn.*, XIII, 323; John Page to Jefferson, Rosewell, Aug. 23, 1785, Boyd, ed., *Papers of Jefferson*, VIII, 428.
[74] *N.C. Hist. Rev.*, XXXII (1955), 7.
[75] "Journal of Benjamin Mifflin on a Tour from Philadelphia to Delaware and Maryland July 26 to August 14, 1762," ed. by Victor Hugo Palsits, N.Y. Pub. Lib., *Bulletin* 39 (1935), 437; William Parker Cutler and Julia Perkins Cutler, *Life, Journals and Correspondence of Rev. Manasseh Cutler* (2 vols., Cincinnati, 1888), I, 237.
[76] Franklin P. Dexter, *Biographical Sketches of the Graduates of Yale College with Annals of the College History* (3 vols., New York, 1885–1912). It is not always possible to determine whether currency or sterling is meant. The median of some 76 estates evaluated between 1740 and 1800 was about £280.

Suffolk County probate records show that ministers there were generally substantial rather than large property owners. Still, they usually left estates valued at over £500, being as a rule considerable land owners. Southern clergymen were paid more and acquired more. One South Carolina minister left a personal estate of £5,117 sterling, including 76 slaves, while another owned 70 slaves, a library of 300 volumes, and £24,549 currency (about £3,500 sterling).

The income of doctors varied more than did that of ministers but apparently averaged about the same. Even trained physicians made little in country towns. In Hartford, wrote Peter Colt, the practice would not support a family, so that one doctor decided to open an apothecary shop, as more profitable.[77] Perhaps doctors would have prospered had they been paid promptly, but they received little cash. One physician averaged only about £4 specie a year during a six-year period; while others complained that they did not receive one-third of what was due them.[78] The able and widely known Samuel Holten of Danvers, Massachusetts, estimated that his work was worth 7s per day, which would have brought him an income of £110, about the same as that of a well-situated clergyman, if he collected his money. Probably that sum was typical of the respectable small-town physician.[79] The earnings of some city doctors, however, were far greater, and exceeded the salaries of even the most

[77] Peter Colt to Jeremiah Wadsworth, Hartford, Dec. 28, 1783, Wadsworth Papers box 135, Conn. Hist. Soc.

[78] Robert Stanton Account Book, 1755–1783, Conn. Hist. Soc.; Dr. Thomas Williams, Account Book, N.Y. Hist. Soc.; La Rochefoucault-Liancourt, *Travels*, II, 39.

[79] Samuel Holten Papers, Lib. Cong. The managers of the Philadelphia Dispensary paid one doctor £100. *The Independent Gazetteer, or, the Chronicle of Freedom*, Jan. 2, 1787. An Ipswich, Massachusetts, Loyalist claimed a loss of £333 annually but testimony lowered this to £100. *Loyalist Claims*, 173.

highly paid clergymen. One Boston physician had an annual income of £700 sterling.[80]

Tax lists emphasize the predominantly middle-class character of the doctor's earnings and the low estate of many country practitioners. The only doctor in Goshen, Connecticut, in 1771 was assessed for £27 (one cow, two horses, four acres) as compared with a median of £40. In Milford, where the median was £50, the doctor's property was rated at £34. The £30 assessment in Winchester was below average and the New Town, New York, doctor paid taxes on £24, much less than the median of £40. One of the two doctors in Ashfield, Massachusetts, paid an assessment for only a horse, owning no other farm animals, no house, and no land; the other had a house, four acres, a cow, and two pigs, paying a very low tax. A Worcester physician in 1789 paid only his poll tax (he was boarding with a widow). The doctor of wealthy St. Paul's parish, South Carolina, had no land and only one slave, while in Prince Frederick, an upland parish, the doctor owned no land and no slaves.

These poor men were balanced by others who were among the most prosperous of their community. The Groton, Connecticut, physician, also a trader, was in the top 5 percent. The doctor in Fitzwilliam, New Hampshire, owned 200 acres, which placed him near the top. Hadley's doctor was one of the town's wealthy men. The same was true of the Concord, New Hampshire, doctor, while one in Concord, Massachusetts, had the second highest assessment.[81] Both extremes were exceptional. In most towns the doctors ranked well down from the top of the list but much farther

---

[80] Shipton, *Harvard Graduates*, IX, 429. Several Loyalists claimed between £500 and £800.

[81] Norton, *Fitzwilliam*, 180–185; Judd, *Hadley*, 423–424; *Concord Town Records*, 1732–1820 (Concord, N.H., 1894), 548–552.

from the bottom, owning perhaps three or four times the average amount of taxable property, on a level with the ministers, shopkeepers, and substantial farmers.

Probate records show the same wide variation. Side by side in a Suffolk County Will Book are a "physician" whose entire estate consisted of £4.2.9 in personal property, and a doctor whose books alone were worth four times as much, forming part of a £850 total inventory. Suffolk County doctors generally averaged about £400 in total property. Elsewhere, especially in South Carolina, they had considerably larger estates. In the country as a whole about 30 percent had £500 or more in personal property, and one out of five left less than £100, the median being about £280. Probably most of the wealthy doctors had college educations, whereas the poorer ones had little or none.

Information concerning the income and estates of lawyers is much more limited, partly because the records seldom identify them as such, and because they were fewer in number. But if the precision made possible by many illustrations is lacking, the general situation is clear enough: the law was the most profitable of all professions. Lawyers might earn ten times as much as did doctors and ministers, as much as all but the very wealthiest merchants and planters, with less risk, and greater odds in favor of acquiring and retaining fortunes. Thomas Burke of North Carolina studied medicine, practiced, and "made a proficiency equal if not superior to most gentlemen in these Climes." But he found "that in this Country it was not a Field in which the most plentiful Harvest might be reaped. I therefore determined to study Law which promised much more profit and yet less Anxiety." [82] Burke was correct. When

[82] To Mrs. Sydney Jones, c. 1778, Thomas Burke Papers, U. of N.C. Lib.

lawyers became bankrupt it was usually because, like James Wilson, they used the great profits of their profession to speculate in land.

Of course not every lawyer was rich. The New Haven, Connecticut, lawyer, Amos Botsford (Yale 1763) received from the British government £225 annually, which was his average annual clear income.[83] However, most lawyers of record made more than this. James Allen of Pennsylvania earned £300 to £400 in 1773, £600 in 1775, and would have increased this in 1776 but for the war. Jaspar Yeates, as a beginning lawyer, earned about £35 per year per county court, attended in eight counties, and received income from other sources as well. Virginians complained about their small returns, but Paul Carrington earned nearly £600 in ten months and Arthur Lee, like Burke, turned from medicine to law because it was the "most lucrative and honorable" profession.[84] After the Revolution a French traveller in Virginia wrote, "The profession of a lawyer is here, as in every other part of America, one of the most profitable." John Marshall, he asserted, made during some years $4,000 to $5,000 (£1,200 to £1,500).[85] Yet this was less than the usual income in South Carolina, where lawyers earned more than £3,000 sterling a year. Josiah Quincy noted in his journal that Charlestown, Massachusetts, lawyers made £2,000 to £3,000 sterling annually. Small wonder that Governor Bernard of Massachusetts recommended a minimum salary of £500 for government attorneys or that South Carolina's

[83] Dexter, *Yale Graduates*, III, 10.

[84] "Diary of James Allen, Esq., of Philadelphia," *Pa. Mag. Hist. Biog.*, IX (1885), 183, 185; Diary, Yeates Papers, Hist. Soc. Pa.; Lucille Griffith, "English Education for Virginia Youth," *Va. Mag. Hist. Biog.*, LXXIX (1961), 7–27.

[85] La Rochefoucault-Liancourt, *Travels*, II, 38–39. See also John Caile Account Book, 1766–1770, and John Mercer Account Book 1736–1767, Mercer Papers, both in the Va. Hist. Soc.

House of Representatives allowed £1,800, plus expenses, to each of the men who digested the laws of the state.[86]

Such inventories as can be identified are uniformly of high value. Most instructive are those of the Yale graduates. Nearly half of the estates probated before 1800 were worth more than £2,000 and two-thirds were evaluated in excess of £1,000. All of the known lawyers' estates in South Carolina exceeded £2,000 in value—and this was only personal property. Obviously the majority of the lawyers were well-to-do and many were rich.

The earnings of government officials varied greatly. Many of the salaries were small, and their recipients either left little property or supplemented their earnings with other work. But on the whole the servants of King or people did well. The judges, treasurer, and secretary of Massachusetts earned £250 to £375 annually,[87] while the Governor earned about £2,300 before and £1,100 after the Revolution. Connecticut paid less, but even clerks made enough to bring protests from farmers: the member of one board was accused of earning 18s per day, "the whole being more than the nett proceeds of any ten farms in the state." [88] Rhode Island's clerks and other white collar employees of the legis-

[86] George R. Rogers, jr., *Evolution of a Federalist: William Loughton Smith of Charleston (1758–1812)* (Columbia, S.C., 1962), 123; Mass. Hist. Soc., *Proceedings*, XLIX (1915–1916), 447; Leslie J. Thomas, "Partisan Politics in Massachusetts During Governor Bernard's Administration 1760–1770," PhD. dissertation, University of Wisconsin, 1960, p. 553; Journal of the South Carolina House of Representatives, Feb. 4, 1784. Loyalists claimed anywhere from £100 to £2,000, averaging £500. *Claims*, 26, 40, 63, 86, 115, 119, 168, 175–177, 275, 282, 302, 311, 338.

[87] Salaries before the war were lower but fees and plural office holding raised them considerably. *The Boston Magazine*, Dec. 1786.

[88] "A Farmer," *The American Mercury* (Hartford), Aug. 27, 1787. If he worked the usual six day week, his total income was about £280.

lature charged 6/ per day, while her delegates to the Continental Congress received four times as much, or £435 annually.[89] Yet most of the other states paid their representatives considerably more. The Mayor of New York received nearly £600 in fees, while the states' special commissioners charged 16/ per day, equivalent to £240 per year. Pennsylvania's public officers earned between £400 and £2,000 after the war.[90] South Carolina's payroll was comparable, and those of North Carolina were nearly as large. Even the clerk of a superior court in Maryland was paid £100 before the Revolution, while sheriffs might collect £200 to £300, county clerks £115 to £250, and major officials perhaps £600. Henry Knox's salary as Secretary of War was £700 (which he called "but a slender support").[91] Judges received between £300 in the poorer states to £1,000 currency in Pennsylvania. Military officers in Connecticut and Rhode Island earned from £48 for lieutenants to £240 for generals, plus another £26 for billet, and of course, food. Other colonies paid higher sums. Such salaries generally were below the income of lawyers, but decidedly above the amounts received by other professsional men.

To turn from public officials to farmers is to move, on the average, far down the economic scale, but averages mean little with respect to a group so diverse. One would suppose that over 4,200 inventories would permit confident generalization concerning the property of the typical farmer; but in fact the median varied greatly from place to place, and farmers were found at every economic level

[89] *Rhode Island Acts and Resolves, passim,* and Feb. 1786, pp. 38–39.

[90] Memorandum of Feb. 28, 1788, James Duane Papers, N.Y. Hist. Soc.; *Independent Gazetteer,* Dec. 11, 1786.

[91] Donnell Maclure Owings, *His Lordship's Patronage: Offices of Profit in Colonial Maryland* (Baltimore, 1953), 30–34, 56–58, 67–71, 83; Knox to Washington, Boston, March 24, 1785, Knox Papers, XVIII, 11, Mass. Hist. Soc.

from poor to rich. When farm incomes are examined, therefore, it is not surprising that the facts differ.

The one generalization which seems to be valid for all sections is that the great majority of farms produced only a small cash surplus, and that the return on the value of the property, according to the usual estimation of its worth, was low—probably seldom over 4 percent. This is, of course, all found: after the family had been supported, to a considerable degree, and represents therefore a true income much higher than the cash earnings. The figure also does not include the rise in farm values.

New England's farms were principally of the subsistence type, and their surplus was small. A farm of above average size in Hampton, New Hampshire, near the coast, was valued at £3,592 in 1761, and estimated to be worth £151 annually. It is possible that the currency used in the first figure was different from that in the second, but apparently the rate of return was 3 percent and the income perhaps £22 sterling. Another eastern farm in the same colony, assessed for £6,389 in 1754, was worth £100 per year—only 1½ percent, the sterling profit being about £14. A Rhode Island tenant's farm, supposedly a good one, yielded £103 per year, netting £31.14.5 after rent and laborers' wages had been paid.[92] A writer in a Connecticut newspaper postulated a typical 40-acre farm costing £200 plus £110 for improvements, which he thought would earn about £54 after labor costs had been subtracted. But this was, like many such estimates, probably hopeful, since the projected yield per acre in this case is higher than the actual average. Another writer believed that the best farms in the state would net less than £28.[93] The nature of the source suggests that this

[92] Douglas S. Robertson, ed., *An Englishman in America 1785 Being the Diary of Joseph Hadfield* (Toronto, 1933), 219.

[93] *Conn. Gazette* (New Haven), Feb. 7, 1767; *American Mercury*, Aug. 27, 1787.

may be an understatement, but clearly ordinary farms produced a much lower return.

About the same average net incomes are indicated by assessment lists. The Massachusetts records of 1771 estimated, supposedly, the average annual value of the real estate. The median income varied from £3 to £13, depending upon the town, but usually stood at £7 or so. Probably most of those men who had incomes from real estate of only £1 or £2 were not really farmers but had a little land for part-time work or a speculative lot. If this is the case, then the median for farmers was about £8. The question of course is whether these assessment lists undervalued the property. The answer surely is yes, for the median value of farm property according to inventories in Suffolk and Worcester Counties was £425, which one would expect to produce more than 2 percent. Probably the median annual income was between two and four times the assessed value. Certainly most of the farms in Massachusetts provided only a slight profit, since over 90 percent were assessed for less than £20.[94]

Probably farms of the middle colonies were somewhat more profitable, though it is hard to generalize. It has been estimated that a small farmer or tenant in New York had a yearly cash income of only £9 to £11. On the other hand a writer in a Philadelphia newspaper estimated that 4 percent was the usual profit of a Pennsylvania farm.[95] If such a

---

[94] Assessed value of Massachusetts farms, select towns:

£3–4	28%
£5–9	40
£10–19	24½
£20–29	5½
£30–49	1½
£50+	½

[95] George Dangerfield, *Chancellor Robert R. Livingston of New York, 1746–1813* (New York, 1960), 427; "Timoleon," *Independent Gazetteer*, Jan. 3, 1787.

farmer were worth £400—which one observer guessed was average for New Jersey—then his income would be £16.[96] Four hundred pounds is a little below the value of Suffolk County farms as shown by inventories, and since Pennsylvania was richer, agriculturally, the equivalent income was perhaps nearer £25. One Pennsylvanian postulated £30 as the usual cash profit for that state.[97] Four hundred acres near Lancaster were reputed to have brought £60 per annum "clear of all expenses," but this was so exceptional as to occasion particular notice, and the farm was much larger than the average.[98] Delaware assessment lists suggest that incomes there were about the same as in Massachusetts. It is impossible to separate the farmers from the rest of the population as given in these lists. However the general median for Sussex and Kent, which were almost entirely agricultural, was about £4. It is necessary to subtract farm laborers, which perhaps may be accomplished by eliminating those whose estates were valued at only £1 or £2 (about 32 percent of the whole number); but the median still remains less than £5. Even if the figure is doubled or tripled, the income must have been quite low. To that sum must of course be added the supplies produced by the land which the family used: most of the food, firewood, furniture, and the house itself.

Farther south, farm incomes were much higher. One writer estimated that a 289-acre farm on the eastern shore of Maryland would return £170. The perceptive traveller Schoepf reported that an acre of good land produced a hogshead of tobacco worth £18 Pennsylvania currency (about £10 sterling). Few planters, he wrote, made more

[96] *Address to the Freeholders of New Jersey* (Philadelphia, 1763), 106.
[97] *Pa. Gazette*, Oct. 15, 1788.
[98] "John Penn's Journal," *Pa. Mag. Hist. Biog.*, III (1879), 295.

than fifteen hogsheads, most not over five or ten.[99] This price may be too high. Thomas Jones of Virginia, a prosperous planter, received only £7 per hogshead during the years 1764–1772 and even less during the next two years. His hogsheads commonly weighed less than 1,000 pounds in England (whatever they may have weighed in Virginia), some tobacco was damaged, and he had to pay a variety of charges. His property was near the coast, where perhaps the land was less productive than that farther west. The tobacco sold by John Norton and Sons averaged £10 for 259 hogsheads in 1771 and a little over £7 each for 390 hogsheads the following year.[100] If £7 to £9 is the more usual average, then the cash income from tobacco, according to Schoepf's estimate, varied from £35 to £80 with few men earning more than £125 sterling. An average North Carolina farm, according to one patriotic resident, earned £45 to £60 from surplus corn alone. The figure is probably currency, and the lower estimate was based on the usual value of corn (3s per bushel) whereas the higher one assumed an extraordinary value, so that the true profit was probably £25 sterling, plus the income from other products of the farm such as lumber and naval stores. On the other hand, 300 acres in the same colony were assumed to be worth no more than £20 sterling cash.[101] The latter figure is surely more accurate. Probably the cash income in local money averaged about £16 in New England, half again as much in the middle colonies, and £50 or thereabouts in the South outside of North Carolina.

Other sources confirm these rough generalizations. An

---

[99] Brooke Hindle, *The Pursuit of Science in Revolutionary America* (Chapel Hill, 1956), 359; Schoepf, *Travels*, I, 353.

[100] Figures for over 200 hogsheads, Jones Family Papers, boxes 13–21, Lib. Cong.; *John Norton & Sons*, 164, 213.

[101] *American Museum*, II, 131–133; *N.C. Hist. Rev.*, II (1925), 235.

advertiser in Pennsylvania hoped to attract a farmer who "understands all kinds of country business, especially carting, plowing, and mowing, and more particularly breaking steers to draught and hauling logs to a mill," by offering £25 sterling per annum in addition to food and lodging.[102] Overseers in the South were paid anywhere from £15 to £60, which presumably equalled or surpassed the income which they might expect as farmers.[103] Many Virginia farmers were wealthy, but these are balanced by those who, like the tenants, were usually poor and frequently unable to pay their debts.[104] A contemporary believed that only half of those who borrowed money succeeded in repaying it.[105] Still, the average farmer who owned his land, though he did not earn a large income, might live in comfort. A Rhode Island commentator truly observed that "the Profits arising from Agriculture are indeed not great, but they are certain." [106]

The property accumulated by farmers confirms the conclusion that their income, while moderate, afforded a chance to save, and that their economic status improved as one went south. In Massachusetts, the median estate in personal property was about £100, and most of the farmers owned between £50 and £200, though one out of five had

---

[102] *Pa. Packet*, Feb. 22, 1773.

[103] *The Gazette of the State of Georgia* (Savannah), July 3, 1788; "Diary of Col. Landon Carter," *Wm. and Mary Qtly.*, XIV (1905–1906), 250; *Md. Hist. Mag.*, XIII (1918), 60; Washington's *Diaries*, III, 67n; *American Husbandry*, 80, 176, 286; Galloway-Marcoe-Maxie Collection, Galloway papers box 5, Lib. Cong.

[104] Willard F. Bliss, "The Rise of Tenantry in Virginia," *Va. Mag. Hist. Biog.*, LVIII (1950), 434–440.

[105] St. John de Crevecoeur, *Sketches of Eighteenth Century America* (ed. by Henri L. Bourdin, Ralph H. Gabriel, and Stanley T. Williams, New Haven, 1925), 91.

[106] *Newport Mercury*, Dec. 21, 1787. See also *Life of Manasseh Cutler*, 252; *American Husbandry*, 49–50.

less. Their land was worth fully three times as much as their personal property, the median being about £350 in Suffolk and £280 in Worcester. A majority owned between £100 and £500 worth of real estate, the variation being wider in Suffolk than in Worcester, where smaller farms predominated. The median for all types of property was about £425. In Worcester County, most farmers were worth £100 to £500, while in Suffolk there were a greater number of estates valued at over £500. These Massachusetts farmers had acquired nearly twice as much property as had the artisans and nearly as much as professional men.

New Jersey inventories listed only personal property. Farmers there owned about £260 (£160 sterling) which was roughly twice as much property as their Massachusetts prototypes. Even if the New Jersey landholders had no more real estate than did Massachusetts farmers, the majority were worth not far from £600, or £350 sterling. Since farms in New Jersey were considerably larger the figure is undoubtedly low. Virginia inventories indicate about the same personal property there as in New Jersey—less in the southern Piedmont, more in some of the eastern counties. South Carolina's farmers were evidently much wealthier, the median being no less than £900. This valuation is probably correct for the eastern parishes but much too high for the western ones. Combining all this data, and ignoring sectional differences, we can estimate that farmers owned personal property worth about £200, the usual range for small landholders being £50 to £500. Their total property probably averaged £300 to £500 sterling.

Large landowners made far greater profits. About one out of twelve farmers had personal estates of £1,000 and perhaps one in twenty or thirty were worth £2,000. The merchant Charles Ward Apthorp had real estate valued at £13,600, which produced £672.5 (about 5 percent).[107] Robert Livingston's "manor" produced an income of nearly £850 annually from real estate, excluding a farm at his manor and a house in New York City, while his cousin reputedly made even more. James Delancey's land furnished him an income of more than £1,200 a year, and Frederick Philipse's supposedly brought £2,400 currency (£1,340 sterling) in rentals plus the profits of his unrented land.[108] Charles Carroll of Carrollton earned £1,800 annually, net.[109] The great southern planters did especially well. Every young and healthy Negro produced a profit, the estimates of which vary from £10 all the way up to £100 per hand.[110] The higher figures may be in inflated money, or perhaps refer to an exceptional case; probably costs are not subtracted. Apparently £10 to £20, net, is not far from the mark. Therefore the average planter who owned twenty working slaves made roughly £200 sterling, clear. Estimates of profits per acre varied from £5 to £12 or £14.[111] On a plantation only a small number of acres would be intensively cultivated, probably not over four acres per hand. One traveller believed that a 500-acre estate in the Shenandoah Valley would yield £485 annually, while a rice plantation of 200 acres, 130 of which were in rice, employing forty hands, would earn £700.[112]

[107] Suffolk County Probate Records, vol. 87, p. 8.

[108] Dangerfield, *Livingston*, 29; *Loyalist Claims*, 146, 241.

[109] *Md. Hist. Mag.*, XII (1917), 27.

[110] Smith, *Bondage*, 27; Schoepf, *Travels*, II, 143, 157–160; J. F. D. Smyth, *A Tour in the United States of America* (2 vols., London, 1784), II, 95; La Rouchefoucault-Liancourt, *Travels*, I, 595–596, 622–623; Gray, *Agriculture*, I, 284, 294.

[111] *ibid.*, I, 182, 218–219, 294; Schoepf, *Travels*, II, 159–160, 162.

[112] *The Journal of Nicholas Cresswell 1774–1777* (New York, 1924), 195–196; W. W. Abbot, *The Royal Governors of Georgia, 1754–1775* (Chapel Hill, 1959), 23–24.

Some of these estimates may be optimistic. A Georgia
writer believed that a planter who had twenty workable
hands (out of forty or fifty slaves) would make £360 from
his rice, and would spend nearly £160. This figure includes
depreciation on the Negroes at £50, but not the family's
living costs. Probably such a plantation would also produce
a surplus of lumber, and perhaps of indigo or other crops,
but the profit would still be less than £200. This lower
figure is confirmed by John Page's estimate that for five
years his expenses, with "the most strict Oeconomy" had
exceeded his average net proceeds of 14,000 lbs. of tobacco.
If Page's tobacco sold at 2d per pound, his income averaged
about £116.[113] Yet the wealthy South Carolina planters
might clear £1,000 sterling.[114] In general it appears that the
income of a large southern planter varied from £100 to
some hundreds of pounds sterling, not including provisions
and the like supplied by the land, and exclusive of interest
payments. The large properties which many accumulated
proves that they rivalled the merchants in economic status.

The revolutionary class structure can now be described
in terms of occupational groups. Each occupation had its
exceptional men, but in general the laborers were poorly
paid and acquired little property; artisans earned somewhat
more and became small property holders; most farmers were
in the same position, though some became wealthy; professional men and shopkeepers received good incomes and had
substantial estates; while merchants were characteristically
well-to-do or rich.

The revolutionary lower class, consisting of one-fifth of
the white population, was made up of the rural and urban

[113] *State Gazette of Georgia,* July 3, 1788; *John Norton & Sons,*
172.
[114] Carl Bridenbaugh, *Myths and Realities* (Baton Rouge, 1952),
67–68.

laborers together with some artisans and a few farmers. These were usually landless and owned little property of any sort. The middle class of small property owners included over half of the whites. They were principally artisans and farmers, though a few professional men (especially schoolteachers) and shopkeepers must be added. An upper middle class of substantial property owners included the larger farmers, most professional men and shopkeepers, and some merchants; while the upper class was made up primarily of merchants, lawyers, and large landowners.[115]

So far we have demonstrated that economic classes existed in every section of the country. These differences in property and income are, however, meaningful only when

[115] The following table is based upon personal property recorded in over 5,000 probated estates. The first column includes only those estates; the second adds indentured servants; assumed to include 10 percent of the white men; the third adds adult male slaves. Percentages are approximate because the number of estates used is too small for precision, and above all because the currencies varied. Figures are local money, not sterling.

£2,000+	3%	3%	2½%
£1,000–1,999	7	6	5
£500–999	10	10	9
£100–499	40	36	31
£1–99	40	45	52½

The same inventories furnish the comparisons below.

	All Estates	Laborers	Teachers	Artisans	Doctors	Ministers	Traders & Shopkeepers	Farmers	Merchants
£2,000+	3	0	0	0	8	7	5	4	28
£1,000–1,999	7	0	0	4	7	3	10	8	15
£500–999	10	0	0	8	15	15	10	12	12
£200–499	20	0	20	20	30	35	40	25	25
£100–199	20	2	20	20	20	15	15	20	10
£50–99	20	48	20	20	10	15	10	16	3
£1–49	20	50	40	28	10	10	10	15	7

we know how much money the people had to spend in order to survive and to live in comfort. The different standards and styles of living illuminate the class distinctions during the revolutionary era.

CHAPTER IV

Standards and Styles of Living

THE COST OF LIVING during the revolutionary period depended, as it does today, upon income and desires as much as upon the actual price of necessities. Most people probably spent little more than the basic sum needed for food, clothing, and shelter. Some, in "middling" circumstances, required a much larger amount of money to uphold their standards of living, while a few lived luxuriously.

The single man who lived alone needed not over £10 to £13 annually for food. A shilling (lawful) a day was universally allowed when one was not found and was more than ample. New England jailers were authorized to spend between 4/6 and 5/ lawful money weekly for the support of debtors in prison. Of course this represents a minimum, and the shilling a day (£18 lawful per year) probably was a more usual outlay.[1] Clothing and lodging cost about £10.[2] Thus a bachelor could survive on £25, though the well-to-do merchant or lawyer might pay £40 or more a year for

[1] *Rhode Island Acts and Resolves,* June, 1765, p. 33; Henry Harrison Metcalf, ed., *Laws of New Hampshire . . .* III, 472, IV, 468; *Vermont State Papers, being a Collection of Records and Documents . . . and the Laws from the Year 1779 to 1786, inclusive* (Middlebury, 1823), 482. The cost in New Jersey seems to have been as low as 3/6 currency (*Session Laws,* 1769, p. 89), but in Virginia it was over 6/. William Waller Hening, ed., *The Statutes at Large; being a collection of all the laws of Virginia . . .* VIII (Richmond, 1821), 528–529. Georgia permitted the warden of the work house to spend 6d sterling a day for provisions for each slave. This sum was equal to a 4/8 per week in New England money. *Col. Rec. Ga.,* XVII, 562–563.

[2] Bureau of Labor Statistics, *Bulletin* 499, pp. 23–24; *Conn. Gazette,* Feb. 7, 1767; Galloway-Marcoe-Maxie Collection, Galloway Papers, vol. 4, Lib. Cong.; *Columbian Herald,* Nov. 20, 1786; Aaron Leaming diary, July 1775, Hist. Soc. Pa.

room and board alone.[3] However the unmarried laborer usually lived with a family and was charged perhaps £12 for room and board.[4] Clothes cost little: a pair of coarse laborer's shoes could be bought for 7/6; breeches came to £1 and lasted two years; good blankets were worth a guinea and felt hats 5s. The average annual cost of an adult's clothes was not over £2½ sterling.[5] All told, the laborer who was found probably needed only £5 or so in cash.[6]

The family man of course needed much more. A wife was an economic asset, for she could make many articles which the bachelor had to buy, but small children were liabilities. The minimum annual cost of food and clothing for the man and wife was probably not far from £20. A child cost £4 to £6 to feed, while clothes cost about £2.[7]

[3] Samuel Holten Papers, Bills, Accounts and Receipts 1780–1789, Lib. Cong.; Brissot de Warville, *New Travels*, 159; Clark, *Manufacturing*, 136; *Va. Herald*, June 19, 1788.

[4] *Col. Rec. N.C.*, vi, 99. Probate records furnish interesting data. There was great variation in the charge for board, the lowest being £4. Chesterfield County Year Book, vol. 4, p. 54, Va. State Lib.

[5] Newspaper advertisements contain much information concerning the price of clothes. Examples are, *Pa. Journal*, Jan. 18, 1770; *Pa. Gazette*, July 14, 1763; *Va. Gazette* (Rind), June 2, 1774; *The Freeman's Journal: Or, the North-American Intelligencer* (Philadelphia), July 18, 1787; *Independent Gazetteer*, April 24, 1787; *New Hampshire Gazette*, Sept. 16, 1768, Aug. 12, 1785; *Essex Gazette*, Aug. 16, 1768; *The Carlisle Gazette, and the Western Repository of Knowledge*, April 19, 1786. See also Col. Soc. Mass., *Transactions*, xxviii, 303; Clark *Manufacturing*, 140–141; Gottlieb Mittelberger, *Journey to Pennsylvania in the Year 1750 . . .* trans. by Carl Theo. Eben (Philadelphia, 1898), 66; Burnaby, *Travels*, 93; *The Diary of Matthew Patten of Bedford, N.H.* (Concord, N.H., 1903), 134; Daniel Dibble Account Book, Conn. Hist. Soc. (Dibble was a shoemaker). See values set for tax purposes in *Laws of New Hampshire*, iv, 438 (1782).

[6] New Hampshire granted totally disabled veterans £18 currency (£13.10 sterling) for their livelihood. A single man could just exist on this. *Laws*, v, 221. See also Hening, *Statutes*, xii, 132, and *The Statutes at Large of Pennsylvania*, xii, 113–116.

[7] Probate records contain much material concerning the cost of maintaining children, especially in reports of the guardians. For

Schooling and medical bills were very small for families of this subsistence level. The usual total expense was about £10 for a child of school age, £6 for the younger ones. The cost of maintaining each Indian boy in a school was £7 for food and lodging, £2 for clothing, and £1 for books and paper.[8] As more children were added, the per capita cost went down. The five orphan boys of John Skinner, Esquire, needed only £3 each per year for food over a four year period. Their clothes cost a little more than did their food; however, they were better clad than the average child, actually paying a tailor for fashioning their garments. Medical costs came to £8.14.6 for four years. The total amount spent was £6.15 apiece annually.[9] Probably a family of seven required something like £50 currency in the country and £60 or so in the towns to maintain themselves at the subsistence level. Food would cost £30, clothes £12, medical expenses and schooling £5, firewood, taxes, and miscellaneous essentials a few more pounds. House rent might add another £5 or £10. These estimates assume that the family provided none of its own food or clothing.

Various contemporary estimates confirm these figures. A

example, Halifax County Deed Book, vol. 2, p. 29, Va. State Lib.; Suffolk County Probate Records, vol. 66, p. 206.

[8] Kemp, *Support of Schools*, 224. There was naturally quite a variation. Typical are the following. An Essex County, Virginia, schoolboy cost his guardian £10 per year, exclusive of medical care (vol. 14, p. 27). Another orphan in Halifax County cost £18.14.6 during twenty months, or about £11½ per year, and two children there cost almost the same (vol. 2, pp. 137, 29). See also C. G. Chamberlayne, ed., *The vestry book of St. Paul's parish, Hanover county, Virginia, 1706–1786* (Richmond, 1940), 408, 502, 523, 578 (bastard child, £5); *New Jersey Archives*, xxxiii, 52 (two very small children for four years, £50); Barker Account Book, 1761, Conn. Hist. Soc. (a schoolgirl cost £15 per year); *Pub. Rec. Conn.*, v, 419 (a baby and a two-year-old, £13 and £9 respectively); Suffolk County Wills, vol. 64, pp. 252–253; Worcester County Probate Records, vol. 9, p. 224, vol. 10, p. 117.

[9] Suffolk County Probate Records, vol. 85, pp. 33–36.

Connecticut family, number of children unknown, got by for £42.[10] Probably typical was a Marshfield, Massachusetts, family which spent £38 for food and £4 for clothing during each of two years; they also had debts and of course taxes, doctors' bills, and other costs not itemized.[11] A Georgian felt that £55 per year was "no more than a Competent sufficiency." [12] An Acton, Massachusetts, minister barely got by on £70 sterling, while a Charleston, South Carolina, artisan complained that no one who earned less than 30s or 40s a week (£67 to £89 sterling per year) could support his family. Such support included house rent of probably £10 and £3 sterling for cordwood. Another estimate for a later period, when prices had risen somewhat, puts the minimum family cost at £60 including £5 for house rent.[13]

One could easily spend twice as much, and many did so. Anyone who wished to live in some comfort required at least £100. This was the sum regarded as a "sufficient Support" by the Society for the Propagation of the Gospel in Foreign Parts, and as the expected housekeeping cost of a planter's family by the author of *American Husbandry*.[14] An income of 10s a day (£150 a year, allowing for a six-day week) maintained a Boston family "in credit." A Mary-

---

[10] *Pub. Rec. Conn.*, XIII, 485.

[11] Lawrence B. Romaine, "Family Expenses during the Revolution," *Hobbies*, LIV (1949), 53.

[12] McCaul, "Education in Georgia," *Ga. Hist. Qtly.*, XL, 111.

[13] Shipton, *Harvard Graduates*, IX, 334; Walsh, *Charleston's Sons of Liberty*, 43; E. V. Wilcox, "Living High on $67.77 a Year," N.Y. State Hist. Assn., *Proceedings*, XXIV (1926), 197. Residency in Pennsylvania could be established by leasing a house with the yearly value of £10. *Statutes*, VIII, 84. I suspect that this was ordinarily the minimum cost. Houses in Philadelphia were never advertised for so low a figure.

[14] Frank J. Klingberg, *An Appraisal of the Negro in Colonial South Carolina* (Washington, 1941), 79; *American Husbandry*, 293.

land "gentleman" could support his family with the same income, and £150 was also assumed to be the usual cost of a
Georgia "planter." Presumably most of the food was supplied
by the farm.[15] Boston in 1784 raised the salaries of its teachers
to over £200 "to support their own Children & Families and
in the Exercise of that Cardinal Virtue, Prudence, to lay up
for them such a Moderate Overplus, as every industrious &
provident Inhabitant wishes to do for his own Family at the
period of Needfulness or Life." [16] There certainly was no
difficulty in spending that amount. The cost of a schoolboy
might reach £32 a year if he was supported at the rate of
£15 and provided with good clothes, for a decent winter
suit alone could come to £3.3.4.[17] An academy usually
charged £15 a year for board, which was also the upkeep
for a Connecticut schoolgirl,[18] and tuition would be from
£2, as was true of a Lebanon, Connecticut, school, on up to
£10.[19] Thus three schoolchildren even in New England
might require £60 including clothes. An adult might spend
£5 or more for clothes and £2 for shoes.[20] Dorchester's
schoolmaster spent £12 for clothing in 1791.[21] A respectable house cost anywhere from £25 to £50 or more annually.
Wood might come to £4. If only the head of the family
kept himself in liquor, he could spend £5 on rum.[22] Still to
be added are food for the parents, the maintenance of a

[15] *Mass. Centinel,* March 11, 1786; Owings, *His Lordship's Patronage,* 2; *State Gazette of Georgia,* July 3, 1788.
[16] Kaplan, "Teacher's Salaries," 375–376.
[17] Suffolk County Probate Records, vol. 82, p. 790.
[18] Barker Account Book, 1761. See Chapter VIII for details.
[19] Isaiah Tiffany Account Book, 1766, Conn. Hist. Soc.
[20] Abiel Abbot Account Book (Wilton, N.H.), 1759–1776, Winterthur Library 57.17.1, for example. A writer in the *Pennsylvania
Journal* assumed a general average of £4 currency per person annually, including children. Jan. 18, 1770.
[21] Small, *New England Schools,* 135.
[22] *Cumberland Gazette,* March 9, 1787.

servant, medical costs, furniture, and the always expensive miscellany, the whole certainly more than £150 sterling and approaching £200, especially if there were more than three children. The latter income was considered in New York City to be "sufficient to support a family in a genteel manner, and yearly to lay up something for posterity." [23]

The standard of living which a well-to-do family maintained was discussed in Boston newspapers at an earlier date (1726).[24] The three writers assumed that the family consisted of nine persons, including a servant, and that they "lie in a Medium," "of middle fashion," "of but middling figure"; but the prices given are obviously for a standard considerably above even the normal middle income range for colonials. The writers supposed food to cost between £177 and £219 (one insisted that £200 was the minimum, for a "Gentleman cannot well Dine his Family at a lower rate than this"). A maid, everyone agreed, must be paid £10 to £11. Clothes cost £10 for each person; three or four pairs of shoes apiece came to another £10. Candles and washing added about £12. In addition there would be rent, which at this level might cost £100, luxury foods, liquor, tobacco, entertainment, charity, pocket money, books, pen and ink, paper, medical costs, nursing, schooling, and the buying and repairing of household utensils. The total, no matter which of the three writers was more nearly correct, came to between £450 and £500—obviously the standard of a man of means.

Indeed the well-to-do American lived at this level if not above it. The wealthy artisan of Charleston, South Carolina,

---

[23] *Ecclesiastical Records of New York*, VI, 3,855. To be precise, a minister was paid £300 currency (£180 sterling), plus the perquisites of marriages and burials.

[24] Carl Bridenbaugh, "The High Cost of Living in Boston, 1728," *New Eng. Qtly.*, V (1932), 800–811.

Thomas Elfe, spent £313 sterling in 1769 and £546 in 1770, including the cost of schooling for two boys.[25] Charles Carroll of Carrollton's "Household Expenses & tradesmans Bills" were £400.14.9½ in 1770, while Landon Carter wrote in his diary, "I find it has not for some years been less than 400l the year that has maintained my family in everything, tools, &c." [26] Both of these gentlemen were planters who could supply most of their own food. The author of *American Husbandry* reported that in New England, "Four or five hundred pounds a year is a great estate—not that there is not much larger, but it is sufficient for all the comforts and conveniences of life, and for such a portion of the luxuries of it as are indulged in by any neighbour, though their estates may be larger than his." [27] Truly wealthy men who lived in the cities might spend far more, especially in New York and Philadelphia, where, one writer believed, the cost of living was much more expensive than in New England, so that the £375 received by an assistant judge in Massachusetts equalled £600 or £700 in Philadelphia.[28] Walter Livingston of New York spent £570 in 1783, £740 in 1784, £1,1227 the next year exclusive of £387 for furni-

[25] Account Book, *S.C. Hist. Mag.*, xxxv (1934) and subsequent volumes.

[26] *Md. Hist. Mag.*, xii (1917), 349; *Wm. and Mary Qtly.*, xiii (1904–1905), 158.

[27] *American Husbandry*, 68.

[28] "It was always much cheaper living there than here. The residence of Congress and the great officers under them; of the [French] minister; of the multitude of strangers, and of our exiled friends from New-York, Carolina, &c. the interruption of our trade; the greater safety of the New-England navigation, with a variety of other circumstances, have effected much greater differences than ever between the expence of living in those two states." *Pa. Packet*, Apr. 23, 1782. Gerardus G. Beekman, a New York merchant, reported to his brother that one could live like a gentleman for £300 New York currency, or £170 Sterling—but he had no family. Jan. 30, 1764, Letter Book, N.Y. Hist. Soc.

ture and repairs, £1,400 in 1786 and £1,600 in 1787. Thomas Lee Shippen of Philadelphia spent $1,615.43 (£602) including a doctor's bill of $50, a trip to New York ($251), play tickets to "Hamlet," "segars," a child's maid, a footman, a cook, a washerwoman, a chambermaid, and a personal servant. In subsequent years his family expenses were £710, £1,227, and £696.[29]

Such a standard of living was not unusual. Alexander Contee Hanson, a Maryland judge, itemized nearly £600 which he wrote "by no means, supposes a splendid, magnificent style of living—It affords not equipage, costly entertainments, or sumptuous fare—It provides a comfortable subsistence; but not even that, without a strict attention to expenditures." House rent came to £75 and food for ten including five servants cost £220, which corresponds closely to the 1726 Boston estimates; while clothing for five required £120, medical bills were £15, the liquor cost £40, firewood £50, candles £8.15.0 and the five servants had been hired for £60. "There is no allowance made for casualties, or for what is called pocket money." Thus the expenses of a judge, when one added the cost of travelling, came to nearly £700.[30] Presumably Hanson was using the Maryland currency, so that his sterling expenditures were about £400. Carroll and Carter certainly would have spent as much had they not been able to provide their own house rent, firewood, and much of their food. Henry Knox wrote to Washington that the salary of the war office, $2,450 (£755) was "but a slender support," and in fact he considerably

---

[29] Account Book, Robert R. Livingston Papers, N.Y. Hist. Soc.; Account Book, 1793–1797, Shippen Papers, box 2, Lib. Cong. The figure is Pennsylvania currency.

[30] *Md. Gazette*, March 29, 1787. One could certainly spend £75 annually for house rent, but a good home could be obtained for less. Governor Franklin of New Jersey was regularly granted £60 currency. *Session Laws*, 1766, p. 5.

exceeded it, spending £1,304.16. The Knoxes, who had five servants, managed to stow away £365 (New York currency) in food and £180 in wine, winning quite a reputation for size, and allowed £120 for entertainments.[31] Finally, Joseph Pemberton spent £4,476 in eight and a half years, averaging £526 per year and bankrupting himself in the process.[32] Thus £500 seems to have been the minimum income needed by a well-to-do colonial.

The cost of living for a Revolutionary family varied all the way from £50 to £500. The American's economic situation and way of life therefore depended upon his income, the degree to which he could supply his needs without cash, and the manner of living to which he aspired. Negroes generally lived at a subsistence level. The total spent to maintain the average slave varied from £3 to £8, the former figure being more common.[33] Good shoes could be bought for 3/6 or 4/, or sometimes less when purchased in quantity. On one South Carolina plantation the total cost of clothes, including blankets for 32 slaves, came to £18.3.8. The doctor's bill was £4.14.6 by prior agreement. A newspaper correspondent assumed that £1 per slave was a usual expense for clothing.[34] Certainly the owner spent no unnecessary money. Young slaves were sometimes allowed, or required, to run around naked, to the great scandal of northern visitors.[35]

[31] Boston, March 24, 1785, Washington Papers, vol. 232, no. 47, Lib. Cong.; Knox Papers, xx, 172, Mass. Hist. Soc.

[32] Pemberton Papers box 28, 1775–1776, pp. 111–114, Hist. Soc. Pa.

[33] Gray, *Agriculture*, i, 364.

[34] *American Husbandry*, 286; *State Gazette of Georgia*, July 3, 1788.

[35] Lida Tunstall Rodman, ed., *Journal of a Tour to North Carolina by William Attmore, 1787* (The James Sprunt Historical Publications, xvii, no. 2, Chapel Hill, 1922), 44; William Duane, and Thomas Balch, eds., *The Journal of Claude Blanchard, commissary of the French Auxiliary Army sent to the United States during the American Revolution. 1780–1783* (Albany, 1876), 163; "Journal

Adults wore strong coarse trousers and shirts during the summer; and in the winter strong cheap shoes, a woolen jacket, and breeches were added. The food, almost entirely provided by the master, consisted largely of hominy, with sometimes a little pork or fish twice a week.[36] Robert Carter allowed his field hands a peck of corn and a pound of meat per week. Carter and doubtless other planters allowed the Negroes to raise their own vegetables and perhaps even hogs and poultry.[37] Masters or companies with large incomes could afford to spend an extra sum on the slaves. For example, slaves working for the Potomac Company were to receive salt pork and beef or even fresh beef and mutton, plus a "reasonable quantity of spirits when necessary."[38] On the other hand, farmers who were themselves poor, or large landowners having a bad year, were unable to provide adequately for their Negroes.[39] The slave quarters, of course, were inexpensive small cabins, one of which might contain several families.[40]

The treatment of the slave varied greatly. House servants were "better clad, more active, and less ignorant,"[41] while

of Ebenezer Hazard in North Carolina, 1777 and 1778," *N.C. Hist. Rev.*, xxxvi (1959), 364, 377; John Spencer Bassett, *Slavery and Servitude in the Colony of North Carolina* (Baltimore, 1896), 42.

[36] [Thomas Anburey], *Travels through the Interior Parts of America; in a Series of Letters* (2 vols., London, 1791), ii, 295–297, based on Smyth, *Tour*, i, 44–47; Schoepf, *Travels*, ii, 147; Gray, *Agriculture*, i, 364; Morris, *Government and Labor*, 32.

[37] Fithian, *Journal and Letters*, 51, 128; *N.C. Hist. Rev.*, iii (1926), 616; Weld, *Travels*, 114–115.

[38] *Md. Gazette*, Nov. 25, 1785.

[39] "Trade has in general been very dull this fall: the planters most wretchedly poor, numbers of them not able to purchase necessaries for their negroes." Thomas Rutherford to Messrs. Hawksley & Rutherford, Richmond, Dec. 6, 1786, Rutherford Letter Book, Va. Hist. Soc.

[40] Klingberg, *Negro in South Carolina*, 106.

[41] Brissot de Warville, *New Travels*, 284–285.

particular skilled workers were given special care—they were, after all, twice as valuable as a field hand, and brought a good return when rented or sold.[42] There are numerous instances of slaves being well cared for. One traveller believed that the kindest treatment was given by poor farmers, who "share with them the toils of the fields, and who, although they do not clothe and feed them well, yet treat them, in this respect, as well as they do themselves."[43] But many large planters were kindly too, and observers who had seen slavery in the West Indies testified that the North American Negroes were far better provided for and happier. Some of them showed real affection for their masters.[44] Nevertheless many, perhaps most, Negroes not only worked hard but, as Anburey said, fared hard, working long hours for no return except a bare livelihood, without hope, and unable to prevent cruelty when it occurred.[45]

[42] Examples of the cost of skilled workers are, Warren B. Smith, *White Servitude in Colonial South Carolina* (Columbia, S.C., 1961), 35; S.C. Inventory Book A, William Hopton, 1786. Slaves rented for £12 a year as a rule. *Md. Journal*, March 1, 1785.

[43] La Rochefoucault-Liancourt, *Travels*, II, 69. On the other hand, another traveller lamented the fate of those who "are unfortunate enough to fall into the hands of the lower class of white people." Weld, *Travels*, 116. "Lower" here might have a moral rather than an economic connotation.

[44] "A Frenchman Visits Charleston in 1771," *S.C. Hist. Mag.*, LII (1951), 92; Chastellux, *Travels*, II, 195–196; Kalm, *Travels*, 208; Robert Lewis Diary, May 15, 1789, Va. Hist. Soc.; Henry Laurens to William Bull, April 23, 1785, *S.C. Hist. and Gen. Mag.*, XXIV (1923), 6. When Washington rented some land, he was required "not to move the Negroes out of the County, and a clause is to be inserted in the lease that, in case of my death and they should by my successor be maltreated in any respect, a forfeiture of the lease shall be incurred." *Diaries*, III, 114–115.

[45] Fithian, *Journal and Letters*, 123; Samuel McKee, Jr., *Labor in Colonial New York 1664–1776* (New York, 1935), 124; Anburey, *Travels*, II, 295–298; Smyth, *A Tour*, I, 40, 43–48; Burnaby, *Travels*, 150–151.

One newspaper advertised frankly that a healthy Negro wench, pregnant, was to be sold "with or without a child, which she now has, about three years old." [46]

Northern slaves, most of whom were house servants, were better treated. Like such servants in the South, they were often regarded with affection, well clothed, well fed, and well housed, though of course they remained slaves still, unable to rise from their status and permitted only to make the best of their situation. The anti-slavery movement accompanying the Revolution gave some their freedom and ameliorated the lives of others. [47]

Free Negroes were in a status midway between that of the slaves and the free laborers. In the South they were ordinarily semi-skilled workers or small farmers, occupying at every level an economic rank below that of the equivalent whites. Seldom did they own any property other than a little land and a few personal possessions, though a Negro in Prince Frederick parish, South Carolina owned 130 acres and five slaves in 1786. [48] Their position in the major cities seems to have been better than in the country. In Charleston, Negro workers were reported to be gambling, drinking, and profaning the Sabbath, as well as selling produce and undercutting white wages. [49] Their situation was similar

[46] *The Maryland Gazette: or, the Baltimore General Advertiser,* July 4, 1783.

[47] For general status see Lorenzo Johnston Greene, *The Negro in Colonial New England 1620–1776* (New York, 1942), 218–225, and Eugene Parker Chase, trans. and ed., *Our Revolutionary Forefathers: The Letters of François, Marquis de Barbé-Marbois* (New York, 1929), 156. For particular aspects see John Watts to General Murray, New York, July 4, 1763, "Letter Book of John Watts," N.Y. Hist. Soc., *Collections,* LXI (1928), 151; and *Md. Journal,* Oct. 7, 1777.

[48] Tax list, S.C. Archives. For the poor condition of free Negroes, see Wright, *The Free Negro in Maryland,* especially pp. 30–35.

[49] Journal of the House of Representatives of South Carolina, Aug. 6, 1783; *S.C. Gazette,* Aug. 27, 1772.

in the North. Those among them who had good positions as servants, or kept shop, or owned farms, were careful to behave decently and attained moderate economic success. They could not rise much above this level because whites would not loan them money, educate them, or in general give them an equal chance.[50] As a consequence most of them were poor. According to one observer, "you do not see one out of a hundred that makes good use of his freedom, or that can make a comfortable living, own a cow, a horse; they remain in their cabins where they live miserably, barely raise some corn, but do not rise to any thing." [51] But they did vote, often were literate, went to church, elected their own "King" (at least in New England), and had their own decent, though inferior, society. In the cities Negro servants attended elegant balls, consumed conspicuously, and compensated for their lowly lot just as did the whites.[52]

White indentured servants were less numerous than slaves but still comprised a significant proportion of the population. Pennsylvania, Maryland, and Virginia in particular contained large numbers, for they were often skilled workers and required less cash outlay than did a slave. The average price of a slave including women and children was perhaps £36 before the Revolution and £50 after it, whereas a servant bound for four years might be purchased for £10 or so. Washington bought an Irish shoemaker and a tailor, to serve for three years, for £12 sterling each; and a German family, the man a miller

[50] Brissot de Warville, *New Travels*, 282–284; Jeremy Belknap to Ebenezer Hazard, Boston, Jan. 25, 1788, "The Belknap Papers," Mass. Hist. Soc., *Collections*, 5 series III (1877), 12; *New Hampshire Gazette*, April 20, 1786.
[51] Cazenove, *Journal*, 8.
[52] *Laws of New Hampshire*, III, 564; La Rochefoucault-Liancourt, *Travels*, II, 386; Cazenove, *Journal*, 8.

and good farmer, the woman healthy and strong, with four and a half years to serve, together with a four-year-old daughter bound till of age, were advertised for £35.[53] Once purchased, they cost little more than a slave to keep, and less than a free laborer, who had to be paid £15 a year or more.

The character of the servants who immigrated during the colonial period left much to be desired. They were, according to Abbot Smith, "for the most part men of low grade, lazy, unambitious, ignorant, prone to small crimes and petty evasions, an unsavory and sometimes a dangerous class especially in those regions where there were many transported criminals."[54] But by the time of the Revolution they were of much better quality.[55] Many respectable farmers and artisans indentured themselves, and the accounts indicate a large number of skilled workers among

[53] *Diaries*, III, 70; *New York Mercury*, Dec. 1, 1766. The price varied, of course. Kalm reported that the usual cost of a German in Pennsylvania was £14 currency, or about £9 sterling, for a person who was to serve four years (*Travels*, 205). According to the data given in Gray (I, 370), the cost ranged from £2 to £4 (currency?) per year of service, skilled artisans bringing £15 to £25. A shipload of one hundred servants sold in Alexandria for at least 10 guineas (£10½ sterling) each. Timothy Parker to Peter Colt, Aug. 7, 1784, Wadsworth Papers, box 136, Conn. Hist. Soc. See also for detail on this point, records of indentures, 1771–1773, Pa. German Soc., *Proceedings*, XVI (1907). Abbot Smith sets the price of male convicts at £10, £25 for skilled workers (*Colonists in Bondage*, 122).

[54] *ibid.*, 245, 287–288.

[55] Smith writes, "There can be no doubt that towards the end of the colonial period better servants came, and the large migrations of 1773 did not bring nearly as much riff-raff, proportionately, as did the smaller movements of a century before. . . . The point was, of course, that the colonies had settled down into a stable existence; men could go there not as on a wild gamble, but with fair certainty of making a decent and even a comfortable living. It had become a reasonable project for the sober and industrious farmer, or the ambitious laborer." *ibid.*, 288–289.

the servants.[56] Out of twenty runaways advertised in a Virginia newspaper during the year 1775, eleven had some skill, including a barber, a gardener, two blacksmiths, a wheelwright, and a painter; two were only boys, and one of the four convicts was a "pretty good scholar."[57] Most of the servants in South Carolina were poor Protestants or Irishmen rather than convicts, and a fair number eventually became farmers or artisans.[58] Whatever may have been the situation earlier, by revolutionary times a high proportion were advancing in status after their terms were up.[59]

Although the life of the servant was far from ideal, especially if he had not been bred a farmer, disliked hard work, or could not adapt himself, most of them "worked out their time without suffering excessive cruelty or want."[60] In the South they might work with the Negro slaves, but they lived separately, were better clothed, and were more often allowed to raise food of their own.[61] Servants in the North were sometimes treated as members of the family. John Hancock, renting a house in New York City, insisted that his servants be provided with "decent Rooms,"

[56] William D. Hoyt, Jr., "The White Servants at 'Northampton,' 1772–74," *Md. Hist. Mag.*, XXXIII (1938), 126–133; *Va. Gazette* (Pinkney), March 16, 1775; *Va. Gazette* (Purdie), Oct. 13, 1775.
[57] *Va. Gazette* (Purdie), Aug. 4, 1775, to the end of the year.
[58] Smith, *Servitude in South Carolina*, 69, 88.
[59] Kalm, *Travels*, 205. The view that indentured servants were often of good quality even in the seventeenth century is strongly supported by Mildred Campbell, "Social Origins of Some Early Americans," in James Morton Smith, ed., *Seventeenth-Century America* (Chapel Hill, 1959), 63–89. *The Boston Gazette, and Country Journal* for Jan 1, 1770, contained the following advertisement: "To be Sold for £20 Lawful Money, for Five Years. The Time of a hearty young Man, who is a good Sailor.—He also understands Gardening and Husbandry very well, is a good Cook, and handy to any Sort of Business, and will bind himself to any whom he may suit for said Term."
[60] Smith, *Bondage*, 258, 278.
[61] *ibid.*, 256, 291.

for they "Lodge and Eat at home as well as I do my self." [62]
Probably they lived nearly as well as did the free laborers,
although they could not for the moment acquire property.

The economic condition of a free worker depended upon
whether he had a family. If he did not, his position was
good. The usual wage for a person of that sort was about
£15 sterling "found," and since he needed only £5 or so in
cash, the thrifty man might save as much as £10 a year.
Expenses "not found" were considerably higher but earnings rose proportionately. This surplus of income over expenditures explains the general belief of contemporaries that
wages were high, one writer indeed complaining that "the
Wages they receive for the Labour of one Day, will support them in Intemperance for Three Days"—which was, in
fact, true. In America the workers were able, in a few years,
to save up money enough to buy a small farm or shop;
whether they actually did so is another matter.[63] It is true
that there was periodic unemployment due to heavy immigration or competition from farmers' sons; but the single
man was mobile and there were always jobs in the back
country.[64]

On the other hand the family man was in trouble. It is
obvious that the wage for an unskilled worker, not found,
of 3s currency per day was inadequate. If he were fully
employed he might earn £45 currency a year, which would
barely suffice; but full employment was rare. A writer in
the *New Hampshire Gazette* inquired, "How many industrious Tradesmen are there of this Town, who have
large Families to Support, and whose Dependence is intirely
on their daily Labours, are often unemploy'd . . . ?" while

[62] To Henry Knox, Boston, March 14, 1787, Knox papers, xx, 21,
Mass. Hist. Soc.

[63] *Md. Gazette*, Nov. 16, 1769; *American Husbandry*, 52; Dwight,
Travels, I, 193–194.

[64] McRobert, *A Tour*, 9; *New Hampshire Gazette*, Nov. 26, 1766.

a Philadelphia contributor remarked that "mechanics in the country depending intirely on accidental employment, and having their families mostly idle, are generally poor." [65] Still, as he went on to point out, the worker might go West, family and all. This was indeed a principal reason for the comparatively high wages.

Obviously the unskilled worker, even if he were single, had to accept a low standard of living if he hoped to save, while the married man could do little but survive. The city laborer probably lived in a tenement, and the farm worker in someone's home. According to probate and tax records, very few men of this class owned any real estate. Information about urban rentals is scarce, but £10 is near the bottom.[66] Doubtless families doubled up. The rooms were furnished scantily—even an entire house would have only £20 worth of furniture.[67] The whole estate of William Call of Boston, a poor baker, came to £24.14.2, of which £10 was in household equipment, £6 in clothes, and £2 in one luxury item—a silver watch.[68] The entire family wore clothes of their own making except for shoes. The great advantage which the worker enjoyed over his European counterpart (aside from mobility) lay in his food, which even in the towns was abundant. Most laborers had to content themselves with what was provided for them, and none could have luxury items other than liquor, which seems to have

---

[65] *ibid.; The Pennsylvania Chronicle, and Universal Advertiser*, March 27, 1769; and see *The New Jersey Journal* (Chatham), May 7, 1783.

[66] In Philadelphia, for example, a two-story brick tenement rented for £28. *Pa. Packet*, Oct. 27, 1778. Benjamin Clark, a Boston brazier, rented out houses for £12. Account book, Winterthur Lib. Houses cost as little as £20, however.

[67] Thomas Pownall, *A Topographical Description of the Dominions of the United States of America* (rev. ed., Lois Mulkearn, ed., Pittsburgh, 1949), 45.

[68] Suffolk County Probate Records, vol. 82, p. 19.

been part of the "diet." Poor city folk sometimes suffered for lack of wood, but this was usually provided for them through philanthropic societies.

As the laborer's skill increased, his standard of living rose. The artisan who hired himself out by the day, and was of only average ability, received 4/ sterling per day, or perhaps £60 currency a year. The foremen of distillers, remarked one writer, received £40 or £50 sterling and were, in addition, allowed to sell the finished product, with which they enjoyed "as comfortable a living as most of the best tradesmen are able to obtain." [69] Presumably those who had their own shops and hired these skilled workers enjoyed a higher standard of living. Probably the average artisan family spent about what it earned. Forty pounds would furnish food, consisting of corn, rye, pork, beef, sugar, butter, a little cheese, salt, coffee, fish, spices, and cider. Included also were rum or an equivalent—evidently a necessity, since everyone bought it—and vegetables which would be raised in the garden and cost practically nothing. Many artisans produced much of their basic foods. Clothes could be kept down to £12 if the wife made everything except hats, shoes, a good suit and equivalent dress, and a great coat. Candles, wood, medical bills (£2), taxes, and miscellaneous supplies required about £6 or £7. Therefore the ordinary skilled worker lived comfortably but did not accumulate a surplus, while the master craftsman, especially the owner of a shop, could save money.

The great majority of artisans in Massachusetts, and probably of those elsewhere, were homeowners. Three-fourths of the Suffolk and Worcester County artisans owned some real estate. Usually the house and lot cost at least £100, though the poor man could find older ones for less, and many doubtless built their own. His home con-

[69] *Boston Evening Post*, Aug. 8, 1763.

tained £50 worth of household articles; four beds alone might cost a quarter of that sum. Undoubtedly some men inherited their houses or furniture, but many of them must have had to borrow money during their first years of business. Evidently most artisans lived near the margin, were vulnerable to depressions, and could purchase few luxuries. On the other hand they had plenty to eat and drink, were adequately clothed, warmed during the winter, lighted at night, and they owned their own homes. Moreover they could, and many did, become prosperous.

Rural craftsmen almost certainly earned less than did the townsmen but reduced their cost of living considerably. Their houses were less expensive and they had more land. Probably their food bill would be cut in half at least, and they did not need to pay for wood. These lower costs compensated for the reduced cash income and probably resulted in a standard of living equal to that of the ordinary urban artisan. The inventory of Ebenezer Kezar, blacksmith-farmer of Sutton, Massachusetts, is typical except that he had more real estate (£287.10) than usual. His personal property was worth £50. This included £3.9.6 in blacksmith's tools, about £5 in other implements, two cows, a calf, six sheep and a pig, one colt and a mare, and £6 or so in clothes (his wife's not included). Henry Stone, a Stoughton, Massachusetts, blacksmith, owned £80 in real estate including a small dwelling house with four acres valued at £24, an orchard with his blacksmith's shop on it, a wood lot of 150 acres (£27), and one-fourth of a saw mill (£9). His wearing apparel and books were valued at £1.14.9, four beds with their furnishings at £13.18.7. He had one horse, two cows, two swine, and personal property totalling £59.11.7.[70]

[70] Kingsbury, *Sutton*, 243; Suffolk County Probate Records, vol. 83, pp. 658–660.

Village blacksmiths like Kezar and Stone earned most of their money shoeing horses and oxen. They also sharpened shears, hoes, and axes; mended plows, scythes, forks, and chains; and made a few simple implements. In addition they cut and sold wood, farmed, and perhaps marketed a small agricultural surplus. In return they received goods and services. Artisans kept books on each other and settled periodically. The blacksmith shoed the doctor's horse in return for medical care. Farmers and their oxen ploughed the land and harvested the crop, and were credited accordingly.[71] The rural artisan's life was much like that of a small farmer, with perhaps this exception, that the craftsman seldom rose beyond this level.

In the city, on the other hand, artisans became well-to-do or even wealthy, and multiplied their expenses accordingly. Even the poor ones often had a few luxury articles. Nathan Simpson of Boston had only £10 worth of equipment in his blacksmith's shop, ate off pewter instead of silver, and owned only £50 worth of personal property; but he did have a clock worth over £10 and a saddle horse which he kept in a stable near his house. The tailor Ephraim Copeland was typical of many artisans of moderate property. He had a house and land worth £266.13.4, a silver watch, silver buckles, a pair of gold buttons and two gold rings, six silver spoons, and furniture, including china and glass, worth over £75. The successful artisan is typified by Captain Andrew Sigourney, the Boston distiller. His real estate was valued at £1,400. His stills cost £310 and he had on hand £666.13.3 worth of molasses. The "mansion house" contained furniture appraised at £238, not counting £116 in plate. Sigourney had spent £30 of clothes and £7 for books; his

[71] Joseph Cook, Account Book, 1771–1793, Conn. State Lib.; Abiel Abbot, Account Book, 1759–1776, Winterthur Lib.; Daniel Dibble, Account Book 1774–1785, Conn. Hist. Soc.

three slaves were estimated at £100; and he was well supplied with £156 worth of rum and spirits.[72] There was every temptation to buy the innumerable luxury articles which the town offered. Newspapers were filled with complaints "That *Tailors, Shoemakers,* in fact all mechanicks dressing in *silk stockings* and *lace ruffles will ruin the country.*" [73] Benjamin Clarke, a Boston brazier, paid as much as £4 in a year to a perukemaker for "dressing and Shaveing." He hired workers, paying £50 or so a year; had he been in the South he would have invested in slaves.[74] One could also subscribe to a newspaper, contribute to the church, buy more real estate, send children to school dressed in linen, rent a house for £100 (not at all uncommon) or buy a brick one for £500 (quite usual), purchase some good furniture and silver, keep a horse, buy a carriage, hire a maid or two (£10 each), and drink wine instead of rum. Furthermore, one no longer had to attend the shop from five in the morning until six in the evening. Sigourney, Clarke, and other well-to-do artisans could entertain as grandly as the merchants and professional men whom they doubtless emulated.

Although merchants and shopkeepers had large incomes, their expenses were proportionately greater. "A man in Trade," observed one writer, "is obliged to cloathe himself and Family in more costly Apparel, and to live at a higher Rate, than the Farmer." [75] Much of their profit had to be put back into business, for their stock might run into thousands of pounds. To outfit and supply a ship required £80 or so, to pay wages and other charges during a voyage cost more

---

[72] Suffolk County Probate Records vol. 64, pp. 57–58, vol. 65, pp. 216–217, 190–194.

[73] *New Hampshire Gazette*, Feb. 3, 1786.

[74] Account Book, Winterthur Lib. In Charleston, South Carolina, two-thirds of the artisans whose estates were inventoried owned slaves.

[75] *New York Gazette and Mercury*, May 18, 1772.

than £200, and to fill the vessel with goods took £700, or £1,000 all told. Moreover, a large share of the trader's assets consisted of debts, which often ran into thousands of pounds and were of doubtful value.

The country retailer was as financially involved, in proportion to his income, as the wholesaler. He usually purchased, on one year's credit, goods valued at £100 to £500. This stock was almost always sold on credit to his customers.[76] Usually the amounts thus advanced were small, a few pounds to each person, but they added up to a substantial sum and were often impossible to collect; in northern Virginia a firm lost £600 in one year to absconding debtors.[77] It was expensive to bring suit, and often when a trader foreclosed upon a debtor's property he failed to obtain enough to reimburse himself.[78] Therefore the shopkeeper carried his customers from year to year, often for many years, charging interest, and collecting little by little through a variety of goods and services.[79] A Lebanon, Connecticut, shopkeeper not only ran a general store but did work outside (at 4/ per day) while his wife taught private school. He received oysters, sand, clothes for his family,

[76] Glenn Weaver, *Jonathan Trumbull* (Hartford, 1956), 20; *Conn. Courant*, June 11, 18, 1771. A few merchants, like James Schureman and Francis Hopkinson, insisted upon cash. *The New Jersey Gazette* (Trenton), June 27, 1781; *Pa. Chronicle*, May 9, 1768.

[77] W. A. Low, "Merchant and Planter Relations in Post-Revolutionary Virginia 1783–1789," *Va. Mag. Hist. Biog.*, LXI (1953), 315.

[78] *Pa. Chronicle*, Nov. 16, 1767

[79] For these debts see *New Hampshire Gazette*, Dec. 16, 1786; *Conn. Courant*, June 11, 18, 1771; *Vermont Gazette*, July 3, 1783, May 17, 1784, Jan. 31, 1785; Charles C. Crittenden, *The Commerce of North Carolina, 1763–1789* (New Haven, 1936), 101–102; Gray, *Agriculture*, I, 412; Weaver, *Trumbull*, 17–18; Grant, *Kent*, 43; Bidwell and Falconer, *Agriculture*, 133; Thomas Rutherford Letter Book, Va. Hist. Soc.: for example to Messrs. Hawksley and Rutherford, Richmond, June 25, 1786.

food of all sorts, a large number of notes, rum, nails, lumber, cheese, a grindstone, and work such as weaving.[80]

The shopkeepers accumulated, over the years, considerably more property than most other men of their community, and had a higher standard of living. Isaac Thomas, a Hardwick, Massachusetts, trader, owned clothes worth £24.3.4. and a riding chair. He was a farmer with £55 worth of livestock to furnish his family with meat; he was also a miller, iron manufacturer, potash maker, and small-scale land speculator. David Blanchard of Weymouth had fewer interests, but he too had a farm and died leaving £138.18 in personal property. He also owned £57 worth of debts.[81] Country shopkeepers in the South were sometimes poor, like the one in Jacksonburgh who owned only £29 worth of property, but they were more apt to be slaveowners and men of consequence, such as Maurice Harvey of St. George's Dorchester, with £2,905 (£415 sterling) in personal estate alone, including five slaves, and in addition £25,178 currency in debts outstanding.

The city merchants were even more involved in the network of debts. Jonathan Trumbull in 1740 owed £3,258. 8.11 and had £5,169.11 in good and £247.2.8 in uncollectable debts. The Ringgold firm of Maryland had sums outstanding which were as large as £5,000 currency from one firm and £2,700 from an individual; over 500 persons owed money to it. Isaac Holmes, a Charleston merchant, died possessed of £3,428 sterling in debts from 144 persons. The firm of John Norton & Sons was owed £63,856 by 398 Virginians in 1773.[82] The amount of debts became even

[80] Isaiah Tiffany Account Book, 1763–1767, Conn. Hist. Soc.; see also Benjamin Snyder Account Book, N.Y. Hist. Soc.

[81] Worcester County Probate Records, vol. 9, p. 117; Suffolk County Probate Records, vol. 87, pp. 444–449.

[82] Weaver, *Trumbull*, 20; Galloway-Marcoe-Maxie Collection, Gal-

greater after the war, and the network of obligations was so complicated that the merchants' economic position cannot be discovered with certainty.[83] The situation may have been most extreme in South Carolina. Over four hundred inventories between 1783 and 1788 listed about £843,000 in personal property, of which over £250,000, or 30 percent, was in debts. This sum was owned by one-quarter of the men, who had an average of £2,404 each. The largest share was held by twenty persons who possessed three-quarters of the total amount. These men were presumably rich, but since money owed is not shown by the records and since the state's citizens collectively were in debt to British firms, many men who appear to have been creditors to a great amount may have been on the edge of bankruptcy.

Meanwhile they lived very comfortably. They owned £2,000 or even more in personal property and were well supplied with servants or slaves. Merchants probably spent at least £500 a year, purchasing imported clothes, fine foods, good wines (in impressive quantities), carriages for as much as £200,[84] gold watches for £27, costly silver, plate, and furniture.[85] The family expenses of one Baltimore family with two children ran over £600 a year, including dancing lessons, membership in a fishing club, and losses at whist.[86] It was not a hard life. The beginner kept long hours,

---

loway Papers, box 4, Lib. Cong.; S.C. Inventory Book 1763–1767, pp. 84–88; *John Norton & Sons*, 293.

[83] One resident of Carlisle, Pennsylvania, estimated that the storekeepers were owed £25,000. John Armstrong to Gen. William Irvine, Carlisle, Aug. 16, 1767, *Hist. Mag.*, VIII (1864), 18.

[84] *New York Mercury*, Nov. 2, 1767. The usual cost was about £50. E.g., Galloway Papers, 1770–1779, Lib. Cong.; *The Virginia Gazette and Weekly Advertiser* (Richmond), Dec. 6, 1787.

[85] *Md. Journal*, June 9, 1768; Israel Pemberton Papers, vol. 27, 1774–1775, p. 175, Hist. Soc. Pa.

[86] John Davidson Account Books, Md. Hist. Soc.

for the stores were open from sunrise to sunset,[87] but clerks kept store for the established wholesaler, who attended for only a few hours, with plenty of time for coffee and pleasure.

The prosperous merchant often invested in land. Suffolk County contained some who had no real estate—about one-fourth of the whole number—but these were with few exceptions small property owners who scarcely deserved the title of merchant. The true merchants ordinarily owned at least £1,000 and often £2,000 worth of real estate. This property usually consisted of a brick house with land worth hundreds of pounds, perhaps another house which was rented, a store, a ship of some sort, and part of a wharf. The richer ones had land outside the city and often other sorts of real property. Many Charlestonians were merchant-planters, and the combination was common throughout the South: a North Carolina merchant had lots, stores, houses, and wharves in Wilmington, a house and a lot in Campbelton, as well as a saw mill, a grist mill, farm land, perriagues, canoes, and oceangoing vessels.[88] Such properties helped greatly when commercial profits were reduced and enabled many merchants to maintain their expensive households even in periods of depression.

The incomes of most professional men, though lower, were more secure than the earnings of merchants and permitted a comfortable standard of living. Clergymen received anywhere from £40 on up to several hundreds of pounds. But even the minister with £40 in cash, if it was paid, lived adequately. He received a house and firewood; the glebe supplied most of his food; and he might collect something through fees and gifts. Therefore he could spend

---

[87] *Providence Gazette*, April 23, 1768; *Continental Journal*, July 1, 1784.

[88] Crittenden, *Commerce of North Carolina*, 110.

more than usual on clothes—say £20—buy what was necessary of food and essentials, and break even. What made
such a salary seem low was the understandable, indeed
proper, desire to live at a higher level—the level befitting a
college man, a leader of the community, and one who regarded lawyers, doctors, and merchants as equals.[89] Probably most ministers also wanted to educate their children,
which would cost £10 to £20 a year apiece. The actual
standard of living adopted by most ministers, therefore, was
considerably above subsistence and required the £150
which, as observed earlier, would enable one to live like a
gentleman.

There were many poor clergymen, especially in the
country churches, whose salaries did not allow such a style
of life. Woodmason remarked of the North Carolina backcountry preachers that the salary was "not a competent
Maintenance. It hardly subsists them—and those few among
Us who *Shine away* owe their Splendor to their marrying
of Women of Property." Similarly in New Hampshire an
observer commented that "the salaries of our clergy in general, especially in most of the country towns, is scarcely
sufficient for the support of their families in the common
necessities of life, much less for the education of their children."[90] Some of these men farmed, turned part-time doctor (for there often was no other), supplied the need for a
schoolmaster, or took private pupils.[91] However most min-

[89] Practically all clergymen, especially in New England, were
college-trained, though some had been farmers or artisans (one was
a former butcher: Dyer Throop Hinkley, Journal, Aug. 1, 1784,
Conn. Hist. Soc.).

[90] Charles Woodmason, *The Carolina Backcountry on the Eve of
the Revolution* (Richard J. Hooker, ed., Chapel Hill, 1953), 91;
New Hampshire Gazette, July 9, 1783

[91] The Rev. Manasseh Cutler practiced medicine and had a private
boarding school. *Life*, 72–73. Jonathan Boucher did the same. *Reminiscences of an American Loyalist*, 1738–1789 . . . (Boston, 1925),

isters earned enough to live well. Dr. John Peirce of Brook-
line, during a ten-year period beginning in 1802, spent £180
a year. This included the services of a maid, and exceeded
his salary of about £165.[92] Both income and expenses were
higher than the norm for revolutionary times, but prices
had risen in the 1790's so that Peirce's situation may be
regarded as typical of the prosperous clergymen. The average minister's salary probably just equalled his expenses,
since he received the usual £70 (in New England), a house
equivalent to at least £25, wood worth perhaps £5, most
of his food (say £30), plus fees and gifts (£20?). There
were ministers, especially in the South and larger cities in
the North, who lived "in elegant style." Of the Maryland
clergymen we read that "each incumbent has a neat and
convenient habitation, with a sufficient quantity of land,
in proper cultivation, to answer every useful and domestic
purpose; and the emoluments arising from the least benefi-
cial preferment, are amply sufficient to support an appearance, perfectly consistent with the respectability of the
clerical profession." [93] The average clergyman, as we have
seen, was able to enjoy several hundred pounds of personal
property and the same amount of real estate, apart from his
glebe. It was a standard of living neither precarious nor
elegant, but comfortable.

Teachers received incomes which were lower at every
level and which, as a rule, enabled the bachelor to get by
but forced the married man into other fields. Most schoolmasters were young men, often just graduated from college,
who taught while studying law or theology, the much more

41, 48. See also John A. Munroe, *Federalist Delaware, 1775–1815*
(Brunswick, N.J., 1954), 44, 47; Middlekauff, *Ancients and Axioms*,
70.

[92] Dr. John Peirce Papers, Mass. Hist. Soc. He had three children.

[93] Brissot de Warville, *New Travels*, 101n; *Life of Cutler*, 237;
Eddis, *Letters*, 47.

lucrative professions.[94] For the time being they often lived like laborers, receiving about the same income, boarding in someone's house. There was little incentive to excel. "Are there no suitable men employed as schoolmasters?" asked one of them. "Then let the business be considered more reputable—offer a handsome salary." [95] Schoolteachers at this level were often incompetent. "A pedagogue is a term of reproach," wrote "A Friend to Literature," "and there are but very few who will undertake the instruction of our youth, if a subsistence can be procured by any other means, and by this they gain but a bare support, their salary is very low—a prompt payment of it (trifling as it is) might make it more valuable; but even this is not attended to, and our school masters continue in their offices 'till their cloaths are worn out, and their credit exhausted—then they are obliged to quit, and trust to public faith for the payment of their arrears!" [96] William Plumer has left a gloomy picture of the school in Epping, New Hampshire, where the illiterate selectmen hired such men as would accept the lowest wages. The situation was no better in the rural South. Here also schoolmasters usually needed some supplementary income, so that they took private pupils, received gifts, or were primarily ministers.[97] The future Anglican minister, Devereaux Jarrett, started as a young uneducated teacher in

[94] La Rochefoucault-Liancourt, *Travels*, I, 530; *The Massachusetts Spy* (Worcester), June 4, 1778.

[95] *Independent Gazetteer*, Dec. 15, 1786.

[96] *New Hampshire Gazette*, Feb. 15, 1783; *Mass. Spy*, Feb. 27, 1783; see also *Md. Gazette*, Feb. 15, 1770; Whitfield J. Bell, jr., "Some Aspects of the Social History of Pennsylvania, 1760–1790," *Pa. Mag. Hist. Biog.*, LXII (1938), 289–290.

[97] Autobiography, p. 9, Lib. Cong.; McCaul, in *Ga. Hist. Qtly.*, XL (1956), 111. Teachers who lived by tutoring students had difficulty in collecting their money just as did the public school masters. For example, *Gazette of the State of Georgia*, Oct. 30, 1788.

Virginia's backcountry earning so little that he had to go into debt for a suit of clothes.[98]

A single man who saved his money could make a profit while preparing for a more remunerative career as minister, lawyer, or merchant. The schoolmaster of Dorchester, Massachusetts, received £45 and spent £19.10 for board and £12 for clothing, which ought to have netted him £10 or so.[99] For the bachelor who served as a tutor or taught in an academy, the life was not a bad one. Wealthy merchants or planters took the tutors into their homes, promised to treat them as one of the family, provided them with all the essentials, and paid them £30 besides.[100] John Harrower, an impoverished Scotsman, left his family at home and indentured himself in Virginia to serve four years as a schoolmaster for bed, board, washing, and £5. His contract was bought by Colonel Daingerfield, who at once had his clothes washed and gave him pocket money. Harrower taught for eight hours a day, and was allowed to teach other students for 5s currency per quarter. He ate with the family, had his own room, slaves to clean his quarters and make his fine feather bed, and money enough to buy rum when he wanted it, though not enough to support his family back home.[101]

Teachers in academies and colleges earned much more, but only a small fraction of them made enough to support their families above the subsistence level. Many must have been like Jonathan Sewall, schoolmaster of Woburn and

---

[98] Douglass Adair, ed., "The Autobiography of the Reverend Devereaux Jarratt, 1732–1763," *Wm. and Mary Qtly.*, 3 series IX (1952), 346–393.

[99] Small, *New England Schools*, 135.

[100] *Va. Gazette* (Dixon and Hunter), Aug. 8, 1777; Fithian, *Journal and Letters*, 8.

[101] Diary, *Am. Hist. Rev.*, VI (1900–1901), 65–107.

Salem, Massachusetts, who could not afford to buy luxuries such as wine, beer, and tea.[102] Their standard of living was, on the whole, not only below that of other professional men, but less than that of many artisans. The ablest ones were tempted to accept the higher salary of a minister, for which profession they were often trained. A Bostonian observed that even Harvard professors could not live on their "slender" incomes of £600 Old Tenor, and speculated that they were all in the country preaching. Any geniuses among them, he thought, would have poor inducement to stay at Harvard, since they could earn twice as much elsewhere.[103] As a rule it seems that teachers were a peripatetic lot, acquiring little real property, spending what they earned for a subsistence-plus style of life, and saving little.

The term "doctor," in early America, was applied to or used by two quite different types of men. "The proper sense of the word," wrote a newspaper essayist, "signifies an able, learned man, eminently distinguished from mankind in general, by a uncommon acquaintance with some art or profession. The common or vulgar acceptation of the word denotes either a *physician*, a *chuirgeon*, a *bone-setter*, an *apothecary*, or any person performing chuirgical or medicinal operation." [104] The first was always reputable; the second frequently a quack, sometimes a barber with a few lethal implements. The distinction was not always clear, for few doctors were well educated, and those who were not, be their intentions ever so good, were in fact often mere quacks.

Doctors' bills were sometimes considered excessive, and

[102] Shipton, *Harvard Graduates*, XII, 307.
[103] Elsbree, *American Teacher*, 92; *Boston Evening Post*, Feb. 27, 1764.
[104] *Conn. Gazette* (New London), March 18, 1774.

poor men complained of them,[105] yet many physicians had small incomes and a low standard of living. A South Carolina doctor left only £4.9.4. Thomas Steel of Mendon, "Phisitian," died in 1767 with no real estate, £7.18.8 in instruments and medicines, £4.9.10 worth of books (he was not a quack: this was a substantial amount), clothes valued at less than four pounds, and £25 in notes and accounts, for a total estate of £63.6.1.[106] The rural doctor was paid by an astonishing variety of goods and services. Dr. Thomas Williams of Deerfield, Massachusetts, accepted pigeons, cranberries, bees wax, considerable wood, turnips, bricks, turkeys, and a lamb, and was paid also in ferriages, cartage, weaving, farm work of all sorts—and cash.[107] The country doctor did not in fact live at a much higher level than did most members of his community. A Massachusetts doctor asserted that he was obliged to visit his patients at night as well as by day, regardless of the weather. In the winter, he might require half a day to travel a mile and give advice, for which he charged only 8d and had trouble collecting that. Common laborers, he observed, earned 1/8 at that season, while a shoemaker in a day could easily make two pairs of boys' shoes at 3/8 each, and the blacksmith charged 5/ for shoeing a horse.[108]

On the other hand there were doctors who earned a large income and lived well. The college-educated man usually settled in the towns and enjoyed a large practice. If he had been trained in Edinburgh, the cost of his education certainly justified the charging of high fees. Only the rich

[105] *S.C. Gazette and General Advertiser*, Nov. 22, 1783. "A Mechanic" protested that a carpenter who received $2 a day had to pay $2 for a bottle of physic, one bottle each day for a sick child.

[106] Worchester County Probate Records, vol. 9, p. 439.

[107] Account Book, N.Y. Hist. Soc.

[108] *Boston Evening Post*, Feb. 15, 1768.

could afford such a preparation and even they found the cost burdensome. Walter Jones of Virginia started with the idea that he could live on £90 a year in Scotland, but found that "less than 100 £ perhaps will not maintain a Gentleman in Edinburgh," and ended by spending £118 annually for three years, which he wrote was less by £30 or £40 than any of his acquaintances had required "who have kept up a tolerable genteel character." He then had to stay on for more than a year longer and invest an additional £200 in medicines and costs after that—spending a total of £700 or more. The whole process nearly bankrupted his brother who financed the venture.[109] Once having started practice, however, the skillful doctor was assured of a good living. An eminent Boston practitioner, who charged fat fees, saved a thousand pounds sterling in a few years.[110] Some Suffolk County doctors had no real estate but an equal number held £500 worth of land, while purchasing also £200 in personal property. A South Carolina physician died worth £6,789, not including real estate, of which £5,683 was in debts; while another, a happy man, owned 52 slaves, a fiddle and bow, many music books, and other volumes including a set of Molière.

Little need be said about lawyers other than that most of them belonged to the wealthy class. Even the beginning clerk received £60 plus accommodations,[111] and within a few years one could become rich. Not everyone did. Some backcountry lawyers, especially those with little legal training, had small incomes, while in the city one occasionally found a lawyer like John Pickering of Portsmouth who,

---

[109] Walter Jones to Thomas Jones, Edinburgh, Aug. 15, 1766, June 18, 1769; James Russell to Thomas Jones, London, July 16, 1770, Jones Family Papers, box 15, 17, 18, Lib. Cong.

[110] Shipton, *Harvard Graduates*, XII, 187.

[111] Diary of Jaspar Yeates, 1764–1769, Nov. 12, 1764, Hist. Soc. Pa.

wrote an admirer, "does more business . . . than any other
in the State; but obtains much less money from his practice
than some little contemptible pettifoggers. . . . He is very
moderate in his fees. Of the poor he claims nothing; of
those in easy circumstances he often trusts to their generosity, and frequently suffers thereby." Most of his fellow
attorneys, however, grew rich and lived splendidly, characterized, wrote one critic, by the neatness of dress, especially of the head, gallantry to females, and vanity.[112]

Such qualities were not characteristic of the farmers, who
were reputed to be honest, virtuous, and industrious.[113]
American farmers included a wide range, varying from the
substantial landowner of the seaboard, who perhaps deserved such praise, to the pioneer, who often did not. Eastern farms raised a surplus of men, who had the choice of
learning an entirely new trade in the town, with low pay, or
of moving West where they would at least be following a
familiar occupation. Here they were joined by European
immigrants, peasants who naturally inclined toward the
land.[114] Such men were almost always poor, and many
were deservedly so. Descriptions of the frontiersmen of the
revolutionary era, even when written by those who had no
ax to grind, were generally uncomplimentary. James
Duane's representative on his land in western New York
warned him to "enquire the Surcomstance and Caracture of
the Strangers that Come her for Land as I understand some
are so poor so verry poor that has Nothing at all whatsom-
ever thair some a gain of but Endiferent Caractour." The
newcomers on the Pennsylvania frontier included some

[112] William Plumer to John Hale, Exeter, Sept. 18, 1786, Col. Soc.
Mass., *Transactions*, xi (1906–1907), 389; *Independent Chronicle*,
March 9, 1786; *N.Y. Journal*, Nov. 17, 1785.
[113] *N.J. Gazette*, Feb. 27, 1786.
[114] "Angelus Americanus," *Pa. Chronicle*, March 27, 1769; Gray,
Agriculture, i, 122–123.

"simple and honest" men who were "good sober industrious hands," but others were "generally a pack of drunken lazy gluttons." A traveller to South Carolina's Ninety-six district gladly left the country "to the present rude Inhabitants, who are made up of the Scum of the Universe." [115] Everyone agreed that they were poor, and that they were obliged to start life in debt for land and other essentials. Therefore during the first years, so long as their home was a frontier, they merely subsisted, just maintaining their families.[116] Rents were usually quite low, since high rents would drive farmers to other unoccupied land. Therefore the debt contracted was not very great, but the income was so small that poverty inevitably ensued.[117] At best the pioneer raised enough surplus to buy the essentials and pay his taxes and debts, "a rather scanty yet tolerable subsistence." [118] A one-room cabin sparsely furnished, home-made clothes, a gun to supply meat, a couple of cows and a horse, and a few essential tools were his possessions.

Even after the frontier stage was over, many farmers pro-

[115] John Myers to James Duane, May 26, 1785, Duane Papers, N.Y. Hist. Soc.; "Extracts from the Journal of Samuel Preston, Surveyor, 1787," *Pa. Mag. Hist. Biog.*, XXII (1898), 363; S. F. Warren to Doctor Warren, St. James Santee, Jan. 22, 1766, misc. mss., South Caroliniana Lib.; John McDowell (?) to Henry Knox, Pittsburgh, July 25, 1786, Knox Papers, XIX, 2, Mass. Hist. Soc.

[116] Instructions of Orange County to its representatives, 1773, *Col. Rec. N.C.*, IX, 701; Bliss, "Tenantry," *Va. Mag. Hist. Biog.*, LVIII (1950), *passim*; Jedidiah Morse, *The American Geography* (2 ed., London, 1792), 313–317; Dieter Cunz, *The Maryland Germans* (Princeton, 1948), 114; *Md. Gazette*, July 30, 1776; *Pa. Packet*, March 12, 1785; *American Husbandry*, 90; [William Whiting], *An Address to the Inhabitants of the County of Berkshire* (Hartford, 1778).

[117] *American Husbandry*, 48; *Vermont Gazette*, March 19, 1787; H. C. Groome, *Fauquier during the Proprietorship* (Richmond, 1927), 74–75; Robert Livingston to James Duane, Manor Livingston, Nov. 9, 1764, Duane Papers, N.Y. Hist. Soc.

[118] Gilbert Harris to James Duane, Kingsbury, Jan. 2, 1787, *ibid.*

duced little beyond their own requirements, and comprised "that class of husbandman, whose farms are small, but barely sufficient to support their families." [119] The limitations on marketing can be imagined when one remembers that oats, barley, wheat, or corn sometimes had to be carried on one's back to and from the mills, which might be miles away: settlers in some New Hampshire towns had to walk about forty-six miles with the bags of grain.[120] Fortunately the small farmer needed very little cash. He "could do anything, as indeed the countryman in America generally can, himself supplying his own wants in great part or wholly," so that his small holdings furnished "all the necessities, most of the conveniences, and but few of the luxuries of life." [121] There was some exaggeration here. The farmers did indeed furnish most of their own food, but they had to buy salt, molasses or sugar, and rum. Rum was not, perhaps, an essential article in the diet, but if it (or its equivalent) is to be removed from the food list it might well be added to the medical costs. Matthew Patten replenished his supply whenever his wife had a baby, which was annually, perhaps for himself, though probably his wife needed it most. On November 25, 1766 he noted, "I got 2 Quarts of New England Rum . . . and my wife was a little Easyer." Usually each baby required a couple of quarts, but in September of 1767 he bought three gallons.[122] Even if rum were eliminated from the "diet," the family needed a few pounds for food which they could not produce themselves.

Most of the clothing was made at home. It might consist

[119] *Independent Chronicle,* Feb. 8, 1781.
[120] Cochrane and Wood, *Francestown,* 61–62. General descriptions in Gray, *Agriculture,* I, 441–442; Morse, *Geography,* 313–314.
[121] Schoepf, *Travels,* I, 30; Morse, *Geography,* 240.
[122] *Diary,* Nov. 25, 1766, Sept. 1767.

only of "cotton rags" among the poor southern families, or of "strong decent homespun," [123] but it was usually adequate for protection from the weather even though it did not satisfy an aesthetic sense of taste for luxury. Shoes, however, had to be purchased, and hats also. Fullers and weavers were often encountered in the backcountry and had to be paid. The farmer was also obliged to pay the miller, the tax collector, the shopkeeper, the blacksmith, his creditor, his doctor, and the Justice of the Peace. Some surplus was essential.

Fortunately most of these purchases required no cash outlay. The cordwainer received food, the miller a portion of the grain, the blacksmith a few days' labor, the Justice of the Peace a barrel of cider, the doctor a day's work with the ox team. A small amount of circulating money sufficed to transact the complicated business of a rural village. Matthew Patten wrote in his diary for April 30, 1755, "Got four bushel of Indian corn Ground into meal and bought the Toal from James Moor but Could not pay him for want of Chang the Toal came to 6/3 Old Tenor and paid James Macdugal 55s/6d silver which he overpaid me in a peice of gold of 33 £ also and gave John smith one dollar and 5 £ in paper money for 4 bushell of Indian corn and for 40s I owed him for swingling Flax and the remainder he promised to return as soon as he Got Change." [124] A few acres producing some grain crop probably paid for everything that the farmer needed, so that he might proudly record in his diary, "I owe no Body only Elijah Henman 3 Pound for Boards." [125]

Most farmers raised their standard of living considerably beyond this bare minimum to a subsistence-plus level. At

[123] Smyth, *A Tour*, 1, 104; Morse, *Geography*, 288.
[124] *Diary*, 15.
[125] David Hickok diary, Conn. State Lib.

the same time the small farm did not enable the husbandman to purchase freely, nor was it easy to pay debts. These might amount to £50 or more, requiring £4 at least in annual interest.[126] A farmer who had ten acres in wheat produced perhaps 120 bushels at 3s sterling, or £18 cash, which was about the average income.[127] He might spend £5 for rum and food, £3 for clothes (mostly shoes), and £2 for other essentials, leaving £8 for debts and taxes. Despite the low cash income of farmers, their standard of living was quite comfortable, though it required continuous hard work to maintain it.

The ability of farmers to accumulate wealth varied greatly. In the subsistence farm areas the ordinary yeoman earned little more than his immediate needs. He ended life with about £100 worth of personal property and £200 worth of real estate, not so much by paying cash as by improving the land with his labor. He had perhaps a horse, a few cattle, a couple of pigs, and a few acres under cultivation. Joshua Hubbart of Franklin, Massachusetts, owned a dwelling house, barn, and eighty acres of land valued altogether at £400. But his soil was not very productive, for he possessed less than £90 in personal estate. His clothes were valued at £9.14.6, including a hat, great coat, "strate bodied" coat, jacket, breeches, shirt, stockings, and shoes. He owned a great Bible and other books (£1.10.6), two guns, and £22 worth of implements such as axes, tubs, and carpenters' tools—the necessary household and husbandry equipment of the self-sufficient farmer. His land had pro-

---

[126] Romaine, "Family Expenses," for one example. A farm ordinarily cost more than this to rent. Thus Richard Henry Lee rented 100 acres for £6. To Thomas Jefferson, May 3, 1779, Boyd, ed., *Papers of Jefferson*, II, 263. On the other hand a number of 100-acre tracts in Sussex County, Delaware, each with a house, rented for an average of £4 annually. *Pa. Journal*, Nov. 10, 1763.

[127] Schoepf, *Travels*, I, 45; Hart, *Valley of Virginia*, 10.

duced 20 bushels of Indian corn, valued at £4 (rather too high), and supported a pair of oxen, three cows, two heifers, a mare and two colts, but no pigs or sheep.[128]

Commercial farmers enjoyed a much larger income which permitted a higher style of living. Southerners especially (except in North Carolina) had a higher standard and bought considerably more property. Samuel Carne, a typical South Carolina planter, left a personal estate of £2,418 current money, or £347 sterling. He owned two Negro men, a "wench" with child, a wench with two children, a young wench, and a young girl, the whole amounting to £2,050. He had twenty-four cattle, though these were worth only half as much as the New Englander's seven, seven horses of the same relative value, and six hogs. His land had produced 70 bushels of rice, 150 of corn, and 12 of peas, worth about £10 sterling. Otherwise the Southerner and the Northerner owned about the same property: sparse household furnishings and a minimum of clothes. William Townsend, also a representative Carolinian, had fewer slaves, but a much higher standard of living if his personal possessions are evidence. He owned, for example, an easy chair, a dozen walnut chairs, two dining tables and a sideboard, a mahogany desk, looking glasses, napkins, fifteen silver spoons, and a pair of gold sleeve buttons.[129] The small planter Theophilus Faver of Essex County, Virginia, who held eleven slaves and raised corn and tobacco, had pewter rather than silver, but he did own a desk, a sugar box, candle sticks and snuffers, eight old chairs, table cloths, and a pair of sheets. His property was typical of the medium-sized farmer. He had plenty of food: 18 geese, 26 "Fat Hogs" and 19 other pigs, some honey, three pecks of

[128] Suffolk County Probate Records, vol. 82, pp. 139–140.
[129] Inventory Book x, 256–257, 257–258, S.C. Archives.

beans, bags of fruit, onions, and 75 gallons of brandy (at 4/6 per gallon), though his entire "waring apparrel" came to only £3.2.[130]

The small slave-holder, with his comfortable life, might ultimately become the great planter who lived in luxury. Such a one was hardly a farmer at all but "a writing farmer, a gentleman farmer, a farmer who leases his thousands of acres to his tenants."[131] A large landowner might have 200 acres in wheat,[132] which, allowing only 12 bushels to the acre and a minimum price of 3/ per bushel, would gross £360; tobacco land produced as much as £12 per acre. Thus a wealthy farmer had hundreds of pounds to spend. This posed no problem. A slave cost £30 to £50, or £12 to rent. One could buy on credit, but the price then rose by as much as 50 percent.[133] The maintenance of a slave was £3 to £6 annually. Indentured servants required less initial capital but it was necessary to spend more on them thereafter, while free labor was still more expensive, costing

---

[130] Essex County Will Book 13, pp. 443–444, Va. State Lib.

[131] "A REAL FARMER," *New York Journal* (Poughkeepsie), Jan. 25, 1779.

[132] "Extracts from the Journal of Samuel Preston, Surveyor," *Pa. Mag. Hist. Biog.*, XXII (1898), 354.

[133] *Newport Mercury*, July 16, 1785; Schoepf, *Travels*, II, 203. According to South Carolina probate records, slaves cost £40 before the war, £50 or more after it. See also *The State Gazette of South-Carolina*, March 5, 1787; *Columbian Herald*, May 16, 1785; *American Husbandry*, 293–300. The price in Virginia was £30 before the war, £40 after it. Louis Morton, *Robert Carter of Nomini Hall* (Williamsburg, 1941), appendix table 12; Gray, *Agriculture*, I, 368–369; Ludwell Papers, Va. Hist. Soc.; Ballagh, ed., *Letters of Lee*, I, 46–47; Richard Adams to Thomas Adams, July 5, 1769, *Va. Mag. Hist. Biog.*, V (1897–1898), 133; *Md. Hist. Mag.*, XII (1917), 27; probate records. The price in the North was higher, e.g. *New York Journal*, Jan. 26, 1775; *Rivington's New York Gazetteer*, Sept. 30, 1773; Kalm, *Travels*, 207–208.

(according to one estimate) one-fourth of the crop.[134] The large landowner was also tempted to buy more land. Since the initial price of a large plantation was about £2,000, there might well be debts to pay or to avoid.[135] A Virginian in London wrote home to his brother that he was "an honorable Exception to the generality of our Countrymen; who the merchants all declare are not only unwilling to Pay their Debts but guilty of a Breach of Word."[136] These debts were economically sound if contracted to buy good land or needed field slaves, but too often they resulted from high living.

The rich landholders could afford a style of life which

[134] Aaron Leaming diary, July 6, 1750, Hist. Soc. Pa. Leaming, a substantial New Jersey farmer, estimated the cost of harvesting in detail.

[135] Gray, *Agriculture*, I, 541. By the time of the Revolution good land cost anywhere from 20s to £10 sterling per acre. Large tracts sold for an average of £2 per acre. A lottery advertised in Virginia included a 500-acre estate, complete with an eight-room brick house, other buildings, and an orchard, valued at £2,000; another asked £750 for 1,200 acres in the Piedmont, with houses and some cleared land. *Va. Gazette* (Purdie and Dixon), Sept. 17, 1767, Sept. 21, 1769. Horatio Gates informed Charles Lee that a 2,400-acre tract of excellent Shenandoah land, with a mill, could be bought for 30s sterling per acre, after which Lee would need to spend £1,000 sterling more. He would then have a "fine living." July 1, 1774, N.Y. Hist. Soc., *Collections*, 1871, pp. 124–125. Northern farms were more expensive, averaging £4 to £5 per acre, but one could buy smaller tracts than in the South. Highly cultivated estates were even more valuable. Governor Belcher's 336-acre farm near Boston cost £3,600 sterling. Joseph Peirce to Henry Knox, Boston, Jan. 15, Feb. 15, 1783, Knox Papers XI, 50, 128, Mass. Hist. Soc. A southern Rhode Island plantation of 1,100 acres averaged £8.17. *R.I. State Recs.*, X, 72. Large farms in the Philadelphia area of a couple of hundred acres rented for £100 currency or so. *Pa. Gazette*, May 7, 1772, April 23, 1783; *Pa. Journal*, Nov. 28, 1771, April 23, 1777.

[136] Walter Jones to Thomas Jones, London, July 23, 1769, Jones Family Papers, box 17, Lib. Cong.

other colonials might well envy and try to emulate. In Massachusetts there were farmers with £4,000 or £5,000 worth of property. John Caldwell, Esq., of Rutland owned 1,131 acres and 50 cattle. James Gordon, Esq. had an estate of over £4,000 including nearly 4,000 acres, and the Loyalist John Borland held 1,200 acres, most of which was rented, valued at £6,400 sterling. William West of Scituate, Rhode Island, requested leave to sell by lottery 1,757 acres, 227 of which he had bought for £1,703. In New York, Robert R. and Robert Livingston together enjoyed £850 annually from real estate besides profits from a mill, while Israel Pemberton's holdings in Pennsylvania and New Jersey were valued at £60,500.[137] In the South there were many estates worth £10,000 sterling.

The great landholder ran a diversified business. He had to supply the food, clothing, shelter, and other essentials and luxuries for fifty or a hundred people. Joshua Grimball's estate on Edisto Island, South Carolina, included corn mills, two lots of carpenters' tools, coopers' tools, fishing lines and net, and agricultural implements for garden, corn, and rice.[138] A considerable capital outlay was necessary before the plantation could be even partially self-sufficient. In addition there were the heavy demands of family and friends for luxury articles: a dressing glass, a silver watch, china, glass, silverware, food and drink appropriate to the glittering table, with clothes to match. High though the income was, it was often exceeded by expenditures.

The different standards of living during the revolutionary era grew out of the unequal distribution of property. In studying the consumption habits and manner of life of the

---

[137] *R.I. State Recs.*, x, 72, 141; Pemberton Papers vol. 29, p. 121, Hist. Soc. Pa.
[138] Inventory Book x, 344–345, S.C. Arch.

early Americans, it is convenient to divide them into three groups: the poor, who had little property; the small property holders; and the rich.

The poor included, as we have seen, perhaps one-fifth of the whites and nearly 40 percent of the total population. They did not own land, and received a cash income varying from nothing to a few pounds. Such an income permitted most of them to buy only a fraction of their necessities. Fortunately, most of their needs were supplied by the master or employer, so that beggars were seen seldom or never.[139] Slaves had a bare minimum standard of living, but we do not read of their starving, freezing or (with perhaps a few exceptions) suffering for want of clothes. Indentured servants were better treated than were slaves. As for the indigent freemen, the wage level ordinarily prevented extreme poverty, and the frontier was within easy reach. Moreover the exceptions were taken care of by boarding them with families who were then reimbursed out of local or general funds, while vagabonds and men temporarily out of work were placed in workhouses. Charleston in 1767 was caring for about 200 persons including 50 in a work house, 31 children maintained by the church, and various transient poor people. Three thousand pounds had been collected in 1775 and the amount was doubled in 1776. After the Revolution the work house was rebuilt, and the City Council spent £1,960 in two years.[140] In 1771 a committee in Philadelphia reported that 286 persons had been admitted to the alms house, 85 more had been committed as vagrant or disorderly, and an average of 321 maintained, nearly two-thirds of

---

[139] Seldom: Thomas Jefferson, *Notes on the State of Virginia* (London, 1787), 220–221; *American Husbandry*, 46. Never: Barbe-Marbois, *Letters*, 71.

[140] "Public Poor Relief in Colonial Charleston," *S.C. Hist. and Gen. Mag.*, XLII (1941), 83–86; *Columbian Herald*, Sept. 14, 1785.

whom were incapable of any service. After the Revolution over £1,500 was raised for the relief of 1,600 families—about one-fifth of the population if the "Liberties" are included—most of whom needed only wood.[141] New York City had its "meaner Class of Mankind, the industrious Poor," and in 1769 an article urged that to assist them was not charity, but justice. In 1782 a Society for Alleviating the Distresses of the Poor was established.[142] Many people in Newport, Rhode Island, were unable to buy wood, so that the town was reportedly "at an immense charge to support their poor." Boston in 1768 set up an establishment for the manufacture of cloth, for employing "the many Poor we have in the Town and giving them a Livelihood." Portsmouth too maintained a society for encouraging industry among the poor. In 1786 there were 49 persons in the alms house.[143] Noting that the number of poor had greatly increased, one writer blamed "extravagance or idleness," but admitted that some were idle for want of employment, and argued that these should "have labour prepared for them," while "*force*" would do for the rest.[144]

Another group of people were also poor, though they did own, or were able to use, land. These included squatters, some of the tenants, and impoverished farmers. The South seems to have contained most of them. Chastellux observed of Virginia, "It is in this country that I saw poor persons, for the first time, after I passed the sea; for, in the midst of

[141] *Pa. Chronicle*, June 3, 1771; *Pa. Gazette*, May 18, 1774; *Independent Gazetteer*, March 20, 1784; *Independent Chronicle*, April 8, 1784; *Statutes of Pa.*, x, 32–33.

[142] *New York Gazette and Mercury*, Nov. 13, 1769; *New York Gazetteer*, Oct. 14, 1782.

[143] *Newport Mercury*, Dec. 14, 1767, March 6, 1771; Morris, *Government and Labor*, 13n; *The New Hampshire Mercury, and General Advertiser* (Portsmouth), April 12, 1786.

[144] *ibid.*, March 8, 1786.

those rich plantations, where the negro alone is wretched, miserable huts are often to be met with, inhabited by whites, whose wan looks and ragged garments bespeak poverty." [145] These men were sometimes called, or considered as part of, the "lower class," and occupied in fact an intermediate position between the true lower class of the very poor and the lower middle class of lesser property owners.[146]

The vendue master of New York City divided the householders into three groups, based on the value of their plate and furniture. These were the "First," averaged at £700 (the rich), the "Middling," valued at £200 (well-to-do, upper middle class), and the "Lower," subdivided into those owning £40 and £20.[147] No such great gaps existed, but the figures do emphasize the difference in standards of living and the existence, in the cities, of many small property owners. The middle class, principally farmers and artisans, included over half of the population. Some of them lived little above the subsistence level, spending nearly all of their incomes on necessities, or supplying their own needs from their own resources. A majority, however, earned enough to buy a few luxuries and accumulate some property. Half of the farmers and two-fifths of the artisans owned between £100 and £500 in personal estate. They had in addition two or three times as much real estate. The majority of colonials enjoyed some comfort. Brissot de Warville wrote of the farmhouses in central Massachusetts (a subsistence farm area, for the most part), "Neatness embellishes them all. They have frequently but one story and a garret; their walls

[145] Chastellux, *Travels*, II, 190.
[146] Smyth, *A Tour*, I, 68; *Independent Gazetteer*, March 28, 1787; Anburey, *Travels*, II, 310–311, 332–333; *The Charleston Evening Gazette*, June 5, 1786; *Md. Gazette*, June 7, 1770; Bernard Elliott's Recruiting Journal, 1775," *S.C. Hist. and Gen. Mag.*, XVII (1916), 98.
[147] Pownall, *Topographical Description*, 45.

are papered: tea and coffee appear on their tables; their daughters, clothed in callicoes, display the traits of civility, frankness, and decency; virtues which always follow contentment and ease. Almost all these houses are inhabited by men who are both cultivators and artizans; one is a tanner, another a shoemaker, another sells goods; but all are farmers." [148] The "mansion house," as the home was called regardless of size, was commonly worth £75, though some houses were worth only £10 and others cost over £100. The barns, which varied in value from £5 to £40, usually cost £15. The rest of the real estate was in land, from 100 to 300 acres, depending on where it was located, ranging in value from a few shillings to £10 or more per acre, but averaging perhaps £4 in the commercial farm areas of the North, £2 for good land in the South, and £1 or less for poorer land. Thus the northern farmer, with his smaller holding, would be worth about the same as the southerner, both owning about £350 in real estate all told.

The one major qualification to the general description of prosperity is the existence of debts. The typical farmer or artisan, if free from debt, was in comfortable circumstances, but a debt of any size endangered that comfort. As has been seen, there is a good deal of evidence that debts were widespread. A typical observation was, "I am sorry to find many of our common sort of people inclined to live above their income, so as to involve themselves in debt." [149] Another writer believed, "It is well known the great part of the inhabitants are debtors," and still another maintained that "the greater part of the yeomanry of these States are more in debt than the value of their personal estates." [150]

[148] *New Travels,* 126–127. See also Burnaby on the Shenandoah farmers, pp. 73–74.

[149] "Eumenes," *New York Journal,* April 5, 1780.

[150] *Independent Chronicle,* May 4, 1786; "A Freeman," *Vermont Gazette,* Feb. 12, 1787.

These remarks may be discounted somewhat because their authors commonly were arguing in behalf of moral reformation or pro-debtor laws, but they are given force by merchants' account books. One Boston firm had 361 debtors in Connecticut, and the storekeeper of Kent, in the same colony, had 140 debtors in the town.[151] A Beaufort, South Carolina, merchant was owed over £20,000 sterling by nearly 500 persons. Probate records and account books alike testify to these debts. However they also demonstrate that most debts were small, usually not more than a few pounds: the total sum was large because of a few big borrowers, most of whom were lenders in their turn. A newspaper correspondent observed that "The merchant who ought not to have run into debt above a thousand pounds, has run into debt ten thousand; and the shop keeper who should not have been in debt above a hundred pounds, is in debt a thousand—and the farmer, tradesman, and consumers in general have run into debt ten pounds when they should not more than twenty shillings, or nothing."[152] The point must remain unsettled, but the evidence suggests that the debts, though unquestionably numerous, were seldom burdensome for families of the middle class. They had been contracted for legitimate purposes, such as the purchase of land, which would presently permit their payment; or they resulted from the universal shortage of cash, and were not beyond the ultimate ability of the borrower to discharge. There are exceptions, and periods of severe currency contraction brought genuine hardship, but these debts on the whole did not alter the basic prosperity of the middle class.[153]

[151] *Conn. Courant*, June 11, 18, 1771; Grant, *Kent*, 43.
[152] *Norwich Packet*, March 16, 1786. For the debts of farmers see also *Pa. Journal*, Sept. 14, 1769; Hart, *Valley of Virginia*, 124.
[153] Robert and Katherine Brown in *Virginia*, Chapter v, emphasize that most of the debts owed by what they call the "middle and

Between the small property owners and the wealthy there were many gradations. The truly wealthy class, with £5,000 worth of real and personal estate, included at most 3 percent of the population.[154] The majority of these were large landowners, while the rest were principally merchants, lawyers, and a very few ministers, doctors, and manufacturers, most of whom also held valuable real estate. Their incomes were at least £500, some of which might be in the form of food and lumber used by the household, and were large enough so that they could, or at any rate did, buy what they chose. They paid £1,000 for a house, furnished it lavishly, supplied themselves with plenty of servants, and ate and drank what they pleased. The Carters of Nomini Hall consumed, with the help of their guests, 150 gallons of brandy in one year.[155] James Duane requested his father-in-law to send the family sloop to bring him from New York City, adding, "If by accident she should not I must hire one, for my Family will be too much incommoded in a Crowd of passengers." [156] Robert Hunter wrote in his journal, after

lower classes" were small, whereas those of the "upper class" were large. The generalizations are undoubtedly correct, though the tables which they give are not as useful as one would like because the upper class is defined as including gentlemen, merchants, ministers, constables, mariners, doctors, lawyers, and surveyors, among others, while planters, artisans, and tavernkeepers are assigned a more lowly rank. The basis for this division is "social status," which the Browns use synonymously with class, and which they determine by the title claimed by or given to the individual. Their earlier discussion of the subject indicates that the correlation between titles and wealth was decidedly imperfect, a view with which I concur; so that their upper class contains (as is obvious from the categories) some men of small property. I do not think that Virginia's society can be meaningfully structured in that way.

[154] A Georgian testified that in the 1760's "A Man . . . would have been esteem'd a Man of great fortune if he had £5,000." *Loyalist Claims*, 60.

[155] Edmund Morgan, *Virginians at Home* (Williamsburg, 1952), 42.

[156] June 1, 1767, Duane Papers, N.Y. Hist. Soc.

a series of parties in Virginia, "Most of the company went away this morning, soon after breakfast, in their phaeton, chariots, and coaches in four, with two or three footmen behind. They live in as high a style here, I believe, as any part of the world." [157] They engaged in conspicuous consumption: "How many Houses are built more for Show than for any Thing else! What Dainties crown the Tables of the Rich!" The houses were richly furnished, the women richly dressed.[158] The men and women had plenty of leisure time for drinking, visiting, dancing, riding, and sporting. The men spent only a few hours at work, while the girls slept late, rose late, and went to parties constantly. "We are," wrote a Virginian, "a Luxurious Voluptuous indolent expensive people without Oeconomy or Industry." [159] Even Boston had its clubs where one could play cards (a quarter limit), dance, and drink coffee, tea, chocolate, wine or punch fortnightly.[160]

[157] *Quebec to Carolina*, 209.

[158] *Essex Gazette*, Sept. 6, 1768. Esther Singleton, *Social New York under the Georges 1714–1776* (New York, 1902) contains excellent descriptions of the consumption patterns of the elite. See Fithian, *Journal and Letters*, xxix–xxxi for a description of a large manor house. There is an excellent description of "Westover," and one of the bedrooms in it, in Thomas Lee Shippen to Dr. and Mrs. William Shippen, Dec. 30, 1783, Shippen Papers, vol. 2, Lib. Cong. John Shippen jr. to John Penn, Philadelphia, Nov. 10, 1771, describes a fine estate near Trenton. *ibid.*, vol. 1. See also Bridenbaugh, *Myths*, Chapter II, and Eddis, *Travels*, 112–113.

[159] James Currie to Thomas Jefferson, Richmond, May 2, 1787, Boyd, ed., *Papers of Jefferson*, XI, 328.

[160] *Mass. Centinel*, Jan. 26, 1785; Anburey, *Travels*, II, 293–294; Smyth, *A Tour*, I, 41–42; *American Husbandry*, 132–133; *Quebec to Carolina*, 184; *Newport Mercury*, May 29, 1769; [Lucinda Orr], *Journal of a Young Lady of Virginia, 1782* (Baltimore, 1871); Griffith J. McRee, *Life and Correspondence of James Iredell, one one of the Associate Justices of the Supreme Court of the United States* (2 vols., New York, 1858), I, 128–148; Diary of Francis Taylor, 1786–1795, U. of N.C. Lib.; Christopher Marshall Journal,

The standard of living of the upper class can be illustrated by William Elliott's estate in South Carolina. Elliott, a rich planter, had a home in Charleston and various plantations. His city house contained furnishings worth over £300. These included 50 pictures, 26 china dishes, nearly six dozen china plates, a good deal of other china, 27 pairs of sheets and 27 pairs of pillow cases, and 333¾ ounces of silver dishes valued at £584 currency (£83½ sterling). He had also in the city 21 slaves. Elliott owned, all told, 223 cattle, 422 slaves, and an estate estimated at £24,000 sterling, not including debts to the amount of £167,009 currency which, if good, would equal the rest of his property.[161]

It is clear that revolutionary America produced enough wealth to save even its poor from suffering, to permit the great majority to live adequately, even in comfort, and to enable a few to live in real luxury. The situation was enviable. What made it even more admired was the ease and rapidity with which the poor man could become economically independent, and the remarkable opportunity for the man of modest property to become rich. Thus economic abundance together with high mobility combined to minimize those conflicts which might have grown out of the class structure and the concentration of wealth.

Hist. Soc. Pa., and many other diaries; James Murray letter in Carl Bridenbaugh, *Cities in Revolt* (New York, 1955), 177.

[161] Inventory Book x, 305–313, S.C. Arch.

CHAPTER V

Mobility in Early America

MOBILITY in the revolutionary era was of two types: movement from place to place ("horizontal" mobility) and movement upward or downward in society ("vertical" mobility). The two were essentially connected, for it was above all a man's ability to move to a new location that gave him a chance to rise.

Horizontal mobility needs little discussion. Americans were of "an unsettled disposition" by inheritance, for everyone was either an immigrant or descended from one.[1] The lure of cheap fresh land, the attraction of the city, the excess of population in long-settled communities, and perhaps certain cultural factors such as the reduced importance of the family kept people moving about. One observer believed that "it is scarcely possible in any part of the continent to find a man, amongst the middling and lower classes of Americans, who has not changed his farm and his residence many different times." The intent, he continued, was not "merely to gratify a wandering disposition; in every change he hopes to make money." [2] Immigrants started as city workers and ended as farmers or country artisans; indentured servants in a farming community obtained their freedom, took up land, followed a trade, or hired themselves out in some other village; the sons of yeomen went west, north, south; entire families departed and others arrived to replace them. Indeed this constant

---

[1] *The Pittsburgh Gazette*, March 17, 1787.
[2] Isaac Weld, junior, *Travels through the States of North America and the Provinces of Upper and Lower Canada, during the Years 1795, 1796, and 1797* (4th ed., London, 1800), 99–100.

movement makes the process almost impossible to study in detail.[3]

One reason for horizontal mobility was the decreasing chance to rise in older rural areas. Even before 1700 good land in some coastal regions was unobtainable except by purchase from individuals. The price of land near the cities and along major waterways rose very rapidly. Mittelberger observed that near Philadelphia, cultivated farms cost £16 per acre and even uncleared land was priced at £5 to £8, so that it was hard for German immigrants to establish themselves.[4] Even in the Piedmont of northern Virginia, according to Schoepf, it was expensive to buy land, "and hence the incessant migrations to the farther regions."[5] The young man, indentured servant, or free immigrant thus found his opportunity restricted in many parts of the country, and moved elsewhere in search of a fortune.

Vertical mobility therefore varied with the place, and must be studied along the eastern seaboard as well as on the frontier. It varied with the individual too. The principal authority on indentured servants believes that they "were much more idle, irresponsible, unhealthy, and immoral than the generality of good English laborers."[6] Land was seldom given to them when their term was up, and one student has found that only about one in ten servants had the qualities necessary to obtain it. Another 10 percent became artisans, but the rest failed—died, became landless workers, or returned to England.[7] These opinions are based upon servants

[3] Schoepf, *Travels*, I, 62; McKee, *Labor in New York*, 51–52; La Rochefoucault-Liancourt, *Travels*, II, 138; Daniel J. Boorstin, *The Americans: The Colonial Experience* (New York, 1958), 156 (quoting Franklin).

[4] Gray, *Agriculture*, I, 117; Mittelberger, *Journey*, 118–119.

[5] Schoepf, *Travels*, II, 36.

[6] Smith, *Colonists in Bondage*, 287–288.

[7] *ibid.*, 299–300; Morris, *Government and Labor*, 395–397.

of the pre-revolutionary years. By 1763 the quality of these immigrants had improved; yet it remains true that the native Americans had an advantage over the foreign born. Probably more important was the degree of skill which the individual possessed. Mobility also varied with the objective, for the young man could easily become a small property holder but few replaced rags with riches. The study of mobility during the years 1763–1788 therefore requires examination of several different problems: the upward progress of the landless servant or worker into the ranks of the small farmer, measured both in settled areas and on the frontier; and mobility into the colonial upper class, rural and urban.

European travellers and Americans all agreed that the young man could easily achieve economic independence. Contemporaries insisted that immigrants, even indentured servants, could "acquire an easy and honest competency." [8] Indeed there are many instances of the sort.[9] Western lands were cheap and so easily obtained that artisans who saved their money could migrate. Even laborers, it was reported, refused to work long for high wages before they took up land.[10] "The labouring man will never be so much lost to a sense of his interest and independence, as to toil for others for small wages, when, by removing a little further off, he may possess, in his own right, perhaps a better farm than any of us do at present," predicted "GENESEA." [11]

[8] La Rochefoucault-Liancourt, *Travels,* II, 679; *Country Journal* (Poughkeepsie), April 13, 1786; Schoepf, *Travels,* I, 103; "Information Concerning North Carolina," *N.C. Hist. Rev.,* III (1926), 218–219; Barbe-Marbois, *Letters,* 119–120.

[9] Catherine S. Crary, "The Humble Immigrant and the American Dream: Some Case Histories, 1746–1776," *Miss. Vy. Hist. Rev.,* XLVI (1959–1960), 44–66; Jacob Cox Parsons, ed., *Extracts from the diary of Jacob Hiltzheimer of Philadelphia* (Philadelphia, 1893). Hiltzheimer himself began as an indentured servant.

[10] Morris, *Government and Labor,* 48.

[11] *N.J. Journal,* May 7, 1783. See also advertisement in *Pa. Packet,*

Observers recorded that one could start as a small farmer and acquire real wealth. Planters in South Carolina, wrote "Mechanic" in 1783, had emigrated fifty years before, many "from the lowest classes of mankind," borrowed money, become rich, and now their descendants had hundreds of slaves and lived lavishly.[12] Travellers recorded astonishing examples. A North Carolina planter owned 1,500 acres worth at least £3,000, which his father had bought for £30.[13] A South Carolinian started with five slaves and ended with an annual income of £5,000 to £6,000.[14] Jonathan Boucher, the Maryland clergyman, arrived with nothing in 1759 and by 1772 was worth £3,500 plus his income as minister.[15] Governor Cadwallader Colden wrote that in New York, "the most opulent families in our own Memory, have arisen from the lowest Rank of the People."[16] The opportunities were well summarized by James Iredell, the Scottish immigrant who became an eminent lawyer. In England, he wrote, he would have remained for some years in a dependent and insecure position, whereas in America he was sure of at least an independent income, and he had "a moral certainty of acquiring such an income every year as will maintain me genteely. A young country is the fittest for a young man without a fortune, and however unpromising or disagreeable it may be at first, a steady attentive perseverance will in all likelihood be at last successful."[17]

July 13, 1772. Robert and Katherine Brown give many examples of artisans and others who acquired land in *Virginia*, 22–25.

[12] *S.C. Gazette and General Advertiser*, Nov. 4, 1783.

[13] Smyth, *A Tour*, I, 113.

[14] "Journal of Josiah Quincy," Mass. Hist. Soc., *Proceedings*, XLIX (1915–1916), 453. The figure is presumably in sterling.

[15] Jonathan Boucher, *Reminiscences*, 60, 77.

[16] To Halifax, Feb. 22, 1785, N.Y. Hist. Soc., *Collections*, 1876, p. 470.

[17] To his father, July 20, 1772, McRee, *Iredell*, I, 116–117. See also John Webb to S. B. Webb, Savannah, January, 1787, in Worthington C. Ford, ed., *Correspondence of Samuel Blachley Webb* (3 vols.,

These individual instances or opinions prove only that a few men made their fortunes in the New World. But how general was such success? Did the landless really acquire property, or were there only a few who by their good fortune created an appearance, while in reality most of the landless remained poor? And at the other end of the economic scale, were the wealthy merchants and landowners self-made men, or did they start with advantages, the sons of merchants and planters and professional men? The answers can be found by examining mobility on the frontier, in settled farm communities, and in the towns.

The records of Lunenburg County, Virginia, afford an exceptionally good opportunity to study mobility on the frontier. Tax lists for 1764 show the number of tithes (white men and Negroes over twenty-one) and the amount of land held by each landholder. White tithes were named. Some held land, some did not. Of the latter, most were listed separately, probably signifying that they were heads of families, but others were listed as subordinate to a landholder, their names being indented below that of the farmer. Among these, many bore the same name as that of the landowner, and were doubtless sons who were as yet dependent upon their fathers; while others had quite different names, and were probably hired workers or indentured servants (the few overseers are identified as such). Eighteen years later the first post-revolutionary tax lists begin. The records of 1782 furnish us with a presumably complete list of landowners and non-landowners in almost all of the counties, with the amount of land, slaves, horses and cattle

New York, 1893–1894), III, 73; *Letters of James Murray*, 18. "Happily for the people of America," wrote one essayist, "property is so easily acquired in this country, that a man may be suspected of being dificient in industry, temperance, or honesty, . . . who is not possessed after a certain number of years, of a moderate share of property." *Pa. Journal*, Oct. 3, 1781.

held. These records make possible an examination of the degree to which residents of a Virginia county moved from one place to another or changed their economic status as measured by the ownership of land—which in agricultural Virginia was crucial.[18]

Lunenburg was settled principally by small farmers. A few well-to-do planters were present, but there had been little large-scale land speculation. Therefore the county was reasonably typical of that great area south of the James known as the "Southside," typical also of part of the northern Piedmont and of equivalent areas elsewhere in the South. Indeed a majority of Virginians and probably most southerners lived at one time or another in similar areas. By 1764 it was rapidly ceasing to be a frontier: two new counties, Charlotte and Halifax, were to be created out of it the following year. More than half of the men had land, as was characteristic of the areas which were recently settled. Among those who were not landholders, half were members of landowning families, while the rest were equally divided between heads of families and dependent workers. The great majority of landholders belonged to the small farmer class—nearly three-quarters held between 100 and 500 acres (the median being 340). Some large planters were already present, and there were six estates of more than 2,000 acres, but the wealthiest 10 percent of the men had less than 40 percent of the land, a percentage typical of frontier communities, and there were no large slaveholders. In short, Lunenburg was in an early stage of its development.

Most of the residents of the county were, of course, recent arrivals, and many of them were still on the move. This is especially the case with those who had not acquired land and who did not have relatives in the county. These were men who obviously had started without property, for

[18] Bell, *Sunlight on the Southside, passim.*

if their families had possessed some means, they surely would have purchased land at once. They formed a considerable part of the population—there were, in fact, over 100 of them. Of these more than one-third left the county.[19] They were joined in their emigration by a handful of the landless who did have local family connections; and in addition about 1 out of 12 landowners also went west. Altogether perhaps 1 out of 5 Lunenburgers moved on. The major movement however was into, not out of the county: by 1782 at least 150 men had entered Lunenburg and acquired land, thus increasing the landholding population by 50 percent. Meanwhile the original population much more than reproduced itself, so that the total number of landowners doubled between 1764 and 1782.

What became of the men who in 1764 occupied the bottom of the economic ladder? If one lived in a Lunenburg—that is, in an area recently settled and still being developed, in a society still highly mobile—the chance to rise was excellent. Among the approximately 150 men who had not acquired land in 1764 and whose careers can be traced with some probability, at least three-fourths had done so by 1782.

This estimate is based partly on inference. There is a gap in the records during the revolutionary war years, and when tax lists are again available it is evident that many of the men had gone. No vital records have been preserved, so that it is impossible to determine whether the man not listed had died or moved away. He may have acquired land and then died, or sold it, leaving no trace of the transaction. The only safe procedure is to eliminate such a person from our calculations. In many cases the man himself vanishes, but

[19] Of over 100 persons in this category, 24 apparently acquired property elsewhere, and 25 seem to have died or left the state prior to 1782.

someone with the same surname appears in his stead as a landowner. If the name is a common one in the area, then the relationship is doubtful, but if the name is unusual, probably the landless worker of 1764 acquired a farm, died, and left it to a son (or a wife or daughter) who became the taxpayer of 1782. For example, John Mason had no land in 1764, but Nathaniel and William held 100 acres in 1782. The chances are good that John acquired this property and left it to his children. So also James Vaughn probably inherited his 640 acres from Michael.

The chance for error is greatly increased when we attempt to trace the careers of the men who left the county, or who at all events are not known to its records after 1764. Where a man's name was uncommon, we are probably justified in assuming that one who turns up in the records elsewhere is the same man. The John Broughton who patented 160 acres in Bedford County, or the Philip Poindexter, Sr., who paid taxes on 353 acres in Mecklenburg County in 1782, are in all probability the same men who are missing in the Lunenburg records. In the case of Poindexter, indeed, his son Philip Jr., who was listed with him in 1764, is also recorded. But we can hardly be certain about a man with so ordinary a name as Thomas Hill. The decisive factor in many of these cases is the location of the county: the general course of migration was into adjacent areas and especially into the counties lying directly west. Therefore Thomas Hill of Stafford, far to the north, must be disregarded, but the Thomas Hills of Halifax (100 acres) or of Pittsylvania (400 acres) are strong possibilities, especially when it is discovered that many Lunenburg names are found in those counties. Moreover if some men are in this way considered to have acquired land who did not actually do so, the error is compensated for because other Lunenburgers probably became landholders without our knowing it. Land patents do show what the colony or state sold, and a few individuals can be traced in this way, but private sales cannot always be traced; moreover Lunenburg is not far from the North Carolina border, and undoubtedly some of the drifters ended life as respectable Tar-Heel farmers. Thus the error, if such it is, of counting Thomas Hill among those who acquired land, is counteracted by the equal error of including John Nunn among those who did not, when in fact he may have bought a farm elsewhere.

Altogether, eliminating the men who simply disappear, probably 60 percent of the non-landholders of 1764 became farmers in Lunenburg, and another 14 percent secured land elsewhere. If full information could be obtained, especially about North Carolina holdings and about the number of deaths, we might find the actual total to be nearly 80 percent.[20]

[20] The following table presents the evidence for my conclusions. I have tried to eliminate the non-residents, men who died, men who were young to be polls in 1764, and men whose names were so common that tracing them is hopeless.

MEN WITHOUT LAND AND NO FAMILY WITH LAND

	Certainly Obtained Land	Probably Obtained Land	No Land	Doubtful	Vanished
Tax paid for them					
in Lunenburg	14	8	5	4	10
elsewhere	12	1	2	0	0
Paid own tax					
in Lunenburg	24	6	4	4	13
elsewhere	9	2	3	0	0

MEN WITHOUT LAND BUT FAMILY WITH LAND

	Certainly Obtained Land	Probably Obtained Land	No Land	Doubtful	Vanished
Tax paid for them					
in Lunenburg	4	3	0	2	6
elsewhere	0	0	0	0	0
Paid own tax					
in Lunenburg	33	27	4	23	2
elsewhere	3	0	1	0	0
TOTAL	99	47	19	33	31

The most interesting men are those who did not have the advantage, as far as names reveal the situation, of any family relationship. These men obviously were on their own, being unable to secure land upon their entrance into Lunenburg, and without a relative to help them locally. Indeed about half of them were dependent workers. Yet of this large group—over 100 persons—very nearly two-thirds had obtained land by 1782. In all but a dozen cases the records clearly show the man himself, or one of identical name, securing land; in the others the relationship is probable rather than certain. Overseers, usually thought to be drifters, were successful in acquiring property: 9 of them did so in Lunenburg and 2 obtained land elsewhere—a total of 11 out of 14.[21] In addition, one who already owned 480 acres in 1764 held 1,172 acres and 2 slaves in 1782.

Mobility occurred among the landowners too. There was a slight movement downward as well as upward, for among the nearly 300 Lunenburg landholders in 1764 about one-fourth vanished from the tax lists and were not replaced by a relative. Most of these had not really lost ground. Some had always been residents of other counties where they continued to own land; some are known to have died; and two dozen or so moved from Lunenburg and acquired land elsewhere, thus holding their own, economically, or even advancing. There remain only 4 landholders in 1764 who appear on the tax rolls of 1782 without land, plus 13 more who are not on the later lists and who could not be traced. Some of them doubtless had died or moved to North Caro-

---

[21] To be exact: 6 Lunenburg men in 1782 had names identical to those of the 1764 overseers. Three Lunenburg men in 1782 had the same surnames as those of the 1764 overseers, there being no other men with such surnames. The 2 who appear in different counties had names identical to those of the overseers. I have examined all of the tax lists for that part of Virginia. Brown, *Virginia*, 50–51, also finds that overseers often became successful economically.

lina. Therefore the number who became poorer was extremely small. The owners of large estates (over 500 acres) were quite apt to lose part of their property—indeed rather more of them did so than retained their land intact. On the other hand a compensating number of smaller farmers increased their acreage. Thus among the landowners, about as many rose as fell, and the great majority held their own.

Accordingly, of the entire population in 1764, landless as well as landed, over half remained in the same status, whether high or low, in 1782; about one out of twelve moved downward; and one-third moved up. Since our records tend to exaggerate the proportion which lost ground, it seems probable that the net upward mobility rate (those who rose minus those who fell) was about 25 percent. But this is not the whole of the story, for into Lunenburg poured a great immigration, creating new large estates to replace the old, and adding over 100 families to the small farmer class. Thus Lunenburg, as it developed out of the frontier stage, created opportunities for many of her native sons to rise, and yet could provide scores of immigrants with farms. Just as some of the landless Lunenburgers moved into Pittsylvania or Charlotte or Halifax and took up land, so the poor sons of Tidewater families found homes and property in Lunenburg.

That the high rate of mobility on the Virginia frontier was the rule is shown by Charles Grant's work on Kent, Connecticut, a typical New England frontier town. Kent was founded before 1740. According to Grant, its society during the first half-century or so contained a very large "middle class" of small property owners, and a small "poor class" of men assessed, for tax purposes, at £29 or less. The latter usually comprised between one-fourth and one-third of the population. Most of the "poor" undoubtedly were landless, for the poll assessment alone was £18.[22] A few of those paying a higher tax probably lacked land also, but these must be omitted from consideration. Grant then divides this poor and presumably landless class into three categories: "poor transients" who left without acquiring land; "poor climbers" who remained and improved their economic status, presumably acquiring land; and "permanent proletarians" who remained but did not succeed.

Four tax lists from 1740 to 1777 show that there were all told 150 persons classified as poor (about one-fourth of the men), of whom 43 percent left, 44 percent rose, and 13 percent remained but did not rise. In Lunenburg, the gap in records between 1765 and 1782 makes precision impossible, but there seem to have been even fewer "permanent proletarians." The proportion who left was about the same, and the proportion who remained and succeeded was somewhat larger in the Virginia county. Grant did not try to follow the immigrants, but he was able to demonstrate that among those who stayed in Kent, 77 percent acquired land. "The most obvious conclusions about the 'hired hand poor,'" Grant observed, "would seem to be these: from 1740 to 1777 they were temporary poor, temporary hired hands. The greater part of them stayed in Kent and soon saved or borrowed enough to buy a farm of their own."[23]

Goshen, Connecticut, is not far from Kent and was settled about the same time. In 1751 the town contained a slightly larger proportion of "poor," using Grant's definition, and perhaps also more landless. At any rate one-third of the men had no land according to the tax list of that year. Goshen was primarily an agricultural community, though

[22] In Goshen, Connecticut, about three-fourths of those assessed for less than £30 had no land.

[23] *Democracy in Kent*, 96–98.

one out of six paid some sort of a faculty tax. Of those who had no land, the majority left before 1771, when another tax list permits comparison. Of those who remained, 71 percent probably obtained land. Among Goshen's landless in 1771 who stayed in the town until 1782 (again most of the landless men departed), as high as 86 percent may have obtained land.[24]

These Goshen lists also make possible conclusions based upon assessed property generally. In 1751, 31 percent of the men paid a tax on less than £30 worth of property (heads, oxen, horses, cattle, swine, acres, and faculty). Twenty years later, over half of them had left, but among those who remained, five-sixths had increased their wealth, one in fact being among the town's well-to-do men. Meanwhile the poor men of 1751 had been replaced in 1771 by nearly twice as many new poor men, about two-thirds of whom had immigrated from other towns, the remainder having been born in Goshen (one of whom had previously owned more property). By 1782 an even larger number had left, while of those remaining, four-fifths rose. Most acquired only small property, but once again a newcomer attained high rank. The native-born residents were naturally much more successful than the immigrants: half improved their positions within the town; while the great majority of the newcomers who had drifted to Goshen drifted right out again. Once more in 1782 those who had left were replaced—but now only just replaced—by another group of poor immigrants. It is impossible to trace those who departed, but records of other frontiers demonstrate that many of them eventually settled down.

[24] Tax lists in Conn. State Lib. Actually the 1771 and 1782 lists did not give landholders. I have assumed, however, that those assessed for £25 or more had acquired land. The error, if it exists, is a small one, and does not affect the major point of a mobility rate on the order of 70 or 80 percent.

When the frontier stage had ended, and society became stable, the chance to rise diminished. All the land worth owning was now occupied, and land prices rose, so that the sons of pioneers and the newcomers could not so easily improve their positions. Mobility therefore diminished as the community grew older. Grant found that by 1796, when Kent had become a well-established, primarily subsistence farm community, the mobility rate sharply declined. Half of the poor left, and of those who remained, half did not improve their position. The final stage of this process is represented by Lancaster County, in the eastern part of Virginia's Northern Neck. Tax lists of 1773, nearly complete, record the names of all men and their land, if any. These names can be compared with the tax lists of 1782 and of subsequent years. Lancaster was not quite typical of the eastern counties in that only 46 percent of the men were landless—a higher proportion than in Lunenburg, but lower than the average. The median farm was 260 acres, smaller than that farther west. Large estates were less numerous than in Virginia generally, and the concentration of property, though greater than in Lunenburg, was less than normal for a Tidewater county, the wealthiest 10 percent owning 45 percent of the land.

The opportunities for acquiring land within the county were limited, especially by contrast with the situation nearer the frontier. In Lunenburg, over half of the landless stayed at home and obtained land there, but in Lancaster, only one-third succeeded in doing so.[25] Moreover Lunenburg was only a step from the real frontier, so that another 14 percent could obtain land in nearby areas; but this was not so easy in Lancaster, where only 3 percent are known to have become farmers farther west. Therefore the mobility rate was half that of the Southside County. There is no

[25] I have here excluded those known to have died.

significant difference in the histories of those whose tax was paid by someone else and those paying taxes themselves.

It is possible that errors in research techniques have somewhat exaggerated the difference between the rate of mobility in the two counties, because for reasons not clear there were more men in Lancaster who disappeared without trace.[26] But to eliminate them from our calculations does not affect the basic situation except to increase greatly the possible rate of mobility: in Lancaster, among those whose futures can be traced with certainty, 52 percent obtained land, while in Lunenburg no less than 84 percent did so. Whatever method is chosen for determining the exact ratio, the proportion of men who acquired land was exceedingly high in both counties, and far higher in Lunenburg.

The rate of mobility among landholders was also much lower in the eastern county. In Lunenburg, nearly as many farmers added to their holdings as lost them, and half of those who disappeared from the Lunenburg records secured land elsewhere. In Lancaster considerably more men lost than gained. Moreover the spectacular influx which occurred in Lunenburg was not duplicated in the eastern county, where there were only 28 more landholders in 1782, a gain of slightly over 10 percent compared with Lunenburg's 200 percent. From every point of view, mobility was enormously higher in the frontier county.

This conclusion is confirmed by comparing the Richmond County quit rent rolls for 1765 with its tax list for 1782. Since only landowners were given in the former, it is not possible to trace the fate of the landless, except by

[26] Perhaps Lancaster men were hit harder by the war, but more likely a larger number than in Lunenburg emigrated to what is now West Virginia or Kentucky. I have not tried to follow them there. The men of Southside Virginia could get land nearby whereas those from the east could not, and so may have been more apt to cross the mountains.

inference, but mobility among those with land can be analyzed.

Richmond is located just west of Lancaster and was similar in its socio-economic characteristics. The concentration of property was about the same, and the proportion of landless differed only slightly in 1782. There were 200 landholders in 1765, of whom the great majority—nearly four-fifths —remained in the county seventeen years later. Whereas in Lunenburg there was considerable mobility among the farmers, nearly 30 percent decisively increasing or decreasing their holdings, in Richmond there was almost no movement at all. The same amount of land remained in the same families. A number of new landholders appeared by 1782, but there were only one-fourth more than before; moreover, some of them (such as Charles and Robert Wormeley Carter) were not in fact mobile, being residents of adjacent counties. Almost none of the 1765 landowners increased their holdings to any extent, but more than two dozen had lost a significant part of their property by 1782.

As to Richmond County's landless, some inferences are possible. The 1782 tax lists included all men, and the proportion of landed to landless at that date is therefore known. Assuming that this ratio did not change much between 1765 and 1782 (and there was no major change in Lancaster), about 150 men did not own land at the earlier period. Some 90 new names appear on the land lists of 1782, but not all of these were landless previously, for we know that some of them had resided outside the county, where they may have been farmers. In Lunenburg, about 30 percent of those who took up land between 1764 and 1782 had lived in the county at the earlier date; all the rest were newcomers. The proportion of those who were residents was presumably higher in Richmond, where there was much less movement in and out. Perhaps it is a reasonable assumption that half of the new landowners in 1782 had been non-landholding residents of the county earlier. If so, then about 45 out of 150 landless men acquired land within the county, or just 30 percent, almost the same proportion as the known 32 percent in Lancaster, and again contrasting sharply with the 55 percent or so in Lunenburg. Richmond and Lancaster alike demonstrate that when an area ceased to be a frontier region and became a settled commercial farm community, both horizontal and vertical mobility declined.

In Lunenburg, at least three-fourths of the landless men became farmers; in Lancaster and Richmond slightly over one-third did so. Chester County, in Pennsylvania, represents a northern equivalent of the Lancaster-Richmond type. The 1765 tax list, like the Virginia records, names all of the adult men, and itemizes their acreage and certain farm animals. There are available tax lists for this and other Pennsylvania counties during the next two decades, a time span equal to that of the Virginia records. As in Virginia these records are incomplete, but again inferences are possible.[27]

Chester County lies in the southeastern corner of the state. The townships selected for examination are in the eastern part (now Delaware County) just west of Philadelphia, and in the southern section bordering Delaware and Maryland.[28] The region had been settled for many decades and was a commercial farm area in 1765. Not quite half of the men were landless. These men were of three sorts. About 40 percent were heads of families, paying their own poll tax, and usually (though not always) owning a few

[27] *Pa. Arch.*, 3 series XI (Harrisburg, 1897), and subsequent volumes.

[28] Haverford, Upper Darby, Lower Darby, Nether Providence, Middletown, Egmont, Upper Chichester, and Concord. I chose these simply because they were the first ones to appear in the records.

farm animals. Another 40 percent were called "Single Men," or sometimes "Freemen." They seem to have paid their own tax but owned no farm animals. Presumably they were free laborers or artisans. Finally, one-fifth of the men were called "inmates." These were evidently servants, perhaps indentured, and the category also included some adult sons of the farmers. The tax lists did not always separate the inmates from the single men (two out of eight studied did not), but the latter were clearly more numerous.

The Pennsylvania records, like those of Virginia, have their serious shortcomings. For most of the counties there are no tax records before the 1780's, so that a man might have acquired land and died, and we be none the wiser. Some men doubtless moved to Maryland, where it has not been feasible to follow them; others may have gone to Virginia and even conceivably to the Carolinas (though from Chester this is most unlikely). There is also the same difficulty with names. Thus William Walter, single man of Haverford, is different from the William Walter of Concord and William Walter of Pikeland, so that it is impossible to know which of them is referred to in subsequent records. We know only that the Haverford Walter did not obtain land in his home town.

The eight townships studied contained 277 men without land in 1765. Of these, 72 disappear or cannot be certainly identified. Twenty percent obtained land within the township of origin by 1784. There was a good deal of local movement out of the township to adjacent towns, which were almost always slightly to the west, and occasionally someone moved farther away. Altogether nearly 40 percent of the landless finally became landowners.

Among the landless men, those who were heads of families had the best chance of rising. About 46 percent of them are known to have obtained land, and if the men who disappear or whose names preclude certainty are eliminated, 61 percent eventually became farmers. Those who did not succeed were sometimes artisans, one of whom, a blacksmith, became an "inmate" much later (if this is the same person); while a storekeeper also apparently failed and sank into the same lower status. Two were schoolmasters and seven were called laborers. These men sometimes moved two or three times, never improving their rank.[29]

The "single men" did not do as well, perhaps because they lacked the incentive of a family. Only 36 percent, or 47 percent of those definitely identified, obtained land. The "inmates" are the most interesting of all, for we are here presumably dealing with indentured servants. Their mobility was least of the three groups, being 29 percent of the whole number, or 45 percent of those about whom it is possible to be certain. This is an unexpectedly high figure, since these servants have been assumed to be of inferior potential. The inmates often were or became skilled workers, and frequently moved around. Out of the 17 who obtained land, 5 were artisans and 1 was or became a schoolmaster. These inmates, when they did obtain land, usually secured only a few acres, though Reuben Roberts owned 170, James Denning 200, and John Russel the same quantity. They were apt to succeed in some town other than that in which they began.

There are other points of interest. The men with some skill other than farming met with a high degree of success. Out of 70 landless artisans in the whole county, between 55 and 60 percent acquired land. Of course others may have prospered without investing in real estate. On the other

---

[29] Samuel Withers started in Egmont, moved to Birmingham, then to London Grave (if this is he), and finally as a weaver to East Marlborough, where in 1785 he was still paying a minimum tax.

hand those without a trade, identified as laborers, succeeded less than half of the time and were especially apt to vanish without trace. Pennsylvania offered great opportunities to the men who had or acquired a skill, but the unskilled were likely to fail, as usual.

The geographical mobility which occurred, insofar as it can be traced, ordinarily consisted of a removal from one town to an adjacent town, or perhaps a few towns away. It was usually, though not always, in a westerly direction. There seems to have been remarkably little migration to Philadelphia even among the artisans. The movement, though limited geographically, was considerable: among over 200 landless men who can be traced, nearly half moved at least once.

The general mobility of Chester County residents was almost identical to that in Lancaster County. Of all the landless, 38½ percent are known to have obtained land, compared with 35 percent in Lancaster; and of those whose success or failure is certainly known, 52 percent succeeded, exactly the same proportion as in the Virginia county. This evidence indicates that the mobility rates which were found in the southern state have a general application.

These scattered case studies show that the American who started without land had an excellent chance of becoming a yeoman farmer. Mobility into the upper class of rural society, however, was much more limited. In order to analyze the social origins of the great landowners, we once again turn our attention to Virginia.

In a previously published article entitled "The One Hundred," I have listed the wealthiest Virginians in 1787 according to tax lists of that year.[30] Actually one of these turns out to have been a Londoner; several ought not to have

[30] Jackson T. Main, "The One Hundred," *Wm. and Mary Qtly.*, 3 series, XIV (1954), 354–384.

been included (such as Patrick Henry and James Madison), and there may have been other Virginians richer than those on the list; but it is reasonably representative of the great planter class. All of these men were large landowners, though several were primarily merchants and others were lawyers. Most of them lived in the Tidewater counties, especially in the Potomac and James River valleys. They all owned more than 4,000 acres, and almost half had 10,000 acres, in addition to nearly 100 slaves. Certainly each held more than £10,000 worth of property

Of the 100, 79 or 80 inherited all of their wealth. These were members of the First Families—the old, established aristocracy of the colony which survived the Revolution intact: the Randolphs, Harrisons, Fitzhughs, Nelsons. Nine more started near the top, as sons of well-to-do though not wealthy men. Examples are David Patterson, whose father was a substantial planter, and who bought 40,000 acres in the west out of commercial profits; Muscoe Garnett, third generation, whose father was a Burgess; and Joseph Jones of Dinwiddie, great-grandson of the immigrant, and member of a respectable, perhaps even prominent, family of planters. Two others inherited part of their wealth and cannot really be considered mobile. There remain at the most 10 men who were self-made. Four of these were immigrants. Roger Atkinson, English-born, married a Virginia girl of good family and amassed wealth in what was then the newly developed southern Piedmont.[31] Nicholas Davis, a Welsh immigrant, became a Richmond merchant and married the widow of a Randolph, herself an heiress.[32] William Ronald, also a merchant, bought large tracts in the Southside; and David Ross, a merchant from Scotland, ac-

[31] *Va. Mag. Hist. Biog.*, xv (1907–1908), 345–346.
[32] ibid., xxiii (1915), 325; *Tyler's Quarterly Historical and Genealogical Magazine*, viii (1926–1927), 140–141.

cumulated a fortune during the Revolution and was for the time being the richest man in the state. The other half-dozen apparently were native born, of humble parentage (unless James Henry of King and Queen is the same person as Judge James of the eastern shore).[33] Practically all of the mobile planters had risen through commercial or legal activities, and centered their agricultural pursuits in the Southside—the Lunenburg County area, where mobility was the rule.

The economic opportunity of the city dweller was somewhat greater than that of the American in an older farm community. The skilled laborer, who began as a journeyman wage worker and aspired to become a master, lived in a rapidly expanding community where there was always more room near the top. The Philadelphia tax list of 1769 contains the names of over 100 men, identified as artisans, who were not assessed for any property although only a small amount made one a taxpayer. Of these about one-fourth had disappeared by 1774 and cannot be found in any other tax records of the colony. Another group of men are untraceable because their names are too common. Of the

[33] Horace Edwin Hayden, *Virginia Genealogies* (Wilkes-Barre, 1891), 439; *Va. Mag. Hist. Biog.*, xxxv (1917), 74. The other newcomers were Adam Hunter, who belonged to an old but not a prominent family; Robert Lawson, apparently of the lesser planter class; John Perrin, who is obscure; Henry Banks, a lawyer of old family who may have inherited property; and Edmund Pendleton, the well-known lawyer. I have classified Cuthbert Bullitt, Peter Jones, Edmund Ruffin, James Southall, James Taylor, Patrick Henry, and Alexander Trent as starting with advantages but not of the old elite. This classification is open to argument. The Jones family illustrates the problem. Peter seems to have been the son of Abraham, who left two or three acres and 23 slaves, but a different Peter, who had a son Peter, left at least 2,000 acres and 41 slaves. Amelia County Will Book 2X, 1761–1777, pp. 133, 137–139, microfilm, Va. State Lib. The family was certainly wealthy and perhaps belongs among the truly prominent.

rest, about 45 percent succeeded in acquiring property, almost always within the city. This rate of success is about equal to that in Chester County, though much less than that on the frontier.

The opportunity of rising into the ranks of large property holders was of course much more limited. Manufacturing during the colonial period was seldom profitable enough to permit an artisan to become truly wealthy, and few men could start from scratch and hope to reach the top. Nevertheless the prosperous artisans consisted to an unusual degree of men who had improved upon their father's economic position. The Philadelphia tax list of 1769 includes nearly 60 artisans who were assessed for £50 worth of property. Probably these men owned £2,000 or more.[34] The economic status of a good many parents is unknown, probably because in many cases it is unknowable; but there remain 31 whose social origins can be identified. These men comprise a fair cross-section of the city's well-to-do artisans. They were engaged in a score of trades, and included the owners of fairly large business enterprises such as distilleries, who perhaps ought to be termed manufacturers rather than artisans. Slightly more than half of this prosperous group had decisively improved upon their fathers' economic position. Few of them were truly self-made: probably not more than half a dozen, about one out of five, started from scratch as Franklin, for example, had done. Characteristically their fathers were artisans, or rarely farmers, who could provide the son with the advantage of a respectable, middle class, usually urban background.[35]

[34] Even the wealthiest men were seldom assessed for more than £1,000, and the property of rich merchants was usually evaluated at £500 or less. Yet such men certainly had estates in excess of £10,000.

[35] Fifty-five percent of the artisans had clearly surpassed their fathers' economic status. The overwhelming majority of the artisans

The opportunities in Boston were about the same. The 1771 assessment list does not distinguish artisans, but that of 1780, though incomplete, can be used. Identified are 48 artisans (including the manufacturers) who were rated at £150 or more. These men belonged to the top 15 percent of all taxpayers. The fathers of 40 can be identified. As in Pennsylvania, the man who started from the bottom was unusual, accounting for only one out of four. However about 60 percent of the artisans had acquired more property than their parents. The superior success rate of the Bostonians may be due to some local factor, but is more probably an effect of the Revolution. In any case the aspiring artisan had reason for optimism.[36]

Merchants, as we have seen, had considerably more wealth than did artisans, and they were less often self-made men. The members of the New York Chamber of Commerce, in particular, were a select group. There were 59 of them during the Chamber's first year of existence (1768–1769). The great majority, perhaps all of the members, were large property owners. Probably most of New York's commercial upper class was included.[37]

About two-thirds had been born in the colonies, principally in New York. Among these the majority, and about 45 percent of the whole number, belonged to the colony's elite families. There were, for example, two Crugers, a Beekman, a Gouverneur, a Low, a Reade, a Van Dam, four

---

were city-born. Nearly half were Quakers and most of the others were Anglicans. Only a few were immigrants, although more than half of the parents were probably foreign born.

[36] Almost all of the artisans were Congregationalists. There were only two Harvard men. As in Philadelphia, nearly all were of urban birth.

[37] *Colonial Records of the New York Chamber of Commerce, 1768–1784 with historical and biographical sketches by John Austin Stevens Jr.* (New York, 1867). As a group, incidentally, they had decidedly Tory leanings, 70 percent becoming Loyalists or neutrals.

Waltons, and a Watts. They were related by marriage to each other, to the large landholders, and to various merchants of lesser origin (Duyckinck, Keteltas, Lynsen).[38]

Some of the natives, though not of the established upper class, began partway up the socio-economic ladder. Examples are Nicholas Hoffman, son of a well-to-do farmer,[39] and Laurence Kortright, whose father was perhaps wealthy but who was not of the elite.[40] The rest, about one-fourth of the natives, rose from humble or obscure parentage. We know of Edward Laight only that his father Edward was an immigrant. The same is true of Elias Debrosses. Isaac Sears' father had only moderate means;[41] John Thurman's was a baker; and there are several so little known that even their birthplace is doubtful.

Among the foreign-born a few had advantages. Theophylact Bache, of English birth, son of an excise collector, had an uncle who was a successful merchant and who left him £300. Thomas Buchanan's father was a wealthy Glasgow merchant, while Peter Hasenclever's was a rich merchant and manufacturer. William Seton's uncle was a banker.[42] However the great majority of the immigrants arrived without a head start; though they may have belonged to

---

[38] Duyckinck: Whitehead Cornell Duyckinck and Rev. John Cornell, *The Duyckinck and Allied Families* (New York, 1908), 180–185. Keteltas: *N.Y. Hist. and Biog. Record*, LXI (1930), 333. Lynsen: Stevens, *Chamber of Commerce*, 147–148.

[39] [Eugene A. Hoffman], *Genealogy of the Hoffman Family* (New York, 1899), 118–125.

[40] John Howard Abbott, *The Courtright (Kortright) Family* (New York, 1922), 33–34, 42. His father was a baker.

[41] Samuel P. May, *The Descendants of Richard Sares (Sears) of Yarmouth, Mass.* (Albany, 1890), 76, 113–117.

[42] Stevens, *Chamber of Commerce*, 41–54; Allen Johnson and Dumas Malone, eds., *Dictionary of American Biography* (22 vols., New York, 1928–1944), I, 464, III, 218–219, VIII, 379; Monsignor Seton, *An Old Family* (New York, 1899), 240–268.

families of status, as far as their colonial experience was concerned they were *noveaux riches*.

The background of these merchants, as far as is known, was almost entirely urban.[43] Probably not far from half had wealthy fathers, almost all of whom were merchants. Another group, perhaps one out of five, came from well-to-do families, and were therefore not really mobile. There remain 40 percent who had risen from well down the social scale. The figure may be too high, for among the men about whose background nothing is known there may be some who started with advantages. However there could have been few such because prominent families are, obviously, conspicuous. Taking everything into account, then, it is certain that between one-third and two-fifths of the merchants in pre-revolutionary New York City were self-made men.

Unfortunately no such select list of New York merchants is available for the post-war period. There does exist, however, a directory for 1786 which identified many of the residents by their occupation. The first 100 men designated as "merchants" were selected for study. The term "merchant" was doubtless loosely applied, and there were probably men so designated who had little property. However a distinction was made in the directory between merchants and shopkeepers, thus presumably differentiating between wholesalers and retailers; so that most of the men included certainly were well-to-do.[44]

[43] Unfortunately the occupation of over half of the fathers is not known, but among the identified parents, only two were farmers, both large landowners. In addition several parents whose exact business cannot be discovered were townsmen. Therefore at least 62 percent of the total and over 90 percent of those known were of urban birth.

[44] See Chapter III above for a discussion of the word "merchant."

The significant characteristic of this merchant class was the much higher proportion of self-made men. Only one-fourth were sons of wealthy landowners or merchants. At most another tenth came from well-to-do families. This contrasts strikingly with the situation prior to the war, when about 60 percent had had a head start in life. Two-thirds of the post-war merchants had made their way up. Among these, roughly two out of three were natives of the state. Some of them came from artisan families, but a majority were farmers' sons. The rest—about one-fourth of the whole number—were apparently immigrants, for there is no trace of their surnames in the extensive collection of published wills or in genealogies. Some may have come from prosperous backgrounds, perhaps set up in business by a merchant father or uncle; but it is plain that the majority of New York's merchant class—probably 60 percent at the least—were self-made men. Not all of these merchants were successful, for inventories and tax lists testify that there were poor as well as rich ones. However, the degree of mobility is clearly very high, surpassing that of the pre-revolutionary period and incomparably greater than that in Virginia.[45]

The 1791 tax list for the city's east ward has survived, and this combined with other sources makes it possible to identify positively a number of those merchants who were well-to-do or wealthy. Some changes doubtless had occurred since 1786, and the data are incomplete, but a list can be compiled that is comparable with the Chamber of Commerce membership. Fewer members of this post-war elite

[45] The degree of horizontal mobility is also of interest. Only 4 or possibly 5 of Virginia's "100" were immigrants, but at least 14 and probably 24 members of the Chamber of Commerce—between one-fourth and two-fifths of the total—came from outside the colony. Among the merchants of 1786, probably one-fourth were not native-born.

were self-made men than among merchants generally, yet half of them had risen from humble origins. Therefore mobility was higher than the pre-war rate of 40 percent.

A similar list of Boston merchants in 1789, again drawn from a city directory, proves that the rate of mobility was about the same in both these cities, though fewer Bostonians were immigrants.[46] As in New York, only one-fourth of the merchants were members of the established upper class. One out of four Boston merchants started as sons of artisans. These artisan fathers were of all trades: coopers (John Breck, father of Samuel), sleighmakers, brewers, masons, hatters, leather dressers, felt-makers (Benjamin Clark, who sent his son to Harvard), tailors, snuff makers, braziers, ropemakers, cordwainers, housewrights, and potters. Many of the craftsmen's sons had been brought up in the family business and later entered trade.

Other merchants, sons of mariners, began their careers before the mast. A few were sons of innkeepers, and thus engaged in commerce from the start. Five had fathers who were ministers and one was descended from a school-teacher. One or two out of ten began life on a farm. All together one-fourth started near the top, one-third were the sons of artisans, shopkeepers, or mariners, 6 percent came from families of professional men, and the remaining three-eighths were farmers' sons, or immigrants, of humble or obscure origin. Probably seventy percent had risen from lower status.[47]

[46] The word "store" is sometimes used to indicate a merchant in the Boston directory of 1789. There seems to have been no difference between the men so identified and those called "merchant."

[47] The most interesting was Patrick Jeffrey, brother of a famous Scots Judge. He immigrated as the steward or agent of John Wilkes' sister, the widow of a wealthy London merchant, and married her. A. K. Teele, ed., *The History of Milton, Mass., 1640 to 1887* (Boston, 1887), 137–139.

Among the Boston merchants were thirty-two equivalent in income and social rank to the wealthy New Yorkers. As might be expected, far more of them came from wealthy backgrounds than was true of Boston merchants in general: just half were born into wealthy or well-to-do families, usually the sons of merchants. Four were ministers' sons; four were sons of farmers. Artisans rarely reached the top. The backgrounds of four wealthy merchants are unknown, and they were probably immigrants. The rate of mobility—50 percent—is higher than that of the pre-revolutionary New York Chamber of Commerce, and exactly the same as that of the equivalent post-war New York merchants.

Obviously a larger proportion of prosperous artisans and merchants were of humble origin than was the case with the Virginia elite. However in order accurately to compare mobility in the city and country, the Virginia group should be matched with their economic equals. What were the social origins of the wealthiest townsmen, regardless of occupation?

The Philadelphia tax list of 1765 includes 100 men who were rated at £160 or more—probably the equivalent of £4,000. More than half of these were merchants. Nearly one out of five were professional men, mostly lawyers and doctors. Some owned large amounts of real estate, the rent from which was their primary support. Less than one-tenth were artisans or manufacturers. The economic status of 91 of the fathers has been discovered. Whereas in Virginia only one-tenth of the men had achieved wealth primarily by their own efforts, in Philadelphia one-third had accomplished this. About one-seventh were entirely self-made. Characteristically these *nouveaux riches* were born into an urban middle class family, the fathers evidently following some trade. A considerable number of Philadelphia's elite—at least one-fourth—were immigrants, as were more than one-third of the mobile men. Many of the Philadelphia 100 had far less property than did the Virginia planters, but even among those who were truly wealthy, one-third had made their own fortunes.

A comparable list of wealthy Bostonians can be obtained from the 1771 assessment roll. The 60 men who, according to this record, were the largest property owners, consisted principally of merchants. About one-fifth were artisans, manufacturers, and the like, and there was a scattering of lawyers, men of leisure, or royal officials. About 30 percent were Harvard graduates. A majority were Congregationalists, but one out of five was an Anglican (who usually became a Loyalist). All but a handful were born in Boston or Charlestown; in contrast to Philadelphia, where one-fourth or more of the upper class were immigrants, only three of these Bostonians came from across the seas. Between 40 and 45 percent were *nouveaux riches;* indeed one-third were self-made men. Most successful Bostonians were city-bred: only three are known to have come from farm families, though a few others may have done so. Most of these upper-class Bostonians were not truly wealthy. Of those whose property was comparable to that of the Virginia 100, only about 20 percent had made their own way up. Still, this represents a mobility rate twice that of the planter elite.

Revolutionary America was a society in flux. The amount of movement from place to place is striking. In the average rural community perhaps 15 percent of the population left in the course of a decade, and even more newcomers arrived. Probably 40 percent of the population, or thereabouts, moved during a few years' time. In general this movement was economically successful. There were some habitual drifters: perhaps 5 percent of the men wandered from one place to another without ever acquiring land, and on the frontier the proportion might be two or three times as great. However, out of the 30 or 40 percent of the white population who at any one time were landless, over half, and on the frontier three-fourths or more, became farmers or townsmen of equivalent status. Many men who already owned land also moved, and these seem ordinarily to have held their own. This horizontal mobility helped to maintain the very high rate of vertical mobility. The opportunity to rise was good even in older farm areas such as Lancaster and Richmond, where nearly one-third of the landless acquired real estate within the county, or in Chester, where even more succeeded.[48] Moreover if one failed there, opportunities were excellent in the west. In Kent, Goshen, and Lunenburg, all but a handful of those whose history is known improved their economic rank. There is even evidence that the much maligned indentured servants did well. Thus in America the lower class (excluding the slaves) was a temporary status for the overwhelming majority of men. Probably not more than one in twenty whites was a permanent proletarian.

In the cities, the relative ease with which the skilled worker could obtain credit and open a shop, the generally high wage level which permitted such workers to save, and the actual accumulation of property shown by tax lists and inventories—all suggest that the poor laborer could normally expect to become a small property owner if he had the ability to learn a trade. In Philadelphia the chance to rise was indeed a good one. At least one-third and probably

[48] However in northern subsistence farm communities the chances of becoming well-to-do were so slight that the landless men usually left in search of better land. In four towns of Berks County, Pennsylvania, two-thirds of those who remained obtained land, but the great majority (67½ percent) of the landless departed. Some of these died, but most of them must have moved to the frontier. *Pa. Arch.*, 3 series XVIII (Caernarvon, Tulpehockon, Richmond, and Maxatawny).

over 40 percent of the men who paid no tax in 1769 improved their economic position during the next few years.[49]

Mobility into the upper class was much more limited. In particular the landed aristocracy (in Virginia at least) was virtually a closed group by the time of the Revolution, undoubtedly because most of the available good land was occupied. Probably the same sort of elite was developing wherever commercial farming had been conducted for some time. Even the great estates in the west were being purchased principally by men of established wealth. Commerce, on the other hand, was a comparatively open field.[50] Before the war, 30 or 40 percent of New York's mercantile upper class were self-made men, and the proportion both there and in Boston reached 50 percent after the Revolution. These men frequently became large landowners, and indeed most of the *nouveaux riches* in Virginia were merchants who bought their way into the "one hundred." Here the existence of cheap Western land furthered mobility into the elite as it aided mobility at the lower economic levels.

---

[49] The following table presents, first, mobility rates of all non-artisans who paid no tax in Lower Delaware and Middle Wards during 1769, and second, of all artisans paying no tax, all wards. These men were traced through the 1782 Philadelphia tax lists and also in other counties using the index to the *Pa. Arch.*, third series. The number of men who disappeared is regrettable but the general situation is fairly clear. The higher rate of success among non-artisans is, I think, owing to the fact that they included some men whose family had means and who were just getting a start.

	Non-artisans	*Artisans*
Rose economically	41	29
Perhaps rose	5	5
Did not rise	44	41
Probably did not	3	7
Disappeared	28	37

[50] The law may have offered opportunities to the poor man just as did commerce, but the point remains to be proved. The educational requirements may have hampered the poorer men.

The chance to rise in the revolutionary era varied with the circumstances. The frontier offered almost unlimited opportunity. After the frontier stage passed, the mobility rate was reduced. Subsistence farm areas still afforded a fair chance to buy land, but that land was not very valuable and most of the landless men moved on. In commercial farm areas economic opportunities were also diminished because the good land was claimed, land prices rose, and the land-holding elite became increasingly exclusive. Farmers seem seldom to have risen into the highest ranks: the way to wealth was primarily through trade or perhaps the law. The social structure of the cities was much more open, especially during a period of rapid expansion such as the war years, though when stagnation set in merchants and artisans had trouble maintaining themselves. But even at such times the city people could join the men from subsistence and commercial farm areas as they moved on to Lunenburg County, to the west of cheap land, ample credit, and high mobility.

CHAPTER VI

Social Classes
in the Revolutionary Era

THE American's opportunity to improve his economic position was one of the most important attractions of the new country. Perhaps equally important was the chance to increase his prestige. But whereas economic classes are based on objective criteria, on property and income data which are readily available to the historian, social classes are based on opinion, and are therefore impossible to define with precision. Yet the historian can discover in a general way the esteem in which the different occupations were held, much as recent students have done with contemporary society. In addition, the use of titles, which in Europe were significant symbols of prestige, can be examined for clues concerning the American status order.

Slaves and white servants naturally were accorded little respect. The tutor Philip Fithian agreed with Mrs. Carter that the Negroes were of slight economic value, and that industrious white tenants would make more money and be better citizens.[1] Chastellux could only call the slaves "less depraved than those imported from Africa." [2] The pro-slavery argument, based on the assumption that Negroes were innately inferior, was fully developed by revolutionary times. God had ordained, declared the inhabitants of Brunswick County, Virginia, that some people were born to serve others, and they cited the Bible to prove it. Amelia County's residents anticipated that if the slaves were set free, the state would suffer "the Horror of all the Rapes,

[1] *Journals and Letters*, 123.
[2] *Travels*, II, 196.

Murders, and Outrages, which a vast Multitude of unprinci-
pled, unpropertied, revengeful, and remorseless Banditti are
capable of perpetuating." [3] Free Negroes in the North were
disparaged. Brissot de Warville wrote regretfully that
"There still exists too great an interval between them and
the Whites, especially in the public opinion. This humiliat-
ing difference prevents those efforts which they might
make to raise themselves. . . . Though free, they are always accustomed to consider themselves as beneath the
Whites." [4]

Indentured servants were, like slaves, the property of
their masters and were regarded as "idle, irresponsible, unhealthy, and immoral." [5] Though conditions were changing
by the time of the Revolution, opinions as to their de-
pravity had not. They were usually treated with decency,
but looked upon as inferior beings.

Ordinary free laborers were included among the "lower"
or "inferior" sort of people. They might be regarded as the
"industrious poor," but they were much more apt to be
accused of having bad habits, as "Vicious" men who
worked for one day that they might be intemperate for
three. [6] Timothy Dwight wrote at a later date that every
healthy, prudent man could save money and live well, so
that only the "shiftless, diseased, or vicious" were "labourers, . . . who look to the earning of today for the subsistence of to-morrow." [7] In view of the excellent chance to

[3] Petitions May 10, Nov. 10, 1785, Va State Lib.
[4] *New Travels*, 283–284. See also Cazenove, *Journal*, 8; *Delaware Session Laws*, 1767, p. 125. Milton Cantor conclusively demonstrates the low regard of whites for the Negroes in "The Image of the Negro in Colonial Literature," *New Eng. Qtly.*, xxxvi (1963), 452–477. Barbé-Marbois, *Letters*, 156, expresses a different opinion.
[5] Smith, *Colonists in Bondage*, 283–288, 299–300.
[6] *Md. Gazette*, Nov. 16, 1769.
[7] *Travels*, I, 193–194.

rise, such a characterization has force. At best the unskilled workers were regarded with amusement, as when an article poked fun at the illiteracy of sailors, or they were patronized, as when the editor publishing the article gratuitously termed it "a good and tolerably decent specimen of the language of a honest and useful class of people, who have all dangers and indure all hardships." [8]

The artisans occupied an intermediate position in the prestige hierarchy. Dwight, having damned the laborers, hastened to add that "The Mechanics are in all respects of a different character; and are therefore generally prosperous." [9] On the other hand Jeremy Belknap referred to "the tradesmen and other inferior orders of people." [10] The latter was the traditional view, which was being modified by the belief that manufacturing was essential to the country, a belief increased by the obvious requirements of the war, and further developed during the depression of the 1780's when manufacturing was regarded as a patriotic duty which would reduce foreign debts and help the domestic poor. [11] Despite their improved position in the public mind, artisans continued to be attracted by the superior prestige and profits of farming or of trade. Most people entertained "but a mean opinion of working laborious people," and treated mechanics "with contempt." Such a laborer might perhaps earn a competence but seldom would his craft bring him the respect of his betters. [12]

[8] *The Charleston Morning Post and Daily Advertiser*, April 3, 1786.

[9] *Travels*, 194.

[10] To Ebenezer Hazard, Boston, June 19, 1784, "Belknap Papers," Mass. Hist. Soc., *Collections*, 5 series II (1877), 359.

[11] Examples are *New Hampshire Mercury*, March 15, 1786; *Country Journal* (Poughkeepsie), Sept. 16, 1788.

[12] Quotation from *Md. Journal*, Oct. 17, 1785. See also *ibid.*, Aug. 16, 1785; *Providence Gazette*, Dec. 3, 1768; Bridenbaugh, *Craftsman*, 162–163.

Professional men fared better. "The chairmaker or cabi-
net maker is known in his town; a good physician for 100
miles; a lawyer throughout America," wrote an observer,
adding, however, that philosophers, scientists, politicians,
and generals were known throughout the world.[13] But this
was a lawyer speaking, and others disagreed. Indeed the
position of a professional man was ambivalent. On the one
hand he was considered to be necessary; on the other he was
regarded as expensive and dangerous. "The number of professional men in a state should be as few as possible," wrote
one critic, referring to lawyers, doctors, and ministers, "for
they do not increase the power of the state; but live on the
property acquired by others."[14] According to "Democritus," such men had "very little compassion upon the laity,"
and should not be trusted with power. History proved that
the clergy, lawyers, and physicians were "extortioners and
despots." There were, of course, exceptions, and certainly
the government ought to be run by learned men. It was
only necessary to exclude those who thought and acted as if
the laity were their property. Unfortunately, he concluded,
this was a "part of a college education." An irate reply by
"LYCURGUS" pointed out that the leaders of the Revolution were college men and that most of them were lawyers.[15]

The different points of view reflected the social origins of
both critics and their subjects. Doctors were of several
types, the income and status of which varied greatly. Some
were college educated, or trained by college men. These

[13] St. George Tucker to Masters Theodorick and John Randolph,
June 12, 1787, St. George Tucker Papers, Colonial Williamsburg.
[14] *Pa. Packet*, Feb. 21, 1787.
[15] *Mass. Spy*, July 5, 12, 1775. "Mentor" warned, "Elect no man
merely because *he is called* a Divine or Lawyer, for a professional
name is no proof of common sense or common honesty." *State
Gazette of Georgia*, Nov. 27, 1783.

enjoyed large incomes, yet the esteem in which they were held was not always proportionate to their wealth. Other college men, and many persons of the upper class, approved of them as they did of college graduates generally.[16] On the other hand a good many Americans, perhaps a majority, disliked them for the very fact of their education, or their wealth, or the high fees which they charged. The practice of medicine was sometimes labelled "a Profession that does more Mischief than them all," as the merchant John Watts wrote.[17] Thus "A Mechanic" pointed out that it took a day's wages to buy a bottle of medicine, and that the man was happy whose house was visited by doctors only three months of the year.[18] So too "BENEVOLUS" feared that the formation of a state medical society might increase the number of doctors, already too numerous, and of fees, already too high. Such an increase "would necessarily add to that unhappy inequality which is daily taking place among the people." The physicians "have made as large fortunes, and lived in as much splendor and reputation as any gentlemen in the several towns where they have resided." Lawyers and even some of the clergy were, he asserted, doubling their incomes, and concentrating property at the expense of the people.[19]

Had medical practices been entirely in the hands of reputable men, doctors probably would have been accorded high rank, for they were needed, and the good ones were, on the whole, admired. But in reality the majority of "doctors" were incompetent. No one was more aware of the situation than the qualified physicians, and the newspapers

[16] E.g., *Conn. Journal*, May 26, 1769; *Continental Journal*, Feb. 12, 1778.

[17] To Colonel Barré, New York, Nov. 15, 1763, "Letter Book," 198.

[18] *S.C. Gazette and General Advertiser*, Nov. 22, 1783.

[19] *Conn. Journal*, Oct. 27, 1784.

frequently published their articles which bitterly attacked the majority of practitioners. "These appear," wrote one critic, "under the awful names of doctors, surgeons, apothecaries, druggists, manmidwives, oculists, dentists, rupturists, venerialists, nostrumites, balsamites.—With a long etcetera of infallible pretenders, who 'tis fear'd too often serve as auxiliaries to the King of terrors." The result was "that physick in this place, in point of reputation is at its lowest ebb." [20] When the title "doctor" was "indiscriminately applied to the man of knowledge and the inexperienced quack," most people could not distinguish between them, and blamed every member of the profession as a whole for the malpractice of the part.[21] From the physicians' point of view, the only solution was to suppress quackery by law, by restrictive medical societies, or both.[22]

Many men who were not doctors were aware of quackery, and distinguished between those admirable physicians who were skilled and those who were not.[23] At the same time however the majority of people did not know the difference, patronized whoever was nearest and cheapest, damned the expensive physicians, and preferred the practitioners of folk medicine. The medical success of the latter was not much less than that of the former, since in those days the sick person was purged, made to vomit, bled, filled with antimony and mercury, and left half dead even by

[20] *New York Gazette and Mercury*, Feb. 21, 1771.

[21] *Conn. Gazette*, March 18, 1774.

[22] E.g., *Conn. Journal*, Oct. 27, Nov. 17, Dec. 29, 1784; *Vermont Gazette*, Aug. 29, 1785; *Hudson Gazette*, May 31, 1787; *New Haven Gazette*, July 22, 1784; *Columbian Herald*, Feb. 25, 28, 1788; *Md. Journal*, Dec. 13, 1785; *Mass. Spy*, Sept. 30, 1779; for an early act, *Col. Rec. Conn.*, XIV, 208–209.

[23] *Mass. Spy*, Dec. 20, 1781; *Va. Independent Chronicle*, July 18, 1787; *Boston Gazette*, Dec. 15, 1766.

trained men. Small wonder that the profession's prestige suffered! [24]

The same mixture of admiration and hostility confronted the lawyers. On the one hand they were regarded as following "the most respectable and most lucrative" profession, with great influence among the people.[25] Criticisms were met with the forthright assertion that they were essential, politically capable, learned, upright, and well paid because they deserved to be.[26] Yet even some men who felt that lawyers were "as liberal, honest and respectable, as any class of men in the state" believed that "their business must be regarded as a public evil."[27] William Bradford, uncertain whether to enter the law, medicine, or commerce, wrote to Madison, "The grand objection urged against Law is, that it is prejudicial to morals." This was not a necessary consequence, he felt, yet "It must indeed be owned that the conduct of the generallity of lawyers is very reproachable."[28] As in the case of doctors, some of the profession were indeed ignorant harpies, disliked not only by the people but by the learned and honest lawyers themselves.[29] John Jay, for example, warned against "designing, cheating, litigious pettifoggers, who, like leeches and spiders, will

[24] Richard Harrison Shryock, *Medicine and Society in America 1660–1860* (New York, 1960).

[25] Chastellux, *Travels*, ii, 315; La Rochefoucault-Liancourt, *Travels*, i, 536; Cadwallader Colden, "State of the Province of New York," N.Y. Hist. Soc., *Collections*, 1877, p. 7; Boucher, *Reminiscences*, 103.

[26] E.g., *Independent Chronicle*, April 27, May 11, 1786, Jan. 25, 1787; *Essex Journal*, April 5, 1786; *Vermont Journal*, March 15, 1785; *Providence Gazette*, April 30, 1779; *Pa. Chronicle*, June 6, 1780.

[27] *Pa. Packet*, Feb. 21, 1787.

[28] From Abington [Pa.], Aug. 12, 1773, in Hutchinson and Rachal, eds., *Papers of Madison*, i, 91. Madison replied that all three pursuits were honorable. *ibid.*, p. 96.

[29] Thomas Burke to Mr. Williams et al., May 20, 1783, Thomas Burke Papers, U. of N.C. Lib.

fatten on the spoils of the poor, the ignorant, the feeble, and the unwary." [30]

Attacks on lawyers were continuous throughout the period, but the bar became especially unpopular during the years of depression following the war. They were, said their accusers, insolent, petulant, designing, cheating vultures, who picked people's pockets, corrupted other men, evaded the law, intimidated witnesses, took bribes, and like caterpillars left to the honest men little more than the gleanings of their labor.[31] "We have," asserted Governor Cadwallader Colden, "a Set of Lawyers in this Province as Insolent, Petulant and at the same Time as well skilled in all the chicanerie of the Law as perhaps is to be found anywhere else." [32] High fees were a universal grievance, for they enabled lawyers to "riot in Luxury," and acquire wealth "from the Toil and Labour of the Necessitous." [33] The growing wealth of the attorneys was obvious and the feeling that they represented the rich rather than the

[30] To R. R. Livingston and Gouverneur Morris, Fishkill, April 29, 1777, in H. R. Johnston, ed., *Correspondence and Public Papers of John Jay* (4 vols., 1890–1893), I, 134–135.

[31] *N.Y. Gazette and Mercury*, Oct. 15, 1770; *N.Y. Journal*, Nov. 17, 1785, Nov. 29, 1786; *Providence Gazette*, April 3, 1779; *Vermont Gazette*, Aug. 14, 1785; *N.J. Journal*, Nov. 29, 1786; *The Albany Gazette*, Sept. 14, 1786; *Col. Rec. N.C.*, VIII, 76; *Charleston Evening Gazette*, Aug. 25, 1786; *Conn. Gazette*, Sept. 10, 1784; *Pa. Chronicle*, April 22, 1771; *Md. Journal*, Aug. 8, 1786; *Independent Chronicle*, March 9, 1786; *Md. Gazette*, Sept. 5, 1783; John Watts to Sir William Baker, New York, Jan. 22, 1762, "Letter Book," 13; "Diary of John Quincy Adams," Mass. Hist. Soc., *Proceedings*, 2 series XVI (1902), 342–343.

[32] To Egremont, New York, Sept. 14, 1763, N.Y. Hist. Soc., *Collections*, 1876, p. 231. Colden was, however, a prejudiced source.

[33] *N.Y. Gazette and Mercury*, April 17, Oct. 9, 1769. See also *Hampshire Gazette*, Nov. 15, 1786; *Pa. Journal*, Nov. 19, 1770; *Pa. Chronicle*, April 23, 1770; Harvey Toliver Cook, *Rambles in the Pee Dee Basin of South Carolina* (Columbia, S.C., 1926), 213.

poor led to their being accused of aristocratical leanings.[34] Efforts, occasionally successful, were made to defeat them for office.[35] Lawyers comprised about one-eighth of the membership of the lower houses before the Revolution, but their political influence diminished sharply thereafter.[36] The Councils of the late colonial period contained a disproportionate number of them—indeed about 20 percent; but when the Revolution made those bodies elective the ratio declined to 11 percent. Evidently members of the profession were more popular with British officialdom and prosperous colonials than with the common people. Yet some of the most trusted leaders were lawyers, including many who took the popular side. Even men who criticized them grudgingly conceded that the profession might be honorable and useful, and deserved "the Honour and Esteem of every Person of an inferiour Rank." Despite the bitter attacks it seems probable that the general reputation of lawyers was higher than that of doctors.[37]

Judges and justices of the peace were generally looked down upon by the lawyers, and sometimes by other observers too. The justices were considered to be unqualified, and too much under popular influence,[38] while the incomes of

[34] *Independent Chronicle*, March 9, 1786; *Md. Gazette* (Baltimore), Dec. 17, 1776; *Norwich Packet*, Sept. 28, 1786; *Vermont Gazette*, Sept. 25, 1786; *Columbian Herald*, Nov. 26, 1784.

[35] *Md. Journal*, Oct. 1, 1786; Christopher Gadsden to Marion, Nov. 3 1782, *S.C. Hist. Gen. Mag.*, XLI (1940), 50; Samuel Breck to Henry Knox, Boston, July 14, 1787, Knox Papers, XX, 131, Mass. Hist. Soc.; Caleb Strong to Theodore Sedgwick, Boston, June 27, 1786, Sedgwick Papers vol. A, Mass. Hist. Soc.

[36] In Virginia, for example, 15 percent of the Burgesses in 1773 were lawyers, but by 1785 the ratio dropped to 10 percent.

[37] *Boston Evening Post*, Aug. 30, 1773; Brissot de Warville, *New Travels*, 114. Hart believes that lawyers in the Shenandoah Valley were "generally in good repute." *Valley of Virginia*, 53.

[38] *Continental Journal*, Nov. 29, 1781; Gov. Moore to the Earl of Shelburne, Fort George, Oct. 1, 1767, John Romeyn Brodhead, ed.,

the judges were thought too small to attract first-rate men.[39] Trained lawyers therefore refused seats on the bench, which were as a result "very ill filled." [40] Yet most people seem to have preferred justices of the peace to lawyers, while judges who were chosen by the people or their representatives might win popularity. Probably both sets of men were generally respected, and if perhaps less admired than lawyers they were also less feared.

The clergy occupied an intermediate position on the scale of prestige. Their status seems to have declined from the earlier days, when their authority had been very great. The anticlerical aspects of the Enlightenment had crossed the Atlantic, and it may be true, as some contemporaries claimed, that religion during the revolutionary era was in a "low state." [41] Perhaps the multiplication of untrained revivalists during the Great Awakening also had some effect. At all events, the clergy were considered "not as *valuable* an order of men *now* as they used to be." [42] Even

Documents Relating to the Colonial History of the State of New York, VII (Albany, 1856), 979; *New Hampshire Mercury*, Sept. 6, 1786; Robert R. Livingston, "On Country Justices" (1775), Livingston Papers, N.Y. Hist. Soc.

[39] For contrary opinions concerning judges' salaries, *Newport Mercury*, Aug. 17, 1772; James Iredell to Judge John Williams, Edenton, Dec. 14, 1781, *N.C. State Rec.*, XIX, 892. In most colonies and states the judges' salaries were ample to attract all except men of considerable incomes.

[40] La Rochefoucault-Liancourt, *Travels*, II, 50; *Newport Mercury*, June 1, 1782; Turner, *Plumer*, 32; *Independent Chronicle*, March 23, 1786; Judge Samuel Spencer to Gen. Allen Jones, Anson County, Dec. 22, 1778, *N.C. State Rec.*, XX, 771; John Watts to General Monckton, New York, June 30, 1764, "Letter Book," 270.

[41] Thomas Tillotson to Robert R. Livingston, Baltimore, Dec. 1784, Livingston Papers, N.Y. Hist. Soc.; *Va. Gazette and American Advertiser*, Dec. 21, 1782; *The Continental Journal, and Weekly Advertiser* (Boston), Oct. 23, 1783.

[42] *ibid.*, Jan. 7, 1779.

in Connecticut it was reported that "their mutual wran-
glings, and their fierce intolerance" had lost them much of
the high influence which they once possessed.[43] Newspaper
articles accused them of immorality,[44] and it was suggested
that they should be excluded from colleges and denied political influence on grounds of incompetence.[45] One writer
did not understand "why certain members of the community, who are not better than their neighbours, might
not work for their living like I do," [46] while a prominent
revolutionary leader asserted, "it would require much Time
& Paper to point out the many Evils which have befallen
Mankind, in different Periods of the World by the Usurpa-
tions of the Clergy." Moreover "I know of no Men more
Ignorant of the true Principles of Government, than the
Venerable Clergy," so that they should "have nothing to do
with Civil Affairs." [47] The ministers, as we have seen, were
sometimes forced to fight for their small incomes, another
indication that their prestige had suffered; and this economic decline in turn reduced their prestige. Nevertheless
they were still respected, and their influence was considerable especially in New England.[48]

The merchants also had both detractors and defenders,
but on the whole fared rather worse. To many Americans,
the "Spirit of Commerce" was itself corrupt. Its basis was
extortion, they asserted, and upon such rare occasions when
it was found advantageous to the community, it should be

[43] La Rochefoucault-Liancourt, *Travels*, I, 536.
[44] *N.Y. Journal*, Supplement, April 2, 1768; *The South Carolina
Gazette; and Country Journal*, Aug. 16, 1774.
[45] *Conn. Courant*, Feb. 11, 1783; *N.Y. Journal*, Feb. 19, 1786; *Providence Gazette*, April 3, 1779.
[46] *The Falmouth Gazette, and Weekly Advertiser*, Feb. 5, 1785.
[47] James M. Varnum, Jan. 2, 1773, Peck Coll., vol. III, R.I. Hist. Soc.
[48] *New Hampshire Gazette*, July 19, 1783; La Rochefoucault-Liancourt, *Travels*, II, 215–216; Brown, *Virginia*, 254–255.

strictly regulated.[49] Traders were considered to be of little
benefit to the country, and capable of doing infinite mischief.[50] They charged what they pleased and sought only
their own gain, even at the expense of their country.[51]
They were attacked with particular bitterness during the
war, when they were accused of profiteering,[52] but the
antagonism preceded and followed it. William Bradford believed that "As gain is the sole pursuit of the merchant he is
much more likely to contract an inordinate desire of wealth
than the Lawyers, whose pursuit is as much after fame as
Wealth; indeed they are both improper pursuits, yet generosity and Benevolence are the product of the one Extortion and Selfishness of the other."[53] Farmers especially felt
that men in commerce comprised a "set of sharpers, who
are constantly on the watch for plunder and gain," who
thought themselves superior and demanded "rich wines and
costly spices . . . since their appetite has become too delicate to relish the natural productions of their country."
Therefore they cheated the farmers so that they could live a
life of pleasure.[54] The farmers believed themselves to be in

[49] John Adams to Mercy Warren, April 16, 1776, "Warren-Adams
Letters," Mass. Hist. Soc., *Collections*, LXXII (1917), 222–223; *N.Y.
Journal* (Poughkeepsie), Jan. 18, 1779; "A Husband-Man" to Washington, July ?, 1784, Washington Papers, vol. 230, no. 95, Lib. Cong.
[50] Attmore, *Journal*, 40; *The American Herald* (Boston), June 19,
1786.
[51] *The North Carolina Gazette* (New Bern), Dec. 12, 1777; *Continental Journal*, June 12, 1777; *Md. Gazette*, July 4, 1765; *Newport
Mercury*, Jan. 30, 1786; Richard Bland to Thomas Adams, August 1,
1771, *Va. Mag. Hist. Biog.*, VI (1898–1899), 128–129; Walter Jones to
Thomas Jones, Edinburgh, Dec. 5, 1769, Jones Family Papers box 17,
Lib. Cong.; Richard Henry Lee to James Madison, Aug. 11, 1785,
Edmund Cody Burnett, ed., *Letters of Members of the Continental
Congress* (8 vols., Washington, 1921–1938), VIII, 181.
[52] Crittenden, *Commerce*, 146.
[53] Letter cited, *Papers of Madison*, I, 91.
[54] *Cumberland Gazette*, Feb. 23, 1787; *Norwich Packet*, Aug. 18,
1785.

reality superior to the traders: the mercantile class, they insisted, was the weakest and most dangerous part of the community.[55]

Yet the merchants, like the lawyers and doctors, had their defenders. Newspaper articles, probably written by merchants themselves, praised commerce and men in trade. Agriculture and manufacturing depended upon commerce; liberty rose or declined with it. Trade was the principal source of riches, freedom, and safety. It was true that commerce led to wealth, but merchants had benefitted the community and provided essential support to the state. Moreover the merchant was a "gentleman," "ranks with men of quality and distinction," was "tender of his honour," and "a blessing to society." [56] Certainly wealthy landowners had no hesitation in allying themselves by marriage with traders or engaging in trade themselves; merchants had great influence because of their wealth, and it was said that in Philadelphia commerce was "the only road in Pennsylvania to honours and distinction." [57] Still there remained the feeling that commerce, even if a legitimate and certainly a profitable enterprise, was not the most admirable type of human activity. The highest sanction was reserved for agriculture.

It is true that travellers sometimes described farmers in uncomplimentary terms, and that they were upon occasion patronized as the "common sort of people" or even "the rabble." But most Americans, of all classes, regarded agri-

[55] *N.Y. Journal* (Poughkeepsie), Feb. 1, 1779; *Providence Gazette*, Feb. 22, 1783.

[56] *N.C. Gazette*, Dec. 26, 1777, Jan. 23, 1778; *N.Y. Mercury*, Dec. 19, 1763; *Conn. Journal*, Feb. 2, 1770; *American Herald*, June 28, 1784, also in *Newport Mercury*, July 3, 1784, and *U.S. Chronicle*, March 30, 1786.

[57] Griffith, "English Education," *Va. Mag. Hist. Biog.*, LXXIX (1961), 242; Fithian, *Journal*, 203; Bell, "Social History," *Pa. Mag. Hist. Biog.*, LXII (1938), 285.

culture as the ideal occupation and the farmer as the ideal citizen. Yale students in 1784 debated "Whether Commerce ought to be encouraged more at the present day in America than Agriculture," and agriculture won.[58] Urban life was corrupt and unhappy; but the rural dweller was content: "At noon he calls together his servants and labourers, and they all recline themselves on the green turf beneath the shade of some mighty oak"; enjoy the cool breeze, listen to the warbling of birds and murmuring of the brook and take a nice nap, near sunset they cease work and have a refreshing sleep.[59] Farmers might not get rich, but theirs was the good life, "friendly to health, contentment, liberty, and religion." [60] Agriculture promoted all that was good: "In a philosophic view it is great and extensive. In a political view it is important, and perhaps the only firm and stable foundation of greatness. As a profession, it strengthens the mind without enervating the body. In morals, it tends to encrease virtue, without introducing vice." [61] So too Jefferson described (from Paris) the idyllic existence of the average American: "I know no condition happier than that of a Virginia farmer might be, conducting himself as he did during the war. His estate supplies a good table, clothes itself and his family with their ordinary apparel, furnishes a small surplus to buy salt, sugar, coffee, and a little finery for his wife and daughter, enables him to receive and visit his friends, and furnishes him pleasing and healthy occupation. To secure all this he needs but one act of self denial, to put off buying anything till he has money to pay for it." [62]

---

[58] Dyar Throop Hinckley Diary, Nov. 29, 1784, Conn. Hist. Soc.

[59] *New Hampshire Gazette,* June 1, 1786, reprinted in *The Vermont Journal, and the Universal Advertiser* (Windsor), April 23, 1787.

[60] *The New Hampshire Recorder, and the Weekly Advertiser* (Keene), Sept. 18, 1787; *New Hampshire Gazette,* March 30, 1770; *Pa. Packet,* July 21, 1785; Morse, *American Geography,* 240.

[61] *Pa. Packet,* May 16, 1786.

[62] To James Currie, Paris, August 4, 1787, Boyd, ed., *Papers,* XI, 682

The farmer himself, in such an environment, could hardly help but become the ideal American. The yeomanry "are the main prop and support of the State," honest, virtuous, industrious. To them alone could the freedom of the country be safely entrusted.[63] If we may judge from what people said, rather than the way in which they acted, farmers stood at the apex of the prestige order. Next to them were the professional men descending through the clergy, lawyers, doctors. Still lower were the merchants, lower still the artisans, and, at the bottom, free laborers, white servants, and slaves.

When the revolutionary American selected his leaders, this ostensible rank order to which he paid lip service was not always followed. Supposedly merchants, lawyers, and doctors would seldom be chosen, and farmers almost invariably preferred. In practice, however, professionals and men in trade were voted into office more often than their numbers warranted.

This was especially true of the post-revolutionary state Senates. Although a great majority of the voters were farmers, the agricultural interest was under-represented. Even if all those whose occupations are unknown were farmers (which is probably not quite true), the yeomen comprised not over one-third of the membership. In addition about one-fourth of the Senators were large landholders, so that the total farm strength was about 60 percent of the total. Merchants and professional men were elected with a frequency out of all proportion to their actual numbers: one out of six members were engaged in trade, and professional men (including judges) furnished another sixth.

[63] *N.Y. Journal* (Poughkeepsie), Feb. 1, 1779; *U.S. Chronicle*, Sept. 21, 1786; *N.J. Gazette*, Feb. 27, 1786. See also *Vermont Gazette*, Nov. 16, 1788; *New Hampshire Gazette*, March 31, 1763; *State Gazette* (Wilmington, N.C.), Nov. 22, 1786; *U.S. Chronicle*, March 10, 1785; Jefferson, *Notes*, 274; Tench Coxe, *A View of the United States of America* . . . (London, 1795), 7.

The upper house, however, did not always reflect majority views because of property requirements. Yet analysis even of the lower house suggests that farmers had somewhat less prestige than the praise of them indicates. This is especially the case before the war, when the yeomen played only a minor role in the legislatures. New Hampshire, New York, New Jersey, Maryland, and Virginia elected representatives, between 18 and 26 percent of whom were farmers, large or small (the percentage depending upon the assignment of those whose occupations are unknown). Large landowners, as might be expected, were chosen much more frequently, comprising 44 percent of the members. Thus the lower houses were predominantly agricultural. Still, there remain 30 percent of the representatives who were not farmers. Merchants furnished about one-eighth of the delegates, professionals 15 percent.

The composition of the pre-war legislatures may, however, reflect the structure of power rather than the status order of the different occupational groups. Therefore the situation after the Revolution becomes important. That great event apparently altered the location of power, so that the make-up of the lower houses was considerably changed. By the mid 1780's, merchants especially had lost ground. So had the lawyers, whose proportion, indeed, was halved; and the election of a few other professionals compensated only in part for this. Artisans continued to play an insignificant role. Large landowners were far fewer, but the agricultural interest as a whole gained enormously, for the proportion of farmers doubled; and if the delegates whose occupation is unknown were farmers—and they probably were—not far from half of the members were yeomen, who together with their wealthiest neighbors comprised three-fourths of the membership. It is apparent that both merchants and lawyers lost power and quite possibly prestige as a consequence of the Revolution. Nevertheless they still were chosen more frequently than the vocal opposition to them might suggest.

Military leadership was of a different nature. Shopkeepers, merchants, lawyers, doctors, teachers, and clergymen usually followed their trades or professions as civilians, leaving service in the army to artisans and above all to farmers. In the South, higher ranking officers were large landholders. Not until the Revolution were small farmers occasionally promoted, and then only to the lower posts. The ideal even for the rank of Captain, Lieutenant and Ensign was the man "of personal popularity & connections." [64]

In New England, "connections" were much less important and "popularity" foremost, for officers were elected rather than appointed. Whereas in the South the military rank order corresponded very closely with the rural economic class structure even to using slaves for much of the dirty work, in the North equality was more often the rule. There, officers were "habituated to consider themselves more upon a level with their fellow citizens," whereas southern officers were "in general accustomed to affluence, and to consider themselves far above the peasantry in those states." [65] A French officer wrote in astonishment as he travelled between Boston and Rhode Island, "Our innkeeper was a captain, the several military grades being granted here to every rank of people. There are shoemakers who are Colonels; and it often happens that the Americans ask the French officers what their trade is in France." [66]

[64] Blackwell P. Robinson, *William R. Davie* (Chapel Hill, 1957), 296–297.

[65] *Conn. Courant,* Sept. 23, 1783. See also *Conn. Gazette,* Feb. 2, 1776. General Lincoln had trouble getting soldiers to work on the Charleston defenses because "physical labor was the badge of the black man." Shipton, *Harvard Graduates,* XII, 422.

[66] "Diary of a French Officer, 1781," *Mag. Am. Hist.,* IV (1880), 209. See also *Providence Gazette,* Jan. 9, 1779.

A recent writer has concluded that Massachusetts officers came from all walks of life, and that a "levelling spirit" was characteristic of the revolutionary army.[67] This spirit can be exaggerated, for there did exist a marked tendency to elect the large property holders of the towns. However, consistency was lacking. New Ipswich's colonel was the town's wealthiest man, but the fourth richest was a mere lieutenant, and the seventh was a captain; while two more captains, three lieutenants, and an ensign were in the top 10 percent. An ensign was in the third 10 percent, two captains and a lieutenant had below average property, while a captain and two lieutenants were poor.[68] Concord's tax list of 1771 contained the names of fourteen officers ranging from a colonel, who was the second richest man, to a lieutenant with less than average property. Half of the officers were among the town's richest 10 percent. The two wealthiest men of Westborough were a captain and a lieutenant, and a captain was Oxford's richest citizen; but both towns contained officers who were poor.[69] Similarly the officers of Goshen precinct in Orange County, New York, were

[67] Sidney Kaplan, "Rank and Status among Massachusetts Continental Officers [1775-76]," *Am. Hist. Rev.,* LVI (1950–1951), 318–326.

[68] Kidder and Gould, 70–71.

[69] The assessment lists of 1771 for six Massachusetts towns show the following comparison between officers and the general population in their ownership of real estate:

Annual Value	Officers %	General %
None	7+	22
Less than £3	7+	21
£3 to £9	31	38
£10 to £19	36½	17
£20+	18	2

The officers had about three times as much wealth as the civilians. However lieutenants scarcely exceeded the norm whereas captains had far more property.

chosen principally but not exclusively from the larger tax-payers. Roughly one-third were included among the richest 10 percent, and two-thirds among the wealthiest 20 percent; however two paid a tax which was smaller than the average. In general the officers usually were drawn from the upper income groups—field officers almost invariably being well-to-do—but poverty did not disbar one from being chosen, so that the correlation between class and rank was imperfect.

Non-military titles were ordinarily accorded only to men of property. The most common such title was "esquire." Usage of the term varied considerably. In Connecticut one writer believes that the word was reserved for justices of the peace, judges, and members of the upper house, but was not applied to men because of their wealth.[70] In New Hampshire, legislators were not given the title; in New Jersey this was always done.[71] It seems that justices always were referred to as "esquire," but otherwise there was no universal rule, application being individual and perhaps eccentric. The matter could be a touchy one. The editors of the *South Carolina Gazette* felt obliged to assure the public "that whenever we with-hold, or rudely give, the Title of Esquire or Honourable in our Publications, it is not that we assume a Privilege to divest any of those Honours, or to confer them, at our Pleasure, or to answer particular Purposes, but owing to Misinformation, or our receiving Instructions so to do."[72]

Ordinarily the title "esquire" was granted to or secured by men of high economic rank. In pre-revolutionary Massachusetts 23 out of 27 Suffolk County esquires left

[70] Grant, *Kent*, 145.
[71] *New Hampshire Mercury*, Sept. 6, 1786; *N.J. Gazette*, Oct. 25, 1780.
[72] *S.C. Gazette*, June 4, 1772.

estates of £1,000. After the war there seems either to have been a more general use of the title, or some had suffered financially from the upheaval, for now one-third had less than that sum. Over half of Worcester County's esquires were worth £1,000. In South Carolina all but 8 of 46 esquires owned personal property valued at £1,000. Still, the existence of esquires who were not well-to-do negates an exclusively economic explanation, especially since many men of large estates were not dignified with the title. In pre-revolutionary Suffolk, for example, only one-third of those owning £2,000 were so honored. The "esquire" of New England towns usually had considerable property, but there are many exceptions. In Concord, New Hampshire, one was the richest but another had only moderate means. The esquire of Bow in the same state was the town's wealthiest resident, but in Newtown, Connecticut, one ranked seventh, one thirteenth, and another well down the list. Hollis' largest taxpayer was an "honorable," but both esquires were men of modest property. Finally, those of New Castle, New Hampshire, ranked first, third, ninth, and fifteenth, all substantial men but by no means wealthy. Evidently property was a factor, but the position one held, or one's local reputation, were also important.

If it be granted that the title was, to some extent, a reflection of prestige, then there should have been a relationship between the esquires and the status order to which Americans gave lip service. Actually such a relationship did not always exist. In post-revolutionary Suffolk County, which was about half urban, half agricultural, not more than one-fifth of the 45 esquires whose estates were probated were farmers. Instead, half of them were merchants, and there were almost as many artisans as farmers. In South Carolina at the same time over half were planters, but lawyers, merchants, and various other city folk were honored in disproportionate numbers. It is true however that ownership of land was important, for in Suffolk County the non-farm esquires, with few exceptions, had considerable real estate: indeed such property seems to have been essential to the aspiring artisan. If the merchant or mechanic wished the title, he would do well to purchase land.

In a highly mobile society it is not, perhaps, surprising that family background counted for little. One-fourth of Suffolk's esquires came of merchant parentage, but one-fourth were artisans, and about the same number were farmers' sons. There were a certain number of "gentlemen" among the parents, and they seem to have been generally men of standing: deacons, selectmen, representatives, and the like were numerous; but a surprising proportion of the fathers—nearly one-third—were humble men. Similarly in Worcester County, esquires included both some men with wealth and family and others with neither. In New England, it seems, the use of esquire as a mark of great economic and social distinctions (if such had been the earlier usage) was declining, and a man who was mobile economically or even one who had not achieved any considerable wealth might be given the title. The same situation existed throughout the North. The esquires identified in the extensive tax lists recorded in the *Pennsylvania Archives* included many men of moderate property. In Goshen precinct of Orange County, New York, all of the men so designated were above average in wealth, but only 5 out of 16 were among the richest 10 percent, and the 4 wealthiest men produced but one esquire. Apparently in the South the English tradition continued, though even there it was in decline.

The appellation "gentleman" was used even more loosely. The "esquire" was bestowed upon some men of ordinary means, but their average wealth was very high—six or seven times the median. The "gentleman" had only a third as much property. This was still twice the average amount, but no more than ministers owned, less than shopkeepers, and about on a level with substantial farmers and artisans. Apparently in the South (where the title was little used) it continued to have some significance, but in New England it was assumed by or given to ordinary farmers and artisans who had very little money and whose parents were obscure. The word "yeoman" had no social significance except that it identified one as a landholder rather than a laborer; it was synonymous with "farmer." [73]

The "Mr.," once a mark of distinction, meant practically nothing. In Virginia, even before the Revolution it was adopted by "almost any property owner, merchant or tradesman," [74] and after the war the process of democratization continued, reaching the ultimate in a newspaper announcement, "on Sunday Evening died suddenly, Mr. Edward Lee, Labourer." [75] In New England it was used in no set fashion, and was applied even before the Revolution to men in humble circumstances.[76]

The use of titles as symbols of prestige was declining throughout revolutionary America. Many men of substance claimed or were assigned no such title. On the other hand, the rising farmer's or artisan's son might adopt the title "Mr." without exciting comment, might become a "gentleman," and could aspire to the "esquire" as he increased in wealth and local prestige. Even "honorable" was not beyond his reach, for it was attached to miscellaneous persons

[73] E.g., *The New American Magazine*, Jan., 1758, p. 9.

[74] Charles Edgar Gilliam, " 'Mr.' in Virginia Records before 1776," *Wm. and Mary Qtly.*, 2 series XIX (1939), 142–145.

[75] *The Virginia Journal and Alexandria Advertiser*, July 1, 1784.

[76] The Boston papers attached the name to merchants, tailors, blacksmiths, sailors, barbers, printers, and laborers. For example, *Boston Evenng Post*, Sept. 24, 1770, March 15, 1773.

of repute, especially high civil officials, many of whom were self-made men. The sequence: no title—Mr., Gent., Esq., Hon.—did represent a prestige order which corresponded roughly with the economic rank order, but it was flexible rather than rigid, and instead of symbolizing and reinforcing a series of social levels, each separated by a visible gap difficult to bridge, it rather marked the gradual upward progress of the mobile American in an open society.

Social classes existed in early America, but their precise definition is as unclear as the prestige order was flexible. Everyone pretended to exalt the farmers, giving to professional men and still more to merchants an inferior status, and to artisans no status at all. In practice, however, Americans looked for leadership to their professional men as well as to the well-to-do landowners, while in the North merchants were granted high rank. The truth is that the social climber did not have to change his occupation, except of course that he could not simply remain a laborer—or a teacher. Even artisans achieved wealth and (in the North) prestige as symbolized by the title "esquire"; while doctors, lawyers, and men in trade had an opportunity at least equal to that of the landowner to rise socially. Two pieces of advice could be given to the socially ambitious: the acquisition of wealth opened all doors, even in Virginia, but especially in the cities; and the ownership of land did bring with it a special prestige.[77] Perhaps most important to the

[77] Bridenbaugh, *Cities in Revolt*, 140. Robert and Katherine Brown, in their *Virginia*, Chapter II, consider class to mean status order, and emphasize the use of titles as determinants of status. They furnish several examples of men with little property who gained or assumed a title, and stress the fluidity of the social class structure. I agree that the use of titles was becoming fluid, but question whether titles determined status, to say nothing of class. Actually the Browns' evidence demonstrates that titles were losing their meaning, and that a class order based upon them is not useful for an analysis of Virginia's history during the revolutionary years.

average American was the fact that class did not depend upon inheritance but upon property. Since anyone could acquire property, anyone could rise, and the poor man could and occasionally did become a wealthy esquire.

CHAPTER VII

Contemporary Views of Class

COLONIAL SOCIETY was at once equal and unequal. It was equal in that class distinctions were far less than in Europe and in some areas were almost non-existent, equal too in that the opportunity to rise was open to all except slaves. It was unequal, because there were great economic differences—rich and poor, exploiters and exploited—and because in some areas property was concentrated in a few hands and mobility into the highest class was limited. When men viewed their society, therefore, they saw different things, recorded opposite aspects. Europeans might be impressed by the predominantly middle-class nature of the class structure, or they might note the existence of slaves and wealthy planters. Native Americans seeking reform emphasized class distinctions, the unequal distribution of property, and the rise of an aristocracy; others might insist that there was too much equality for comfort, or that everyone ought to admire the absence of classes in the new land. The historian who tries to discover the revolutionary American's ideas about class is confronted with a set of irreconcilable beliefs.

Most of the statements concerning equality come from New England or from foreigners travelling in the North. It was not so much equality of condition that struck the visitor as the general prosperity. Travellers in the rural region of New England, Long Island, New Jersey, or Pennsylvania, to be sure, did comment on the innumerable small farms and the absence of great estates;[1] but they were

[1] *Quebec to Carolina*, 139, 147; McRobert, *A Tour*, 33; Smyth, *A Tour*, II, 365; *U.S. Chronicle*, May 17, 1787.

considerably more impressed by the comfortable circumstances of even the humble, the virtual absence of an impoverished class, and the opportunity of the poor man to
rise.[2] "It was," remarked McRobert, "the best country in
the world for people of small fortunes, or in other words,
the best poor man's country." [3] They were also much impressed by the spirit of equality arising out of this high
mobility and general well-being. "Riches make no positive
material difference," remarked Schoepf, "because in this regard every man expects at one time or another to be on a
footing with his rich neighbor, and in this expectation
shows him no knavish reverence, but treats him with an
open, but seemly, familiarity. . . . Rank of birth is not
recognized, is resisted with a total force." [4] Laborers were
treated as equals; innkeepers demanded respect; "peasants"
thought themselves as good as anyone else. John Penn was
addressed by a Pennsylvanian in a tavern as "the Honorable
Proprietor," but, he complained, "to show how qualified
respect is in this democratical country, this discourse passed
while he, the tavern keeper, and myself were lounging in
three chairs, and I obliged to joke with him about his age." [5]
The same equality of condition, of opportunity, and of behavior was noted, though less often, in those parts of the
South where the social structure resembled that of the rural
North.[6]

[2] Barbé-Marbois, 88–89, 126; Anburey, *Travels*, ii, 251; Mittelberger,
Journey, 117; La Rochefoucault-Liancourt, *Travels*, i, 29, ii, 672;
Kalm, *Travels*, 211.

[3] McRobert, *A Tour*, ix.

[4] Schoepf, *Travels*, i, 99.

[5] "John Penn's Journal," *Pa. Mag. Hist. Biog.*, iii (1879), 284–285;
Barbé-Marbois, 68–69, 99–106; La Rochefoucault-Liancourt, *Travels*,
i, 68, ii, 215, 671–672; Edward H. Tatum, Jr., ed., *The American
Journal of Ambrose Serle* (San Marino, California, 1940), 278; Eddis,
Travels, 128.

[6] "A French Traveller in the Colonies, 1763," *Am. Hist. Rev.*, xxvi

Some native-born northerners also saw equality in their home. In New England there was said to be no leisure class, no "overgrown estates," [7] but a nearly equal distribution of property, particularly of land, "a happy medium between poverty and affluence," especially as compared with the southern states.[8] Ezra Stiles believed that Congress could not be dangerous to liberty "so long as Property in the United States is so minutely partitioned and transfused among the Inhabitants." [9] New Englanders praised their own generally high standard of living, where people "knew nothing of Poverty & want." [10] Residents of Pennsylvania and New Jersey likewise sometimes referred to equality as a characteristic of their society. John Stevens, Jr. insisted that "We have no such things as orders, ranks, or nobility," nor could there even be such except by "an immense accumulation of wealth in the hands of a few people," which he felt was "an exceedingly improbable event." [11]

(1920–1921), 738 (of North Carolina); J. Fred Rippy, "A View of the Carolinas in 1783" [Francisco de Miranda's diary], *N.C. Hist. Rev.*, vi (1929), 364 (of Newbern); Anburey, *Travels*, ii, 434–435 (of Frederick-Town, Maryland).

[7] *Conn. Courant*, Jan. 7, 1783; Morse, *American Geography*, 240.

[8] *The State Journal* (Exeter), Feb. 4, 1777; Thomas Dawes, jr., *An Oration* (Boston, 1787); *New London Gazette*, March 26, 1773; Jonathan Jackson, *Thoughts upon the political situation of the United States of America* . . . (Worcester, 1788), 56; Jeremy Belknap to Ebenezer Hazard, March 3, 1784, "Belknap Papers," Mass. Hist. Soc., *Collections*, 5 series ii (1877), 313.

[9] To Thomas Jefferson, Sept. 14, 1786, Boyd, ed., *Papers*, x, 386.

[10] Joseph Trumbull, quoted in Chilton Williamson, *American Suffrage from Property to Democracy* (Princeton, 1960), 39; *New Haven Gazette*, Sept. 1, 1785; *New Hampshire Gazette*, Nov. 2, 1764; Thomas Pownall, *Topographical Description*, 59; *American Husbandry*, 46.

[11] John Stevens, Jr., *Observations on Government* . . . (New York, 1787), 46; *Pa. Chronicle*, Nov. 16, 1767; *Pa. Packet*, Nov. 17, 1785; *N.J. Gazette*, March 18, 1778, Feb. 27, 1782; *Independent Chronicle*, Sept. 7, 1786. Americans also noted the high mobility rate. For ex-

Observations such as these were not applied to the South and were in fact comparatively few even in the North. The truth was that classes, both economic and social, did exist, and their existence was therefore honestly perceived and described. During the Federal Convention the South Carolinian C. C. Pinkney insisted that the country enjoyed economic equality. Riches and wealth, he asserted, lay in the great body of the people, "among whom there are no men of wealth, and very few of real poverty." Perhaps he was thinking of his own plantation society, where there were a few wealthy whites, almost no middle class, and practically no poor people, since slaves did not count as people. This extraordinary statement was not refuted directly, but the next day first Madison and then Hamilton explained that the people did not constitute one homogeneous mass, but fell into different classes growing out of the inequality of property which was, according to the latter, the "great and fundamental distinction in Society." [12] The Massachusetts minister Jeremy Belknap remarked that a republic could succeed only if property was equally distributed, and continued, "Where shall we look for an equal division of property? Not in the five southern States, where every white man is the lordly tyrant of an hundred slaves. Not in the great trading towns and cities, where cash in funds yields 13 or 16 percent, and in trade much more." [13] There was much of rhetoric in this, but other observers reported the same thing, even in New England. "There is," wrote a contributor to a Connecticut paper, "a wide difference betwixt people, as to riches, titles and preferments." In Massachusetts distinctions were even greater, for "the con-

ample, *Pittsburgh Gazette*, March 17, 1787; *Country Journal* (Poughkeepsie), April 13, 1786; *N.J. Journal*, May 7, 1783.

[12] Max Farrand, ed., *The Records of the Federal Convention of 1787* (4 vols., New Haven, 1911–1937), I, 400–401, 422–424.

[13] To Hazard, March 3, 1784, Belknap Papers, 313.

siderable fortunes acquired by the commerce which is carried on in the numerous parts of the state prevent the general manners of the people from being so strictly republican here as in Connecticut." [14] One cause for Shays' Rebellion, wrote Nathaniel Ames in his diary, was "all property accumulating with greater rapidity than ever known into a few people's hands." [15]

Rhode Island newspapers depicted a society of class distinctions. The *Newport Mercury* reported that citizens of the town had a wonderful time celebrating the repeal of the Stamp Act: "Gentlemen and Ladies, who were in the Street the whole evening, viewing, with the highest Pleasure, the Illuminations and Fireworks, met with no kind of indecent Treatment from the Populace; indeed the People seemed to be ambitious to outvie each other in Civility and Politeness." [16] A year later in Providence, social differences were reported on another occasion: "The poor People, who were entertained at the late Feast of Charity in this Town, on the 14th Instant, beg leave to take this public Manner of expressing their Gratitude to the Authors of the Bounty.— They Eat and Drank, and were filled.—The Provisions were of the best Kind, elegantly dressed, and in great Plenty. The Generosity, the Christian Behaviour, and the Politeness, with which they were treated on that Day, merit their acknowledgement." [17] A Maine editor complained of extensive land speculation, asserted that the result was economic and social inequality, and declaimed, "Some of the United States show . . . a few individuals in possession of large tracts of land, and multitudes subsisting as their beggarly dependents"; while a Boston writer warned, "Rapidly are you divid-

[14] *Conn. Gazette*, Nov. 9, 1787. La Rochefoucault-Liancourt, *Travels*, II, 215.
[15] Jan. 21, 1787, *Dedham Historical Register*, V (1894), 32.
[16] June 2, 1766.
[17] *Providence Gazette*, Aug. 22, 1767.

ing into two Classes—extreme Rich and extreme Poor." [18]
Richard Oswald accurately reported that the rural regions
of New England were characterized by equality, but that
in the cities "the Case is quite otherways." [19]

In the middle states, distinctions were more marked than
in New England, and contemporaries stressed the unequal
distribution of property. "A Farmer" argued in 1776 that a
republic would be impossible in America because of "the
great distinction of persons, and difference in their estates
or property, which cooperates strongly with the genius of
the people in favour of monarchy." [20] The emergence of a
wealthy class was obvious. Cadwallader Colden noted that
New Yorkers were divided into different "ranks," including
the great proprietors owning over 100,000 acres, and
farmers and artisans comprising "the bulk of the people." [21]
A revealing letter from Philip V. Fithian described the rural
society of New Jersey as distinguished at once by equality
and inequality. "Gentlemen in the first rank of Dignity &
Quality," of "high-born, long recorded Families" associated
freely with poor and industrious farmers and mechanics. He
cites two townships in which three men were worth £16,-
000, and the rest of the people were small farmers. "Hence
we see Gentlemen, when they are not actually engaged in
the publick Service, on their farms, setting a laborious example to their Domesticks, & on the other hand we see

[18] *Cumberland Gazette,* June 8, 1786; *Boston Gazette,* April 2, 1787.
See also for references to economic inequality: Hazard to Belknap,
Philadelphia, July 10, 1784, "Belknap Papers," Mass. Hist. Soc., *Col-
lections,* 5 series 1 (1877), 371; *The New Hampshire Spy* (Ports-
mouth), June 26, 1787; *Mass. Centinel,* Nov. 9, 1785; *New Hampshire
Gazette,* Nov. 13, 1767; *Conn. Courant,* June 11, 1782.

[19] Benjamin F. Stevens, *Facsimiles of Manuscripts in European
Archives Relating to America 1773–1783,* XIII (London, 1895), 2,037.

[20] *Pa. Packet,* Nov. 5, 1776.

[21] N.Y. Hist. Soc., *Collections,* 1877, p. 68. See also *Conn. Courant,*
July 22, 1765; *N.J. Journal,* April 5, 1780; *N.Y. Journal,* Feb. 28, 1768.

Labourers at the Tables & in the Parlours of their Betters enjoying the advantage, & honour of their society and Conversation." [22]

Southern society was generally recognized as being far more unequal than that of the North. Fithian wrote the above passage in order to contrast "the Level" of New Jersey with the opposite circumstances in Virginia, where "the very Slaves, in some families here, could not be bought under 30,000 £ [sic]." Visitors from New England and foreign travellers were especially struck by the "great disproportion & distinction of ranks & fortunes" from Maryland down to South Carolina.[23] Ebenezer Hazard noted that there was "a much greater Disparity between the Rich & Poor in Virginia than in any of the Northern States," [24] while another New Englander wrote of South Carolina, "the inhabitants may well be divided into opulent and lordly planters, poor and spiritless peasants and vile slaves." [25] Southerners themselves were less inclined to dwell on these disparities. They considered their slaves as property rather than as a part of society, thereby at once eliminating much of the lower class. Still, Christopher Gadsden and others referred to "the distinctions . . . between the farmer and the rich planter, the mechanics and the rich merchant." [26] Southerners might argue that such differences were greater

[22] *Journal and Letters,* 210–211.

[23] Honyman, *Journal,* 10; John Adams to Joseph Hawley, Nov. 25, 1775, Burnett, ed., *Letters of Congress,* I, 260; *Conn. Gazette,* Feb. 2, 1776.

[24] "The Journal of Ebenezer Hazard in Virginia, 1777," *Va. Mag. Hist. Biog.,* LXII (1954), 414.

[25] "Journal of Josiah Quincy," Mass. Hist. Soc., *Proceedings,* XLIX, 454. See also John Bacon to Samuel Phillips, Stockbridge, Sept. 22, 1785, *ibid.,* I series v (1860–1862), 480–481; Brissot de Warville, *New Travels,* 288; Smyth, *A Tour,* I, 65–68.

[26] Quoted in Walsh, *Charleston's Sons of Liberty,* 53–54; see also *Va. Gazette and American Advertiser,* Sept. 7, 1782.

in imagination than in reality, since no one was in danger of starving; but the disparity in status was obvious. Devereaux Jarrett, the son of a carpenter and farmer, remarks in his autobiography that "We were accustomed to look upon, what were called *gentle folks,* as beings of a superior order." [27]

The Americans of this period described their class structure much as we do ours today. Men could be "ranked" or "classed" according to their occupation. The geographer Morse, writing of the great variety of people in New Jersey, cited national origin and religion as two of the causes, and continued, "Add to all these the differences common in all countries, arising from the various occupations of men, such as the Civilian, the Divine, the Lawyer, the Physician, the Mechanic, and clownish, the decent, and the respectable Farmer, all of whom have different pursuits, or pursue the same thing differently, and of course must have a different set of ideas and manners; . . ." [28] A contributor to a Massachusetts newspaper similarly referred to "men in every rank, whether they be clergy or laity, farmer, trader, mechanic or common labourer." [29] So also a Connecticut writer defined classes as including "merchants, farmers, tradesmen, &c." [30] Ordinarily, however, "class" meant then, as now, a

[27] "Autobiography," *Wm. and Mary Qtly.,* 3 series IX (1952), 361. Richard Henry Lee also contrasted the equality characteristic of New England with the aristocratic distinctions prevalent in the South. *Observations . . . in a number of Letters from the Federal Farmer to the Republican* (New York, 1787), 17.

[28] *American Geography,* 292. The French traveller La Rochefoucault-Liancourt felt that the most significant factor differentiating the manners and opinions of Americans was the distinction between "those who live at a considerable distance from the sea-coast, and those who belong to trading places," between "traders and cultivators." *Travels,* II, 66–67.

[29] *Independent Chronicle,* Dec. 11, 1777.

[30] *Norwich Packet,* March 16, 1786. See also *N.Y. Gazette and Mer-*

segment of society corresponding with wealth, status, or style of living.

Among all of the factors which created social distinctions, property was the most important, and when the men of the revolutionary era referred to classes, they most commonly meant the unequal distribution of wealth. La Rochefoucault-Liancourt remarked that "Wealth makes all the distinction of classes in Philadelphia." Again he wrote, "Though there be no distinctions acknowledged by the law in the United States, fortune, and the nature of professions form different classes." [31] "Property has an amasing influence over the ideas and judgment of mankind," wrote a philosophical Marylander. "It is for the most part a recommendation equal to learning and abilities; and in many points superior to both." He then proceeded to discuss the contest between the "lower class of mankind" and "the rich." [32] So also "A Farmer" defined classes in economic terms and related politics to a class conflict: "Where *wealth* is hereditary, *power* is hereditary; for *wealth* is *power*—

---

cury, Oct. 11, 1773. Class in this sense meant simply "category." This was a common usage.

[31] *Travels*, II, 386, 672.

[32] The writer continues, "The great respect shewn to people of wealth, has annexed an awe to their persons, which the greatest familiarities can scarcely conquer; Hence the lower class of mankind rarely expect justice when contending against the rich. The great distance between the extremes of rich and indigent, prevents that familiar intercourse necessary to create respect; the wealthy are generally deemed tyrants, who in their turn, view the opposite extreme, as an inferior species unworthy the formality of justice.

"Custom, with all its influence, can never bring about that familiarity, between the rich and poor, as will mutually demonstrate their value; all the knowledge they have of each other, is merely superficial: The one, on account of his wealth, imagines himself entitled to some degree of homage; and the other, on account of his poverty, to singular favours. These extremes, in the very nature of things, are irreconcileable, and of course ideal justice is not to be had in their contentions." *Md. Gazette* (Baltimore), Sept. 5, 1783.

Titles are of very little, or no consequence—The rich are *nobility*, and the *poor, plebeians* in all countries—And on this distinction alone, the true definition of aristocracy depends.—An *aristocracy* is that influence of power, which property may have in government; a *democracy* is the power, of influence of the people or members, as contradistinguished from property. Between these two powers, the aristocracy and democracy, that is the *rich* and *poor,* there is a constant warfare." [33]

People were thus divided fundamentally into "those that are very opulent, and those that are dependently poor," and those in between.[34] A Bostonian recorded in his journal that the citizens there consisted of the rich, the "middling people," and "The poor (who always liv'd from hand to mouth, i.e. depended on one day's labour to supply the wants of another)." [35] A newspaper contributor divided men into four classes: those so poor that they could pay no taxes, the rest of the poor, the neither rich nor poor," and the rich.[36] Virginia, wrote a critic (quite incorrectly), consisted of gentlemen of fortune, vassals, and Negroes, without a "respectable" class in between.[37] "Agricola" structured Connecticut's society into the rich farmers, middling farmers, mechanics, day laborers, and poor. Governor Pownall, as has been seen, found that New Yorkers included the "First, Middling and lower Class of the Householders." [38]

Some observers emphasized the importance of non-

[33] *ibid.,* Feb. 29, 1788.

[34] *N.J. Journal,* April 5, 1780.

[35] "Letters of John Andrew," Mass. Hist. Soc., *Proceedings,* 1 series VIII (1864–1865), 344.

[36] *Conn. Courant,* Nov. 13, 1781.

[37] *Providence Gazette,* Feb. 22, 1783.

[38] *Conn. Courant,* Dec. 10, 1782; Pownall, *Topographical Description,* 45. See also *Pa. Gazette,* March 22, 1786, where a distinction is made between the "rich" and the "middling sort."

economic factors in determining class. According to "Phi-lopolis," in large cities artificers, laborers, and servants com-posed the "illiterate and lower order of the people." These men, the "common people," could not be kept under con-trol by ethical or religious motivations, so force was neces-sary. On the other hand, "religion, education and good breeding, preserve good order and decency among the su-perior orders of mankind." [39] Personal qualities were also stressed by a writer in the *Pennsylvania Packet*.[40] In every country, he declared, there were three classes: the highest, middling, and lowest. "With us, the first class consists of commercial projectors; those who make enormous gains of public confidence; speculators, riotous livers, and a kind of loungers, who are to be found in every place but that where their business calls them. . . . These people are so com-plaisant to each other as to call themselves THE BETTER SORT OF PEOPLE." The second class was composed of "honest sober men, who mind their business," while in the third class were "thieves, pick-pockets, low-cheats and dirty-sots." A combination of economic and prestige factors cre-ated the social structure as seen by "The Country Farmer." "The Yeomanry or Farmers," he wrote, were "of great consequence and use to us, and a very necessary link in the chain of government; as having an immediate connection with the gentleman on the one side, and the labourer on the other; . . . and are of especial service in keeping the meaner people to their duty." [41]

Other writers agreed that social distinctions were the re-sult of esteem as well as of property. "The superior in-dustry, frugality and abilities of some will ever procure wealth and respect, while the idleness and dissipation of

[39] *S.C. Gazette*, March 19, 1763.
[40] March 24, 1782.
[41] *The New American Magazine*, January 1758, p. 9.

others must beget contempt and indigence." [42] James M. Varnum believed that "the different classes of citizens" were distinguished by education, wealth, & talents," and therefore naturally divided into "Aristocratical and Democratical," while "Theophilus" defined the wealthy as those enjoying "the adventitious advantages of family and fortune." [43] Finally John Adams eliminated economics entirely. For him, classes were exclusively a matter of social rank: of "laborers, yeomen, gentlemen, esquires, honorable gentlemen, and excellent gentlemen." [44] Few agreed with him, for the paramount influence of property was obvious.

The words used to define classes characteristically combined prestige with wealth. Most common was the combination "rich," "middling," and "poor," but the "first" class or "better" sort were used instead of "rich," as was "lower" instead of "poor." These words indicate that society was usually divided into three classes. However at times the "lower" or "common" people were contrasted with the well-to-do.

Illustrations are abundant. The Virginian Edward Stevens wrote of "the Rich," "the middling Kind," and "the lower sort." [45] A New York essayist referred to the rich, the poor, and the "middle sort or yeomanry," and in the same state Melancthon Smith used the same words.[46] Robert

[42] *The Freeman's Oracle, and New-Hampshire Advertiser* (Exeter), June 23, 1787.

[43] To Samuel Holten, 1787, Peck Collection box VIII, no. 17, R.I. Hist. Soc.; *Md. Gazette* (Baltimore), Jan. 30, 1784.

[44] Quoted by Norman Jacobson, "Class and Ideology in the American Revolution," in Reinhard Bendix and Seymour Martin Lipset, eds., *Class, Status and Power* (Glencoe, Illinois, 1953), 707.

[45] To Alexander Hamilton, Culpeper, Oct. 6, 1791, *Wm. and Mary Qtly.*, 2 series II (1922), 146–147.

[46] "Sydney," Paul Leicester Ford, ed., *Essays on the Constitution of the United States* (Brooklyn, 1892), 307; Jonathan Elliot, ed., *The Debates in the Several State Conventions, on the Adoption of the Federal Constitution . . .* (5 vols., Washington, 1854), II, 248.

Morris's terms were similarly "the Rich," "The middling Rank," and "the Poor." [47] Variant combinations were the "more opulent," "low," and "middling"; "the wealthy," "middling Circumstances" and "lower Class"; [48] and Patrick Henry's "well born," "middle," and "lower ranks." [49]

What would today be called the upper class was then often frankly termed the "rich." Synonymous were "better sort" and "first class" (or "rank"), "Gentlemen of property" or "of fortune," [50] and, after the Revolution, the "well born." [51] These words suggest what kind of persons were entitled to them: they had considerable property, and in addition certain qualities of birth or experience which distinguished them from the rest of the people. John Jay defined what he called "the better kind of people" as meaning those "who are orderly and industrious, who are content with their situations and not uneasy in their circumstances." [52] Above all in revolutionary America it was money that counted: these men were the "Gentlemen of the first Rank and Fortune." [53] The great merchants and the lawyers composed the upper class in Philadelphia, wrote a foreign observer, [54] while obviously the large landholders, south and north, were included. No more accurate description of a revolutionary urban upper class could be written than Benjamin Rush's observations concerning Carlisle,

[47] To Gov. Martin, July 29, 1782, *N.C. State Recs.*, XVI, 371.
[48] *Newport Mercury*, Dec. 21, 1767.
[49] Elliot, *Debates*, III, 140. See also *The Massachusetts Gazette, or the General Advertiser* (Springfield), Sept. 10, 1782; *Mass. Spy*, April 5, 1781; Morse, *Geography*, 292; *N.Y. Packet*, Feb. 16, 1786.
[50] E.g., *Pa. Journal*, Jan. 31, 1785; E. Wilder Spaulding, *New York in the Critical Period* (New York, 1932), 102.
[51] As in Hughes to John Lamb, June 18, 1788, Lamb Papers, N.Y. Hist. Soc.
[52] To Washington, June 27, 1786, Johnston, *Jay*, III, 205.
[53] *Md. Gazette*, March 27, 1766.
[54] La Rochefoucault-Liancourt, *Travels*, II, 386.

Pennsylvania: "Two or three general officers who have served with reputation in our army, four or five lawyers, a regular-bred physician, and a few gentlemen in trade of general knowledge and of fair character compose the society of the town." Such people bought the luxuries of life and lived in a manner far beyond the capacity of the great majority.[55]

The term "common people" was much more indefinite, often including everyone not of the first rank. It seems ordinarily to have meant the middle, rather than the lower class, the yeomen rather than the farm laborer, especially those who could vote—the ordinary citizen.[56] The word "middling" was almost always used to designate that which today would be called the "middle" class. When used in contrast with "poor," it of course had an economic connotation and referred to people in "middling circumstances as to worldly estate"; [57] when used as distinct from "lower" it might have either a precise economic or a vague general connotation.[58] The English usage of the word restricted

[55] To Charles Nisbet, Philadelphia, April 19 (?), 1784, Butterfield, ed., *Letters*, I, 323; Morse, *American Geography*, 259; *Conn. Gazette* (New Haven), July 19, 1765; *Md. Gazette* (Baltimore), Nov. 28, 1786.

[56] Jonathan Jackson, *Thoughts on the Constitution of the United States* (Worcester, 1788), 118–119; *Litchfield Monitor*, Oct. 3, 1786; Paul Leicester Ford, ed., *Pamphlets on the Constitution of the United States, published during its discussion by the people, 1787–1788* (Brooklyn, 1888), 109; *Md. Journal*, May 16, 1788; *N.Y. Gazette and Mercury*, April 8, 1776; Peter Tappen to George Clinton, Poughkeepsie, Sept. 29, 1787, Clinton Papers, Bancroft transcripts, N.Y. Public Lib.

[57] "Democratus," *Mass. Spy*, July 5, 1775. Examples are, *Norwich Packet*, March 18, 1784; *Vermont Gazette*, Oct. 2, 1786; *Va. Gazette* (Pinkney), Dec. 6, 1775; *Pa. Packet*, April 3, 1775; *Conn. Courant*, April 13, 1779; *State Gazette of N.C.*, Aug. 19, 1786; *Md. Gazette* (Baltimore), No. 28, 1786.

[58] Henry Laurens to John Laurens, March 15, 1778, *S.C. Hist. Gen. Mag.*, VI (1905), 105; *N.Y. Gazetteer*, Feb. 18, 1786; Aedanus Burke,

the term to the well-to-do town dweller. This had been common in the colonies too. For example, the discussion of the standard of living in Boston in 1726, described above, employed "middle" and "middling" to mean what we would call "upper middle" and in reality was upper class in Boston then. Instances can be found in revolutionary times, but these were unusual. The word had been adapted to the facts: it meant neither rich nor poor, and as one would expect "yeomen and husbandmen," "honest upright farmers and mechanics," and small property holders in general were assigned to this class.[59]

Obviously the word "poor," which often identified the third class, had an economic meaning. "Lower" was a much more indefinite term. It might refer to anyone not higher or upper class, in which case it became synonymous with "common" and did not then imply inferiority. One writer, for example, could refer to the "worthy lower-class." [60] Sometimes it meant the generality of voters, sometimes the socially inferior.[61] Most commonly it was a term of reproach, used of people who were untrustworthy, susceptible to deceit by popular leaders, men of no importance or

quoted in Charles Gregg Singer, *South Carolina in the Confederation* (Philadelphia, 1941), 32; Elliot, *Debates*, III, 295; *Pa. Chronicle*, Nov. 16, 1767. James High's use of the word in its English sense is probably correct as applied to Maryland during earlier years, and indeed the old meaning may have been retained in that colony and elsewhere after 1776. But long before that date it had ceased to be useful because the English definition would eliminate everyone except the wealthy and "middle" would in America refer to the upper, not the middle, ranks. Therefore its definition was changed to fit local circumstances. James High, "The Origins of Maryland's Middle Class in the Colonial Aristocratic Pattern," *Md. Hist. Mag.*, LVII (1962), 334–345.

[59] Josiah Quincy, "Journal," Mass. Hist. Soc., *Proceedings*, XLIX (1915–1916), 455; *Md. Journal*, Feb. 18, 1777.

[60] Quoted in Williamson, *American Suffrage*, 106.

[61] McRee, *Iredell*, II, 40; Israel Pemberton to Dr. John Fothergill, Philadelphia, Oct. 11, 1764, Pemberton Papers 1740–1780, Hist. Soc. Pa.

of vulgar habits.[62] Such were the ordinary laborers, together with the poorer farmers, the tenants, and the servants, all of whom lived near the margin of subsistence.[63]

Americans of the revolutionary era recognized that they lived in a society characterized by an unequal distribution of property and class distinctions. Yet this was not the kind of society which most of them wished to create. The ideal, on the contrary, was an economic equality in which distinctions based on wealth should be minimized; and social equality, in which invidious discriminations would be abolished. There were too many people in the world, wrote EUMENES, who "by reason of their wealth, or education, or titles, think themselves so much above the common sort of people, that they will scarcely eat with them at the same table, or ride with, or converse with them with any freedom; but would have the common people keep at a profound distance. Such men, so superior in their own conceit, would, if they had favourable opportunity, bring others into subjection and slavery. But equality should be encouraged." [64] The political reforms which accompanied the Revolution also made equality desirable, even necessary. Restrictions on the right to vote and to hold office were reduced, and the power of the people increased. Most people believed that popular government could not last long if there was an excessive concentration of wealth. "A great inequality, as to wealth, already takes place among the citi-

[62] R. R. Livingston to Robert Livingston, Claremont, Feb. 2, 1764, Livingston Papers, N.Y. Hist. Soc.; *Va. Gazette* (Purdie and Dixon), Jan. 20, 1774; Rogers, *Smith*, 46–47; *Mass. Spy*, Nov. 4, 11, 1773; Edward Rutledge to John Jay, Philadelphia, June 29, 1776, Johnston, *Jay*, 1, 67; Anburey, *Travels*, 11, 47; Mass. Gazette, Nov. 8, 1784. For an exception see William Gordon in the *Independent Chronicle, Sept.* 10, 1776.

[63] *Weekly Monitor*, Sept. 10, 1787; Henry Lee to Washington, Sept. 8, 1786, Burnett, ed., *Letters of Congress*, VIII, 463.

[64] *N.J. Journal*, May 10, 1780.

zens of this state," warned a Pennsylvanian.[65] Similarly "A plain, but real, Friend to America" observed that in Maryland too many men entertained "but a mean opinion of working laborious people," yet the state's constitution "knows of no subordination in professions; all are placed on as near an equality in political privileges as possible." Therefore mechanics should not be treated with contempt, especially since "these opinionated mushroom patriots" were probably descended from mechanics themselves.[66] The greatest danger to the United States, "A True Patriot" insisted, was "the unequal division of property in the space of so short a time" [67] and a citizen of Massachusetts agreed that "the inequality that is now arising among the individuals in this and the neighbouring States" was dangerous to liberty.[68]

Thus Americans extolled equality while living in a stratified society. "Rapidly are you dividing into two Classes—extreme Rich and extreme Poor," wrote "Brutus." [69] Especially endangered was the agrarian ideal. Although probate records indicate that in actual fact farmers gained and city folk lost during the Revolution, it was true enough that some merchants had made great fortunes. Events of the 1780's showed that these fortunes were often made of

[65] The writer continued, "It did so at the declaration of independence—Our constitution does not attempt to make any alteration in this circumstance; and indeed the attempt would be unjust, unless the free consent of all concerned were first obtained: yet this very circumstance is not a little contrary to the nature of popular government; and the native influence of it, if not carefully counteracted, will, one day, produce a revolution." *Carlisle Gazette*, Feb. 15, 1786.

[66] *Md. Journal*, Oct. 17, 1785.

[67] *N.J. Gazette*, March 17, 1779.

[68] *The Hampshire Herald; or, the Weekly Advertiser* (Springfield, Mass.), May 17, 1785. See also *State Gazette of Georgia*, Jan. 1, 1789.

[69] *Boston Gazette*, April 2, 1787.

paper, and that the farmers' position was in reality more secure than the situation of men in trade.[70] Nevertheless the war brought protests against profiteers, and the depression resulted in attacks on rich creditors who were accused of betraying the ideal of equality. A Pennsylvanian noted that costly houses were being erected and that merchants had a great amount of debts outstanding. "Two years more in our present course," he concluded, "must sell plantations and change property very fast & very cheap—Some storekeepers—Lawyers & Speculators, must be the nabobs of this country—we cry out against an aristocracy, but are practically laying the foundation of it with both hands!" [71] Even before the Revolution New Englanders were bemoaning the money shortage which injured the "common People" and enabled a few men to buy great estates.[72] Fifteen years later nothing had changed. "Unhappy for America, that her equality is diminishing!" mourned a Connecticut writer. "Grandeur and shew seem to be the wish of the times. Thousands are unnecessarily crowding themselves into the polite stations, while the profitable and beautiful culture of the field is meanly neglected—Physicians, merchants, judges, attorneys, and even some of the good clergy, are seen doubling their revenues (as they are pleased to say) to *support themselves in decency*. Thus property is going into the hands of men in a few particular professions, while the majority must be reduced to poverty, and, perhaps, bondage." [73]

[70] See Benjamin W. Labaree, *Patriots and Partisans: the Merchants of Newburyport 1764–1815* (Cambridge, 1962).

[71] John Armstrong to General William Irvine, Carlisle, Aug. 16, 1787, *The Historical Magazine*, VIII (1864), 18.

[72] *New Hampshire Gazette*, Dec. 29, 1769.

[73] *Conn. Journal*, Oct. 27, 1784. See also "Brutus Jr.," *N.Y. Journal*, Nov. 8, 1787, and *Va. Gazette* (Purdie and Dixon), Nov. 6, 1766, for examples of attacks on social and economic distinctions. A

The society in which Americans lived was unusually equal in that the poor were few in numbers and the rich, with few exceptions, only well-to-do; equal too in the extraordinarily high mobility, the relatively equal chance to rise. Americans took pride in the fact that class distinctions were minor by comparison with Europe. Nevertheless many also believed that the differences between rich and poor were greater than they ought to be, considering the opportunities in the new world. Classes did exist and were recognized as significant. These classes were evident in the manner of living and indeed in the entire culture of revolutionary America.

Massachusetts citizen warned that "the good people of this community will not suffer any particular class of men to raise themselves unjustly to opulence and live in the greatest magnificence, when at the same time it is extorted from the ruins of the people. P.S. The Lawyers may take the greater part of the conclusion if they please." *Hampshire Gazette,* Nov. 15, 1786.

·⊗· CHAPTER VIII ·⊗·

Classes and Culture Patterns

THE INCOME of the American during the Revolution influenced not only his consumption habits and style of
living, but his cultural life as well. The economic factor was
only one of many (religion and inherited values were probably as important), but it was significant because education,
books, and other sources of culture cost money. Incomes
affected the degree of schooling, the number of books
owned, the paintings and musical instruments purchased,
the plays and concerts attended. One's literary and artistic
pursuits were also influenced by geographical location. Each
city served as a culture center, but the settlers who left the
towns or the banks of major navigable rivers and moved to
the uplands or the frontier became increasingly more remote from European influences and from "higher" culture
generally: the pioneer or subsistence farmers were exposed
to the environment whereas the well-to-do artisans (for example) were protected from it and affected rather by Europe. Therefore culture in early America varied with the section. Most important however were the cultural levels which
corresponded with the class structure. The ordinary farmer
or mechanic worked from dawn until dusk six days a week,
and what money he earned had to be spent almost entirely
upon necessities. His life was narrow, his experience limited.
On the other hand the wealthy merchant, lawyer, or landholder worked far fewer hours and expended less energy in
the working, so that he had time and strength for non-
economic matters; and he had of course surplus income to
be spent in acquiring a higher education, buying books,
paintings, or musical instruments, and attending plays or

concerts. His horizons were broader, and he sought to imitate the way of life of the upper-class Englishman. Whether or not he did all of these things depended, of course, upon non-economic factors; but it was wealth which gave him the choice. Especially important was the education which the American received, for his education, economic progress, reputation, and level of culture were all closely, even causally related.

The American's opportunity to obtain a formal education depended upon where he lived and how much money he had. Even an elementary schooling was not always available and seldom free. In New England most of the towns supported a public school of sorts some of the time. The existence and quality of these varied greatly. In Boston they were numerous and good, for the city could afford skilled masters who made teaching their career.[1] On the other hand the poverty of the frontier and subsistence farm communities made it difficult and sometimes impossible to support schools, and even prosperous towns did not always meet the needs of poor children.[2] Yet Timothy Dwight was probably correct in boasting of Connecticut that there was "scarcely a child in this state, who is not taught reading, writing, and arithmetic. Poverty, here, has no efficacy toward excluding any one from this degree of education." [3] This was true not only because of the schools but because most of the parents could read and write. Indeed one correspondent argued that public schools ought to be abolished, since children could learn at home.[4] Moreover in

[1] Robert Francis Seybolt, *The Public Schoolmasters of Colonial Boston* (Cambridge, 1939).

[2] E.g., *New Haven Gazette*, Jan. 20, 1785, for poor children being "destitute of the means of acquiring a good education."

[3] *Travels*, I, 179.

[4] *New Hampshire Gazette*, March 24, 1787. Public schools were "both unjust and illegal—unjust because many of the inhabitants

many towns one could be privately tutored by educated
men for a low rate. Ministers often supplemented their
salaries in this way, charging as little as 22s per year, while
in the larger cities schools designed for tradesmen cost a
slightly higher but still reasonable sum.[5] Any parent who
had ambitions for his child beyond the barest rudiments had
to pay for it, since such public schools as existed were elementary indeed.[6]

Outside of New England public schools at the primary
level were much less common. New Jersey had a considerable number, but most of them were private and charged
tuition. A few of these did admit poor children at no
charge. The S.P.G. subsidized some free schools for poor
people including Negroes and Indians, as did certain other
religious groups. In Virginia there were a handful of free
parish schools.[7] But the great majority of people, especially
in the South, had to meet the expense of sending their children to private institutions. The cost of such schools varied
considerably. The tuition was never very high. In the

---

are obliged to pay for the support of an institution from which
they can receive no benefit—illegal because the law authorizes an
assessment to be made only for the support of one grammar school,
and more cannot be legally assessed without the unanimous consent
of the inhabitants."

[5] Isaiah Tiffany Account book (Lebanon, Conn.), 1766, Conn.
Hist. Soc.; *Essex Journal*, Dec. 13, 20, 1786, Jan. 3, 1787.

[6] For example, Harry R. Warfel, *Noah Webster: Schoolmaster to
America* (New York, 1936), 13–14.

[7] Richard P. McCormick, *Experiment in Independence: New
Jersey in the Critical Period, 1783–1789* (New Brunswick, 1950), 55;
Munro, *Delaware*, 59; Kemp, *Support of Schools;* Thomas Woody,
Early Quaker Education in Pennsylvania (New York, 1920); Guy
Fred Wells, *Parish Education in Colonial Virginia* (New York,
1923). Wells writes (p. 28), "It is clear that with negligible exceptions the parishes in colonial Virginia did not aid in the education
of their children by establishing schools, by paying for instruction
in private schools, or by furnishing community school buildings."

Shenandoah Valley children paid 2/ per month, and the general average was about £3 annually, a sum which was not beyond the means of substantial farmers or artisans provided the child could live at home. Unfortunately this was seldom possible except in the towns, and most people were therefore unable to send their children to school. The cost of board was rarely less than £10 and usually £20 or even more. A fancy boarding school in Philadelphia, limited to twelve pupils, charged £50 per year "for the accommodation and instruction of each Pupil." [8] More usual was an "English" school established in Richmond which offered arithmetic and bookkeeping as well as reading and writing for £14 annually and $2 entrance fee.[9] Another Richmond boarding school offered, besides the three R's, the principles of mechanics and agriculture on Saturday and religion on Sunday. The tuition of £3 included books, paper, ink, slates, and firewood. Lodging cost £5, washing £5, and board £11.[10] Schools like these were designed for the children of wealthy planters. Such men might hire a tutor instead. The rich man paid about £30 sterling a year for a teacher who lived in the house. Less expensive was the solution adopted by some Virginia families which paid a local teacher £2 or so annually for each child. Still, only well-to-do planters could raise such a sum.[11]

Schools at the secondary level were called "academies" or "grammar schools." The larger Massachusetts towns were required by law to support the latter out of tax funds. Some towns paid a fine rather than meet the requirement, or es-

---

[8] Hart, *Valley of Virginia*, 30; *Pa. Chronicle*, Jan. 2, 1773.
[9] *Va. Gazette and Weekly Advertiser*, Nov. 15, 1787.
[10] *The Virginia Independent Chronicle* (Richmond), Oct. 28, 1786.
[11] For example, Jones Family Papers, vol. 24, and William Peachy to Thomas Jones, Richmond County, Feb. 27, 1770, *ibid.*, vol. 18, Lib. Cong.

tablished one which was barely adequate, but at least sixty-five existed before the Revolution. However the other New England states had scarcely a dozen among them, in addition to a few private academies which charged about a shilling a week for tuition.[12] Outside of New England, tax-supported institutions were almost unknown. The private academies were of two types. Most of them were "Latin" schools which prepared the boy for college (although in New England most Latin school students did not continue). They taught Latin and Greek as basic courses, together with grammar, rhetoric, mathematics (often "the practical branches of"), and geography. The "English" schools did not prepare one for college but for the business world. They taught English, applied mathematics such as navigation and surveying, bookkeeping, astronomy, and sometimes modern languages.[13] A third, rarer variety of school taught dancing, fencing, French, and music. None of these were designed for the majority of colonials because few could afford them. The tuition ranged from £3 to £4 for English schools to £5 or even £10 for Latin schools, being higher in the South than in the North.[14] Moreover, as previously noted, most Americans lived far from any secondary school and had to board their children. This could be done in the backcountry for £10 or so,[15] but practically

[12] Middlekauff, *Ancients and Axioms,* 40–51; Small, *Early New England Schools,* 32–57.

[13] For example, *Md. Gazette* (Baltimore), June 14, 1785.

[14] Many schools offered both types of courses, varying the tuition. Examples are, *Albany Gazette,* Dec. 14, 1786; *N.J. Journal,* April 11, 1787; *Independent Gazetteer,* Oct. 15, 1785; *Pa. Gazette,* March 30, Oct. 19, 1785; *Md. Journal,* Aug. 4, 1786; *Md. Chronicle,* Feb. 11, 1787; *Va. Herald* (Fredericksburg), June 19, 1788; *The Virginia Gazette, and Petersburg Intelligencer,* Jan. 11, 1787; *Charleston Morning Post,* May 1, 1786; *Gazette of the State of Georgia,* April 7, 1785, Sept. 11, Oct. 2, 1788.

[15] One school in upcountry South Carolina charged eleven guineas

all of the academies were in eastern towns where the charge was doubled. To that sum must be added the price of clothes, travel, and spending money. Hugh Williamson believed that the five North Carolina boys who attended a New Jersey grammar school would draw at least £400 sterling per annum out of the state. A Princeton master offered to teach a few boys Latin in one year for £40 currency, in addition to the usual cost of £26 for board and £30 for clothes and other expenses. The parent would therefore pay a total of £96 (about £57 sterling) whereas, he pointed out, ordinarily boys required at least four years and a total of £240 currency.[16]

The curriculum of the grammar schools appealed to men who intended their sons for the professions or for trade. One advertisement announced that Latin and Greek would be taught but "as teaching boys only those [subjects] who are to be brought up to trade and business, or the mechanical arts, is rather spending their time to little purpose, they will be enabled to acquire a grammatical knowledge of their own tongue, and taught to read, with propriety, the best *English* authors, Writing, Accompts, Geography the most useful branches of the Arithmeticks, and French." The £5 tuition certainly enabled residents to attend but few could pay the £12 charged for board, although the price was reasonable.[17] The expense of secondary schools was sometimes too great even for merchants and professional men. One academy in Newark, Delaware, changed £5 tuition but when it tried to collect £25 for board found that parents could not pay that much. The trustees then pre-

---

(£11.11) and one in Kentucky cost £6 to £9, of which only half had to be paid in cash. *Charleston Morning Post*, May 1, 1786; *The Kentucke Gazette* (Lexington), Jan. 5, 19, 1788.

[16] To Iredell, Princeton, Aug. 20, 1783, McRee, *Iredell*, ii, 68; *Pa. Journal*, Oct. 23, 1766.

[17] *Va. Gazette* (Purdie), Sept. 12, 1777.

vailed upon the inhabitants to "board, wash and lodge" the children for £18 per year. Even this reduced price surely eliminated nine-tenths of the children.[18] Residents of towns were more fortunate, for most sizable towns had schools of all sorts, and the students could live at home. The major cities had many evening schools which offered practical courses. These schools of course charged fees. They were attended by people of all occupations but mostly by "Gentlemen." [19]

In general people on the frontier and in subsistence farm communities almost never had academies of any sort near them and could not afford to send their children away. Commercial farm areas also frequently lacked such schools (especially in the South), and such as existed were too expensive for most parents. Moreover the curriculum offered by the academies was usually irrelevant to farm needs. Although towns were better supplied with Latin, English, and night schools, yet the expense was still too great for most of the residents. Only the upper class and the urban upper middle class could acquire a formal secondary education.

Colleges might be even more expensive. A Harvard student estimated that his degree cost him £114.3.1¼. This included preparatory school and three years at Cambridge, "in clothes, in College affairs, Books, Jurneying, having the Small-Pox, other Expenses of what name or nature soever." William R. Davie spent $100 (£33⅓) in one year at the University of North Carolina. Probably £30 sterling a year

---

[18] *The Delaware Courant, and Wilmington Advertiser*, July 7, 1787. Parents did get their money's worth, for the student spent eight hours a day in one school and had only seven week's vacation. *Va. Herald*, June 19, 1788; *Md. Chronicle*, April 11, 1787. Philadelphia's public academy lasted for eight hours in the summer and seven in the winter. *Pa Journal*, May 19, 1773.

[19] Robert Francis Seybolt, *The Evening School in Colonial America* (Urbana, Illinois, 1925); Bridenbaugh, *Colonial Craftsman*, 168–169; *Pa. Gazette*, Sept. 20, Oct. 11, 1764, Oct. 9, 1766.

is a fair average, although there are higher estimates.[20] One colonial expected that it would take £200 to £300 to make a lawyer out of his nephew.[21] An education in Europe cost at least £100 sterling annually and might reach four times that amount.[22]

Obviously only a fraction of the revolutionary Americans—perhaps one in ten—could afford to send a son to college. The proportion was higher in New England, where one could attend a free grammar school. Elsewhere the cost of five years' education was certainly £150 and in the South more than that. One recent writer estimates that about 3,000 men graduated during the thirty years prior to the Revolution and concludes that "no American who could afford the fee of ten pounds a year for four years could fail to secure, if he wanted it, the hallmark of a 'higher' education."[23] But £10 did not begin to cover it, and 3,000 is perhaps 1 out of 200 eligible men, the ratio of course varying greatly from place to place. There were certainly some men of small property who secured a higher education, but in general academies and colleges were reserved for wealthy sons.

The fact was recognized and lamented at the time.

[20] Col. Soc. Mass., *Transactions*, XXVIII (1930–1933), 302–305; Robinson, *Davie*, 270; Ernest F. Brown, *Joseph Hawley, Colonial Radical* (New York, 1931), 12; Burnaby, *Travels*, 104; *N.Y. Journal*, Oct. 18, 1786; *Pa. Packet*, March 2, 1785; *Freeman's Journal*, Feb. 7, 1787; *Md. Gazette* (Baltimore), Jan. 2, 1787; Schoepf, *Travels*, II, 80; *Pa. Gazette*, March 12, 1772; *Gazette of the State of Georgia*, June 5, 1788. The College of New Jersey, in response to complaints about the cost of education, reduced the board by requiring cash in advance. The basic cost was £23.13 currency including firewood, candles, and washing. *Pa. Journal*, Nov. 10, 1768.

[21] *Letters of James Murray*, 82.

[22] William L. Sachse, *The Colonial American in Britain* (Madison, Wisconsin, 1956), 52–55; Paul Mahlon Hamlin, *Legal Education in Colonial New York* (New York, 1939), 22, 34.

[23] Boorstin, *The Americans*, 183.

Fithian remarked that in Virginia the owner of a college diploma was rated at £10,000. Students at the College of New York were said to be "in general, the Sons of Gentlemen of independent Fortunes," while a Pennsylvania writer observed that colleges and academies were "not for the humble and indigent classes of the people. They are calculated, chiefly, for the benefit of the affluent and independent part of the citizens of the state." Only free schools, he felt, could extend the "blessings of knowledge" to the "poor and labouring part of the community." [24] One academy frankly charged the unusually high tuition of £10 "that thus children, if not of loose principles, at least of more vulgar habits, may be prevented from intermixing to corrupt the morals and vitiate the manners of his pupils." [25] The teacher Robert Coram asserted that most American legislatures were composed of lawyers and merchants "because the farmer has no opportunity of getting his son instructed, without sending him to a college; the expense of which, is more than the profits of his farm." Coram was wrong about the composition of the legislatures, but unquestionably correct about the great majority of farmers. [26]

The reaction to this situation took two forms: some people declared that colleges and academies were for rich men, and should therefore receive no state support: while others wished to grant such support in order to provide an education for everyone. A Maryland bill granting £2,500 annually to a college excited much criticism on the former ground. "Poor men and men of common estates, among whom often are the brightest genius, cannot send to the university at all," wrote "PLANTER." The people would be taxed so

[24] *N.Y. Gazette and Mercury,* Dec. 7, 1782; *Pa. Packet,* March 28, 1787.

[25] *Va. Gazette and Weekly Advertiser,* Dec. 20, 1787; *Va. Independent Chronicle,* Jan. 2, 1788.

[26] *Political Disquisitions* (Wilmington, 1791), 93.

that "Gentlemen's children" would be educated at public expense. What advantage, enquired a correspondent, would a poor man receive, "who is scarcely able to feed and cloath his family, pay his public just and necessary demands, and teach his children to read the bible and write their names; what are colleges to these? why should they support them?" [27] It would be preferable to pay off the state debt and reduce taxes. It was much better, wrote a Rhode Islander, to teach a farmer's son how to farm, and an artisan's son one of the "mechanical arts," than to teach the "indolent, expensive, and very refined researches of philosophy and the belle [*sic*] letters." Of what use were these to an infant country? [28]

More often the reaction was to urge an extension of the public system. Most Americans believed that an education benefitted everyone. For some, the chance to learn was reason enough: knowledge was happiness.[29] Others felt that children should be taught to use the Bible; schools should "inculcate early notions of piety and virtue"—perhaps especially among poor people who were apt to lack such qualities.[30] Patriotism led men to advocate improvements in America. Even before the Revolution some men urged that liberty could not be learned in England or France, where one was likely to be infected by luxury and libertinism; local schools would inculcate "Patriotick Principles," the "True interests of *their* Native Country." [31] "I believe everybody

[27] *Md. Gazette*, Feb. 11, March 4, 1785; *Md. Journal*, Aug. 19, 1785. See also "An OLD SOLDIER," *Md. Gazette* (Baltimore), April 1, 1785.

[28] *Newport Mercury*, March 4, 1765; see also *U.S. Chronicle*, Oct. 19, 1786.

[29] *Vermont Journal*, Oct. 16, 1786; *Kentucke Gazette*, Sept. 1, 1787.

[30] *New Hampshire Gazette*, Dec. 6, 1771; *S.C. Gazette,* June 8, 1765, Jan. 25, 1770; *Am. Museum*, April, 1787.

[31] *S.C. Gazette and American General Advertiser*, Nov. 20, 1769. See also *Conn. Gazette* (New Haven), Aug. 2, 1765.

begins to laugh at English education," Landon Carter noted in his diary. "The general importers of it nowadays bring back only a stiff priggishness with as little good manners as possible." [32] After independence, the states were urged to defend the liberty which had been won. Free governments encouraged learning; arbitrary governments discouraged it; and a "general diffusion of knowledge among the great body of the people" was "highly conducive to the security of liberty." [33]

The establishment of a republican form of government, in which the common people had power and public officers derived not from an elite class but from the commonalty, also presupposed that the majority was educated enough to judge aright. "Knowledge," wrote John Jay, is "the soul of a republic, . . . and nothing should be left undone to afford all ranks of people the means of obtaining a proper degree of it at a cheap and easy rate." [34] Members of the upper class were inclined to lament the low quality of public officers and of public learning, and to regard better schools as their only salvation.[35] Others were enthusiastic democrats, and considered education to be necessary for a democracy. "The more democratick the state of government," wrote INTEGRITAS, "the more essential to the interests of the body politick, that knowledge be generally diffused." [36]

Similarly it was felt that most people needed the guidance

[32] *Wm. and Mary Qtly.*, XIII (1904–1905), 47.

[33] *Carlisle Gazette*, Aug. 10, 1785; *Conn. Courant*, Jan. 7, 1788.

[34] To Benjamin Rush, New York, March 24, 1785, Johnston, *Jay*, III, 139.

[35] Hooper to Iredell, Hillsborough, July 6, 1785, McRee, *Iredell*, II, 126.

[36] *Mass. Spy*, Feb. 13, 1783. See also *Providence Gazette*, Sept. 29, 1764; *S.C. and American General Gazette*, Dec. 3, 1778; *The American Recorder, and the Charlestown Advertiser*, Feb. 16, 1787; *Columbian Herald*, Nov. 26, 1784.

which education offered. Left to themselves they were ignorant and vicious men who contaminated children of the better sort, disobeyed the laws, and endangered the state. But good schools would save society, for even the poor were rational beings who might be guided rather than driven like beasts. Education would uphold law and order and protect the government.[37]

For the mass of people with small incomes, education offered hope for the future. Education, remarked one colonial, made the distinction between one person and another. It fitted one for political leadership and was, together with wealth, essential for achieving the highest social rank.[38] Moreover if the youth became unable to do manual labor he could support himself; perhaps he might even grow rich through knowledge. The absence of good free schools in New Hampshire, wrote "VERUS," prevented men of genius from becoming useful to the country. "The Loss sustained by the Want of Education is immense: Genii of every Kind are not more scarce here than in any other Part of the World, they only want polishing: But if a Country well stored with unknown Diamonds, lying in their native Crust, may properly be denominated *Poor*, certainly such a Country as this deserves to suffer the Brand of Infamy, if it will not take some Pains to rescue its richest Treasures and brightest Ornaments from perpetual Obscurity." A man's success in life depended, in great measure, upon his education; so that both the individual and the public benefitted from an extensive system.[39]

[37] *Independent Gazetteer*, March 28, 1787 (excellent); *Providence Gazette*, Jan. 19, 1782; *S.C. Gazette and Country Journal*, Dec. 31, 1765.

[38] *Conn. Journal*, May 26, 1769; "LYCURGUS," *Mass. Spy*, July 12, 1775; "PHILANTHROPOS," *Continental Journal*, Feb. 12, 1778.

[39] *New Hampshire Gazette*, Aug. 11, 1769, March 2, 1770; *S.C. and American General Gazette*, Nov. 14, 1769; *Newport Mercury*, Nov. 20, 1769.

What was needed, then, were schools which would provide a universal education, inculcate proper principles, prepare the citizen, and enable children of poor families to rise. Such a system must be quite different from the private schools, which tended "to excite an odious Distinction between those whose Parents can afford the Expence of their attending the private Schools & those who cannot," [40] and which taught useless subjects such as Latin and Greek.[41] A newspaper correspondent enquired "whether Reading, Spelling, Writing and Arithmetic are not of much greater Importance to the Community in general than the dead Languages?" [42] Private academies had "destructive consequences," for the "gentleman" hired the best tutors for his son, and neglected his townspeople, who perhaps might lack a school entirely; whereas if there was no such thing as an academy gentlemen would exert themselves to establish good local institutions. Public schools must concentrate on "useful knowledge"—on reading, grammar, geography, science; "for it must be allowed that grammar, writing, and arithmetick, are of more real use to the respectable mechanick, and industrious husbandman," than decorative subjects such as pure science.[43]

In every state, Americans lamented the lack of schools for the poorer people and sought to establish them. Even in Massachusetts "A TRUE REPUBLICAN" found few public grammar schools. The poor people, he pointed out, had neither time nor knowledge to instruct their children. Only the

[40] Kaplan, "Teachers' Salaries," 375.

[41] Though classical studies had defenders: e.g., *U.S. Chronicle*, Oct. 12, 1786.

[42] *American Herald*, Feb. 28, 1785.

[43] *Mass. Centinel*, March 22, 1786; *Boston Magazine*, March 1784, pp. 176–178; *American Recorder*, Feb. 16, 1787; *U.S. Chronicle*, Feb. 8, 1787. See the interesting article urging a practical curriculum in *American Magazine*, Feb. 1788, p. 160.

rich would not suffer. As a result all offices of the state must fall into the hands of "fortune, figure and education." In the same state "DEMOCRITUS" believed that such men had "very little compassion" upon the majority and were not to be trusted.[44] A Carlisle, Pennsylvania, writer asserted that until the founding of an academy there, the people sent their children into the world with no more than a little knowledge of reading, writing, and arithmetic, for few farmers "could support the enormous and unequal expence of educating their children at schools and colleges at so great a distance as they were then from them."[45] In the South the situation was worst of all, especially in the vast backcountry where, lamented Aedanus Burke, the youth were "brought up deer-hunters & horse thieves, for want of Education."[46] Efforts to found schools for the poor did have some effect, but in general the situation in 1788 remained unchanged. A very small minority of well-to-do and wealthy people received an adequate education, while the vast majority of farmers, artisans, and laborers learned only to read and write.[47]

The shortage of schools for the middle and lower classes did not of itself prevent them from acquiring an education. If books were available, much could be learned, perhaps

[44] *Mass. Spy*, May 4, 1780, July 5, 1775.

[45] *Carlisle Gazette*, Aug. 10, 1785.

[46] To Arthur Middleton, July 6, 1782, *S.C. Hist. Gen. Mag.*, XXVI (1925), 204.

[47] Laments and suggestions: "Journal of Ebenzer Hazard," Nov. 17, 1777, *Va. Mag. Hist. Biog.*, LXII (1954), 420 (conditions in the South); *S.C. Gazette*, Nov. 9, 1769 (concentrates on education for sons of rich planters); Bell, "Social History," *Pa. Mag. Hist. Biog.*, LXII, 295; *Essex Journal*, March 15, 1786; *Va. Gazette* (Purdie and Dixon), May 12, 1774; *Pittsburg Gazette*, March 10, 1787; *S.C. Gazette and Country Journal*, Nov. 17, 1767, Feb. 9, 1768; *S.C. Gazette*, Dec. 27, 1773. There were a few free schools even in the South. Lyon G. Tyler, "Education in Colonial Virginia," *Wm. and Mary College Qtly.*, VI (1897–1898), 1–6, 71–85.

even much achieved: a New Hampshire writer believed that "many who now live in Poverty, might raise themselves to Affluence, if they knew how to improve the Advantages they enjoy." [48] The extent to which people read partly depended, as did their degree of education, upon where they lived and how much money they had. La Rochefoucault-Liancourt remarked of Massachusetts that "knowledge, at least in its first degrees, is very extensively diffused. Not a house is to be found in the most remote corners of the country, where a newspaper is not read; and there are few townships which do not possess little libraries formed and supported by subscription." [49] Booksellers charged two to four times the original cost, [50] yet the prices were not excessive. In Portsmouth one could buy Homer in four volumes for 12s, Shakespeare in eight for a pound, Montesquieu's *Spirit of Laws* in two volumes for 6s, Milton's *Paradise Lost* for 2/6, and Fielding's *Amelia* (two volumes) for 5/. Certainly most of the people, especially in New England, owned books. Out of 500 inventories in Suffolk County after the Revolution, 322, or 64.4 percent contained books. The Worcester County farmers did even better: out of 200 inventories recorded before 1776, no less than three-fourths included at least one volume. Obviously books of some sort were available locally to anyone who wished to read them.

Southerners were almost as well read. A study of 455 Maryland estates between 1760 and 1776 showed that 63

[48] *New Hampshire Gazette*, March 15, 1771.

[49] *Travels*, II, 215.

[50] "Books are an excellent article, they will sell quickly & bring with care 120 or 130 pct. Advance." Thomas Rutherford Letter Book, Jan. 1784, Va. Hist. Soc. A Hillsboro, N.C., firm sold for three or four times the first cost. Elizabeth Cometti, "Some Early Best Sellers in Piedmont North Carolina," *Journal of Southern History*, XVI (1950), 324–337.

percent included books. About one out of six of these men had only a Bible, but on the other hand 22 inventories listed 10 or more volumes.[51] In Virginia exactly the same proportion of the inventories examined contained books, the slightly smaller number of bookowners in the Piedmont being compensated for by a larger proportion in the eastern counties. Shenandoah Valley settlers, just ceasing to be pioneers, did not have as many, yet 44 percent of the families had at least one.[52] Fewer South Carolinians had libraries. In that state only a little more than half of the estates contained books, the proportion increasing slightly after the Revolution.

Much more important than where one lived was one's income and occupation. Men of property everywhere had libraries, but poor people did not; professional men owned many books but mariners had few. In Suffolk County, estates valued at less than £50 rarely contained books. Twice as many—just 60 percent—of the estates assessed at £50 to £499 did so. The possession of £500 in total property apparently placed one in a very different category, for almost nine out of ten such men were book owners, the proportion dropping slightly among the very wealthiest property holders but still averaging 80 percent among those with £2,000. Worcester County, principally a middle-class farming area, was characterized by less variation, but here also the ratio of book owners increased from 62 percent of those worth less than £100 to 89 percent of those with £500 to £999. In that

[51] Joseph T. Wheeler, "Books Owned in Colonial Maryland," *Md. Hist. Mag.*, xxxv (1940), 338.

[52] Hart, *Valley of Virginia*, 167. Hart's estimate for the Piedmont is 63 percent. Out of 197 inventories in Halifax and Lunenburg, both before and after the Revolution, 121 (61 percent) included books. Eighty-nine out of 151 estates in Spotsylvania and Chesterfield (59 percent) and 122 out of 180 in Richmond, Westmoreland, and Essex (68 percent) listed books.

county also a valuation of £500 was crucial, and here too there was a slight decline of book ownership among the wealthiest men.

La Rochefoucault-Liancourt remarked that in Virginia, "a taste for reading is more prevalent among the gentlemen of the first class than in any other part of America; but the common people are, perhaps, more ignorant than elsewhere." [53] The observation is true only in that it correctly identified a class difference, for even the common people might read if they wished. Virginians owning less than £50 worth of personal property were not apt to have books, but he who had more than that usually did so, while the great planter with £1,000 in personal estate almost certainly owned a library—the proportion, to be explicit, rising from 43 percent to 66 percent to 86 percent. Similarly only about one-third of the poorer South Carolinians (less than £100) owned books, but among the men who had £1,000 in personal property, nearly three-fourths had libraries. About half of the middle class who left personal estates of £200 to £500 included books among their possessions, and the percentage rose sharply as one's wealth increased.

The occupation of the individual correlated with the ownership of books even more decisively. Least apt to have them were men whose calling was not identified in the probate records. The great majority of such men were undoubtedly laborers who as we have seen received a low income and left little property. Probably not over one-third of such wage-earners owned books. The same was true of mariners. Those who achieved the rank of ship's captain were better read, but still not over half of them had libraries. Fifty percent of the innkeepers and shopkeepers, and a slightly higher proportion of artisans, were book owners. Therefore the entire non-farm population other than the merchants and the professional men had far fewer books

---

[53] *Travels*, ii, 117.

than the general norm (332 out of 689, or just under half).

In contrast 70 percent of the merchants and 68 percent of the farmers left books among their inventories. The proportion of merchants is lower than might be expected from their wealth, and indeed many with considerable fortunes were not great readers—especially in Charleston. Farmers on the other hand included many men of exceedingly modest property and men who were isolated geographically, yet more of them had books than most city folks. Even those in subsistence farm areas, though less apt to own volumes than the commercial farmers, ordinarily left at least a Bible. The farmers were divided, in this respect, into three or four groups. Barely half of the poorer men who left less than £50 worth of personal property owned books, except in New England, where the proportion was higher. Farmers of medium estate ordinarily did have libraries, while those worth £1,000 in personal property almost always did so.

Professional men comprised a separate category, for virtually all of them were book owners, regardless of what other property they held and irrespective of geographical location. Insofar as inventories reveal the situation, doctors, lawyers, and ministers were well-read men. "Esquires" and "Gentlemen" also nearly always had books, thus distinguishing themselves from the generality. It is obvious that all except the laborer, artisan, or poor farmer had access, in most parts of the country, to at least a few books.[54]

[54] Over 1,800 inventories in Massachusetts, Virginia, and South Carolina show the following situation:

Group	% Owning Books	Group	% Owning Books
Lawyers	100	Artisans	58
Ministers	94	Shopkeepers	51
Doctors	94	Innkeepers	50
Esquires	85	Ships' captains	50
Gentlemen	80	Misc. non-farm	48
Merchants	70	Unknown	37
Farmers	68	Mariners	33

The content of these libraries served still further to separate the classes culturally. The evidence suggests strongly that the small farmers of the backcountry, when they owned books at all, had only a Bible, a few other volumes of a religious nature, and a spelling book. The most interesting study of this subject is based on the records of a Hillsboro merchant in North Carolina's backcountry. The firm sold some histories and copies of Blackstone, but most of its profit came from Bibles and other religious books. A few years before the war the merchants imported a number of novels, essays and poetry. Not one of these sold. During the period 1769–1777 they disposed of 118 hornbooks, 71 spelling books, 59 Testaments, 59 Psalters, 48 Bibles, 45 histories, 30 copies of *Pilgrim's Progress*, 24 primers, and 107 others almost all of which were religious in nature.[55] Inventories of estates are not as informative as one could wish, but in general they indicate that the situation in North Carolina was similar to that in back countries everywhere. Probably most people of small income in the cities had the same sort of reading material.

Professional men and men of wealth owned libraries of a very different sort. They were much larger, for one thing. Wheeler found that in Maryland about one-fourth of the estates containing books listed more than ten. Inventories in Massachusetts and South Carolina often itemized libraries of considerable size. One hundred published Virginia inventories list collections of books ranging from 14 to 659.[56] The content of these is suggestive: religious books comprised only 12 percent of the total, being equalled by scientific and practical works, English literature, and history,

[55] Cometti, "Best Sellers," *Journal of Southern Hist.*, XVI, 324–337.
[56] George K. Smart, "Private Libraries in Colonial Virginia," *American Literature*, X (1938), 24–52. These were not, as the author claimed, representative, for the libraries of farmers and artisans were lacking.

biography, and travel. Half of the libraries consisted of classics, philosophy, and law. The prejudice against novels shown by North Carolina farmers was not shared by men of education. Many such books were advertised in the newspapers, and when a Yale class disputed "Whether reading of Novels be advantageous," the President himself decided "that it is advantageous in some measure, if not too much attended to." [57]

A few illustrations will show the advantages enjoyed by men of means. A Halifax County (Virginia) planter left 69 books including Smollet, Cervantes, Milton, Gibbon, Plutarch, Shakespeare, the *Spectator*, the *Tatler*, and a Bible.[58] A Charleston, South Carolina, lawyer owned about 530 including Locke, the English "Cato," Shakespeare, Pope, Milton, Swift, Congreve, Addison, Puffendorf, Montaigne, and Molière (in French) valued at £834 currency, or nearly £120 sterling.[59] Another Charlestonian owned some 200 volumes among which were Shakespeare, Dryden, Pope, Waller, Addison, Fielding, and Locke, together with 8 books on gardening, 5 on architecture, 30 on law, and many histories, geographies, and travel accounts; while a plantation library of 150 volumes contained books on law, politics, religion and music in addition to 21 volumes of parliamentary debates and assorted London magazines.[60] Lawyers, doctors, and ministers often had extensive collections which ranged far beyond their immediate fields. A minister of St. Helena parish, South Carolina, had over 200

[57] Dyar Throop Hinckley Diary, Feb. 15, 1785, Conn. Hist. Soc. But see an attack on novels in *Pa. Packet*, Aug. 20, 1785.

[58] Halifax County Will Book 2, 1783–1792 (Walter Robertson).

[59] S.C. Inventories 1763–1767, pp. 280–284 (James Gridley). Jefferson felt that a lawyer ought to own a library worth £100. To Thomas Turpin, Feb. 5, 1769, Boyd, ed., *Papers*, I, 24.

[60] Frederick P. Bowes, *The Culture of Early Charleston* (Chapel Hill, 1942), 58–59.

books including Locke and Montesquieu, and one in Charleston owned Shakespeare, Pope, Swift, the *Spectator*, and the *Critical Review*. A country doctor in Purisburgh had Molière and a number of musical works, while one in Boston owned 1,130 volumes valued at £70.15.10 out of a total estate of £210. Such men could of course borrow from one another and many had access to lending libraries.[61] The country gentleman near any city could and in most cases did enjoy the advantages of one near Philadelphia who went to many parties, lived luxuriously and, as an observer remarked, "To this we must add reading, which fills up some hours very agreeably; great numbers of books, including all the new publications, are imported from London at Philadelphia; besides which, that city, which has a college and a literary society itself; employs several printers, and sends forth news-papers every day." [62]

The people whose own bookshelves were nearly empty could occasionally borrow from libraries. The desirability of establishing these was recognized. A newspaper contributor urged that "they will tend to diffuse knowledge more generally, if the farmers and tradesmen in the neighbourhood of them (upon paying a moderate sum yearly) are permitted to have access to them." [63] However only a few such libraries were established and these few were located in the cities and usually cost money to use. Philadelphia was well supplied as early as 1767. In that year a rental library required a deposit of £5 and a fee of $4 per year. Several years later a circulating library was charging only

[61] See Wheeler, "Reading Interests," *Md. Hist. Mag.*, xxxvi (1941), 184–201, 281–301; Bowes, *Culture of Charleston*, 56–58; W. W. Clayton, *Bergen and Passaic Counties New Jersey* (Philadelphia, 1882), 79.

[62] *American Husbandry*, 134.

[63] *Pittsburg Gazette*, March 10, 1787.

$2 for one year or 10s for a half-year, while at least two libraries opened their doors to the public without charge.[64] New York had several libraries prior to the Revolution costing between 10s and 30s per year, or 6d to 2s per book borrowed. There were, however, no free libraries, and apparently the readers were principally well-to-do men. Trenton, Burlington, and Elizabeth Town all had private institutions after the war.[65] Alexandria's library charged $6 per year, and one was planned in Baltimore for a guinea annually.[66] Boston's John Mein started the first circulating library in 1765, charging £1.8 lawful money a year. After the war another was established. A number of towns contained "social libraries," of which the Library Company of Philadelphia was the first and prototype. Shares in these were generally held by the local elite, the cost being too high for most men. Non-members were sometimes allowed to read the books for a fee. There were, however, no free libraries until a much later date.[67] Such social and rental libraries helped some of the artisans and other urban small property holders but most Americans could not take advantage of them.

Whether all classes read the newspapers cannot be certainly known. They had great educational value, printing

[64] Carl Bridenbaugh, "The Press and the Book in Eighteenth Century Philadelphia," *Pa. Mag. Hist. Biog.*, LXV (1941), 19, 29; *Pa. Packet*, Dec. 23, 1771; *Pa. Journal*, March 31, 1768; *Pa. Gazette*, Jan. 3, 1771. See Chester T. Hallenbeck, "A Colonial Reading List," *Pa. Mag. Hist. Biog.*, LVI (1932), 289–340 for the loan book of the Hatboro Library, 1762–1774.

[65] Austin Baxter Keep, *History of the New York Society Library* (New York, 1908); McCormick, *New Jersey*, 61.

[66] *Va. Journal* (Alexandria), May 11, 1786; *Md. Gazette* (Baltimore), May 5, 1786.

[67] *Boston Evening Post*, Nov. 11, 1765; Jesse H. Shera, *Foundations of the Public Library* (Chicago, 1949), especially 31–69, 133–136.

not only laws and political information but a variety of economic, literary, and scientific matter.[68] According to one Virginian, "In the Eastern States the *People* are informed. The Gazettes circulate freely; the laws are promulgated before they are in force; the *People* know their situation, and keep a watchful eye over their servants. Here, you are uninformed; you are bound by laws which you never see,—know nothing of." [69] New Englanders agreed that the people became educated in this way. Rich men, ministers, lawyers, and doctors could air their opinions easily, but the farmers and mechanics, it was claimed, had "no way so cheaply and so eligibly to communicate their Ideas to each other" as through newspapers.[70] Only by reading them could the "lower and poorer sort of people" obtain useful knowledge.[71] Although one commentator believed that their circulation was limited and that they were "comparatively but in few Hands," most people felt that their influence was widespread—an English traveller called it "almost incredible." [72]

Circulation figures support this, especially if we assume that newspapers travelled from hand to hand, as they almost certainly did. Even in the 1780's, when Isaiah Thomas's *Massachusetts Spy* had but 298 subscribers (he had had 3,500 before the Revolution), the paper reached little towns scattered all over rural Worcester County.[73] New Eng-

[68] See in praise of newspapers, "CONSIDERATION," *Va. Gazette or American Advertiser*, Nov. 22, 1783; *Conn. Gazette* (New Haven), Nov. 1, 1765.
[69] *Va. Gazette and American Advertiser*, Dec. 21, 1782.
[70] *Weekly Monitor* (Litchfield), Aug. 6, 1787.
[71] *Essex Journal*, Feb. 9, April 6, 1785; *Pittsburg Gazette*, March 10, 1787.
[72] *New London Gazette*, Aug. 5, 1768; Serle, *Journal*, xxi.
[73] *Mass. Spy*, Dec. 21, 1780.

land was exceptionally well supplied,[74] but by the 1780's all parts of the country had papers, and probably most people could see them if they wished. Magazines, on the other hand, circulated little outside of the urban upper class.

The educational level of the revolutionary American varied with his class and occupation. Slaves and indentured servants had almost no education and were usually illiterate.[75] The poorer farmers, especially those in the back-country, learned to read or write from their parents, or at times from a free school, but they had little further education. If they owned books their learning was still limited to religious matters. Artisans in the towns were somewhat better off because even if they owned no books they were more apt to find an evening school or a library, and they usually saw a newspaper. Substantial farmers and prosperous mechanics had much better opportunities except in the South. They could often send their sons to a private school, they usually had books, subscribed to a newspaper, and lived in or near centers of cultural activity. Most fortunate were men of wealth, for they could and did hire tutors if necessary, send their boys away to college, patronize local bookstores, and accumulate large libraries. These disparities are obvious, but they should not conceal the fact that except for the lower class, most colonials had some education and owned some books. But the time of the Revolution many men of moderate incomes were able to increase their knowedge, and by so doing increase their chance to rise.

The correlation of class with education is paralleled by

[74] Michael Kraus, *Atlantic Civilizations: Eighteenth Century Origins* (Ithaca, 1949), 67.

[75] But not invariably. There are instances of educated slaves, and some schools were established for them. For example, Greene, *Negro in New England*, 240–244.

that with art. Leaving aside religious prejudices and various national traditions, the American's attitude toward and experience of art varied with economic factors, especially upon his income and geographical location. Art generally could not help but suffer in a colonial environment. The Bostonians, observed Brissot de Warville, had produced no great art, but "Let us not blame the Bostonians; they think of the useful, before procuring to themselves the agreeable. They have no brilliant monuments; but they have neat and commodious churches, but they have good houses, but they have superb bridges, and excellent ships." [76]

This emphasis upon the useful, the practical, grew out of the circumstances of colonial life and could be illustrated at length.[77] Slaves and servants could have no art except that which they inherited. Most farmers and artisans were little better off. They lived in houses which they built themselves, constructed the only way they knew how, with no attention to aesthetic qualities—they were not engaged in architecture but in building. They sang and sometimes owned a fiddle but they learned their music from each other rather than from books. They rarely owned paintings and almost never saw a play. On the other hand men of large property did construct their homes according to architectural principles, and did, or at least could, patronize all of the arts. Almost all of the good paintings, valuable furniture, classical music, and theatrical performances were bought,

[76] *New Travels*, 112.

[77] The *Conn. Gazette* for April 27, 1787, published the following disquisition by "Q." The object of preaching, he stated, is "to enlighten and persuade," and the minister should use that language "which affords the readiest way to the head and heart, the seats of the understanding and affections. . . . A simple style, considering simplicity as opposed to affectation, that is, a style that flows naturally, and is easy to be comprehended by ordinary capacities, is best suited to sacred subjects. . . ."

sat on, played, and attended by the upper class, because it had the education to appreciate them and the money to gratify a desire for ostentatious emulation of the European elite.

Music, as an example, existed in two quite different forms. The great majority knew little except hymns sung to old folk tunes, and had no written notes or instruments or formal training. There continued to be opposition even to singing. In New York a proposed concert was called off because the principal performers were afraid of being laughed at for singing songs. "An Admirer of Vocal Music" admitted that "the best kind of music is not polite," though he insisted that God had made our voices and that singing should be encouraged.[78] A European traveller felt that in Boston music "begins to make part of their education," but remarked that it had formerly been "proscribed as a diabolic art," while an article published both in New York and Boston advised that if music were carried to excess, "its charms become unfortunate, and terminate in the enervation of the people at large, as well as to unman particular individuals."[79] At the same time a Yale student decided that music was "merely a sensual gratification" of no advantage to the Community."[80]

Yet music was flourishing in northern and southern cities before the Revolution. The common people participated to some extent: new tunes and hymnals were introduced into the churches, where congregations were encouraged to sing in tune and with harmony.[81] But primarily musical devel-

[78] *N.Y. Gazetteer*, April 14, 1786.
[79] Brissot de Warville, *New Travels*, 95; *N.Y. Journal*, Jan. 12, 1786; *Mass. Centinel*, Jan. 25, 1786.
[80] "The Diary of John Cotton Smith," Conn. Hist. Soc., *Bulletin*, XIX (Jan. 1954), 27.
[81] *The Granite Monthly*, IV (1881), 320–327; *New Hampshire Gazette*, Feb. 3, 1764; *New London Gazette*, May 20, 1768, Aug. 20,

opment was an upper-class affair. There is, wrote a citizen of Newport, "no art that has so great a tendency to refine our passions, soften the ruggedness of our natures, and improve all the delicate feelings of social life," and music should be rescued from the "persons of an inferior class" who were singing in churches.[82] Those who worried about refinement and delicacy could buy musical instruments (a flute cost $3) and books, and even an American-made spinet (in Boston).[83] Concerts, attended by the upper class, were given in private homes or in public buildings, while in Charleston the exclusive St. Cecelia Society, founded in 1762, supported an orchestra.[84] Many years were to pass before the public generally became concerned with such concerts. Farmers and artisans had little free time and less money, nor were they in a position to learn that there was a musical tradition different than their folk art of songs and hymns.

Attendance at the theater was limited almost exclusively to the well-to-do. Dramatic companies were under attack throughout the period, principally on moral grounds,[85] and many men of moderate incomes who could have afforded tickets were unwilling to endanger their souls. Poorer peo-

---

1773; *Conn. Courant,* Sept. 25, 1769; *S.C. Gazette and Daily Advertiser,* June 17, 1785.

[82] *Newport Mercury,* Aug. 7, 1784. See also *Md. Gazette* (Baltimore), July 1, 1785.

[83] *Boston Gazette,* July 16, 1764, Feb. 5, 1770; Singleton, *Social New York,* 286–300.

[84] Bowes, *Early Charleston,* 106.

[85] Ebenezer Hazard to Belknap, Jamaica Plain, Aug. 9, 1780, "Belknap Papers," Mass. Hist. Soc., *Proceedings,* 5 series II (1877), 67–68; *Md. Gazette* (Baltimore), Aug. 26, 1785; *Md. Journal,* March 28, 1783; *Providence Gazette,* April 7, June 9, 16, July 14, 1787; *Pa. Chronicle,* Feb. 9, 16, March 2, 9, 30, April 20, May 4, 1767; *Pa. Packet,* Nov. 8, 1773, April 7, 1787; *N.Y. Journal,* Jan. 14, 1768 (especially good), Jan. 28, Feb. 11, April 9, 1768; *Independent Gazetteer,* Feb. 21, 1784; *Pa. Gazette,* July 31, 1766, Nov. 10, 1773.

ple, few of whom could have spared the price, resented the conspicuous display of the well-to-do theater-goers. The announcement during 1773 in Charleston that a theater was to be built led a newspaper writer to protest that theaters might be justifiable "where the Generality of the People are wealthy, have much Leisure, and little Employment," but not in South Carolina; while the city's grand jury felt that at a time when many people could not buy even the necessities it was wrong to spend so much money in this way.[86] Again after the Revolution the upper-class dominated city council favored a playhouse and were attacked in print.[87] A Carlisle, Pennsylvania, critic feared that the theater would introduce aristocracy.[88] Still, performances were held whether legal or not.[89] In Albany, a petition of 70 inhabitants failed to change the corporation's decision to permit theatrical performances when the aldermen and assistants, most of whom were merchants and lawyers, voted 9-4 not to forbid them.[90] Virginians saw plays both before and after the war, the later company extracting (so it was said) £1,500 from the state. Fredericksburg, Maryland, enjoyed plays during the spring and summer of 1786, though the price of tickets was so high that the company did not profit.[91]

An interesting exchange followed the presentation in New Haven of "a very short Dialogue, with a short Farce." The price of one dollar (6s) was attacked as too high, and attendance was considered to be very improper, especially

---

[86] *S.C. Gazette*, Aug. 25, 1773, Feb. 28, 1774.
[87] *S.C. Gazette and Public Advertiser*, Sept. 3, 1785.
[88] *Carlisle Gazette*, Feb. 5, 1786.
[89] Bell, "Social History," *Pa. Mag. Hist. Biog.*, LXII, 295–297.
[90] *Pa. Packet*, Dec. 30, 1785.
[91] Morgan, *Virginians at Home*, 90; *Va. Independent Chronicle*, Sept. 20, 1786; *The Maryland Chronicle or, the Universal Advertiser* (Frederick-Town), May 10, Aug. 6, 1786.

since frugality was necessary "more especially among common tradesmen, mechanicks, &c. (who almost invariably have the vanity of aping their superiors in every fashionable extravagance)." An indignant reply resented the slur on mechanics, and observed that some of the "most respectable" people of the community had attended. Men's time was their own, and they had the right to spend some of it on innocent amusement, and besides, the money made went to the poor.[92] Everywhere the theater had its defenders who extolled the virtue, educational value, and relaxing quality of plays.[93] The upper class especially was appealed to. Most polite people in Europe attended plays, it was claimed, while Addison was quoted as saying that playgoing helped to refine human society, and was useful to the state "by polishing the Manners, and forming the Taste of the People." [94]

Thus be it educational advantage, literacy, or patronage of the arts, the quality of culture in the revolutionary period varied with the economic status of the people. Despite this generalization, cultural differences between classes were not so great as to exclude what might be called cultural mobility. Obviously the slave could not participate in cultural activities. But as the farmer or even more as the

[92] *Conn. Journal,* Feb. 4, 18, 1778.

[93] *Providence Gazette,* April 21, June 23, 1787; *Albany Gazette,* Jan. 12, 1786, et seq.; *Freeman's Journal,* March 3, 24, 1784, Nov. 30, 1785; *Independent Gazetteer,* Feb. 14, 1784; *Pa. Packet,* Nov. 15, 29, 1773, Dec. 20, 1785; *Pa. Chronicle,* March 5, 1787, Feb. 23, March 2, Nov. 9, 1767; *Carlisle Gazette,* March 1, 1786; *N.Y. Gazetteer,* Sept. 20, 1785; *Md. Journal,* May 28, 1782; *Va. Journal* (Alexandria), Sept. 13, 20, 1787; *Pa. Gazette,* March 5, 1767, Nov. 17, 1773; *Pa. Journal,* Jan. 28, Feb. 11, 14, 18, 1784. One writer traced crimes and licentiousness to the restlessness of the human mind, which needed something to keep it in action; Shays's Rebellion proceeded from "the want of theatres, dances, shows and other public amusements." *Independent Gazetteer,* Jan. 31, 1787.

[94] *Albany Gazette,* Jan. 12, 1786; *Md. Gazette,* Oct. 4, 1770.

artisan increased his income and became a substantial property holder, he could and sometimes did increase his education and artistic awareness. Probably rather few actually did so, for the social and economic obstacles were many, but the existence of a fairly general cultural mobility prevented the development of an exclusive cultural aristocracy and encouraged the democratic tendencies in revolutionary society.

CHAPTER IX

Conclusion

THE STUDENT of revolutionary society must ask two questions: whether or not classes existed, and whether the social structure was democratic or undemocratic. If the word "class" requires the presence of class consciousness, if it can be used only when men are aware of a hierarchical structure and of their own rank within it, then this study indicates that America during the period 1763–1788 was relatively classless. Certainly it was both classless and democratic by comparison with the America of 1900 or with England in 1776. Moreover, rural New England, and the frontier and subsistence farming areas generally, furnish impressive evidence of a nearly equal division of wealth and a relative absence of classes.

If on the other hand the existence of classes does not depend upon class consciousness but implies nothing more than a rank order within which an individual can move up or down without any insurmountable difficulty, then revolutionary America can and indeed must be described in terms of classes. The society of the towns and of most commercial farm areas, the great distinctions between rich and poor, and the concentration of property, are decisive evidence of the presence of an economic class structure. Furthermore, a social hierarchy based upon a consciousness of class distinctions, a prestige order, can be identified, although it cannot be so precisely defined.

Although revolutionary America is seen to have contained classes, the question of democracy remains unsettled. On the one hand the societies in which class distinctions were prominent were aristocratic rather than equalitarian.

In some commercial farm regions and in the major cities, a wealthy, fairly stable upper class had appeared, most of whose members had inherited their position, and who owned over half of the property; while a large lower class, often servile, also had developed. The opportunity to rise was restricted, or even denied altogether. In contrast the new country contained other sections in which most people were small property holders, wealth was equally distributed, and the poor man usually prospered. Revolutionary society was certainly not classless, yet neither was it entirely aristocratic. It contained the essential elements for an aristocracy while at the same time possessing the potential for a social and economic democracy.

There was, of course, a "permanent proletariat" consisting of those who always remained at the bottom. Slaves formed the largest part of this class. They totalled 23 percent of the whole population in 1760 and a little less than that thirty years later. Four-fifths of these were in the South, concentrated especially near the coast. A few sections of the country, then, contained a Negro labor force comprising considerably over half of the population, whereas most of the country had only a small such element, and vast areas none at all. Where slaves were scarce, white indentured servants or wage-workers were used instead. Less numerous than the Negroes, the white laborers usually formed only about one-fifth of the whites, though the proportion was doubled in certain areas. The exact number who remained in the lowest status is uncertain, but certainly fewer than half, possibly only one-fourth of them failed to become small property holders. Therefore out of twenty whites only one or two remained permanently poor. The evidence suggests that by the time of the Revolution even indentured servants had a chance of success nearly equal to that of the free workers. If this is true, then immigrants and native-born alike had reason to be confident about their future, and the few whites who failed were defeated not because of any external circumstance but because they lacked some essential quality. Thus the whole permanent proletariat, white and black, totalled less than 30 percent of the population.

At any point in time, revolutionary society contained a lower class comprising between one-third and two-fifths of the men. If defined by occupation, it included Negro slaves, white servants, and landless laborers employed by property owners such as farmers, artisans, and merchants. If defined by income, the lower class characteristically had almost none, except that they were given food, clothing, and shelter; free workers, however, did receive a money wage which enabled them to save. If defined by property, the men of this economic rank almost always had estates of less than £50, and usually they had none.

The free workers, with their money and opportunities for advancement, belonged to an intermediate category. They were partially independent, owned some property and perhaps some skill, were poor but not impoverished, and often were moving up into the middle class. Many farmers were no better off. There were, for example, numerous landowners in western Massachusetts and southern Delaware, the annual value of whose land was assessed at under £5; and according to the probate records (a more accurate indication of wealth) something like one-eighth of the yeomen had personal estates of less than £50. Many tenants were also poor, while perhaps 30 percent of the skilled artisans, especially many weavers, cordwainers, housewrights, coopers, and tailors, left very small estates. These men probably did earn enough to support their families adequately most of the time. Many of them moved from place to place, generally westward, perhaps improving their position, perhaps always balanced precariously upon the boundary between poverty and success. In England such men, together with the true lower class, constituted a latent threat to the existing order, and were kept under control by an educational system which (if it existed at all) taught them morality, by a religion which enjoined them to accept their lot submissively, and by force. In America, many members of this marginal class were young men with prospects. Discipline was rarely needed except by the slaves; even the uprisings of tenants and the flight of servants were not so much protests against their condition as a testimony to the opportunities which they knew existed.

The middle class in America consisted of small property holders who were usually self-employed. Its members are distinguished, at the lower end of the scale, from servants and slaves or others who had little or no property, and from the wage workers who depended entirely upon their daily labor; while at the other end they merge without any sharp definition into the upper class of men with large estates. Whereas the lower class lived at or barely above the subsistence level, the "middling sort" lived in comfort. The less fortunate among them usually owned at least £200 worth of real and personal property and netted perhaps £10 in excess of the minimum cost of living. The majority held property worth £400 to £500 and earned the £75 to £100 (or its equivalent) which supported their families in decency. The class included probably 70 percent of the whites and may be subdivided into the lower middle or marginal segment discussed above (roughly 20 percent, a middle middle (40 percent), and an upper middle (10 percent).

This largest and most important segment of revolutionary society was made up of several occupational groups. Small farmers were the most numerous element, comprising 40 percent of the whites and one-third of the whole population. If farmers who were substantial but not large landowners are added, the proportion rises to very nearly half of the whites and two-fifths of all the people. These farmers furnished most of their own necessities and earned at least £16 in cash (or credits) which permitted them to pay their debts and taxes, buy a few luxury articles, and save a little. Very few could hope to enlarge their farms without borrowing, but since they generally held 100 or 200 acres their prosperity depended more upon improving their methods and developing their land than upon adding acreage. Most of them could not provide for surplus sons, but the frontier or the towns took care of these. The more fortunate, who had good land in commercial farming areas, cleared much more than £16 and presented an agreeable picture of the ideal American, the prosperous farmer.

Second in number among the middling sort were the "artisans and mechanics" or "craftsmen." These were of two types. Some of them were not entrepreneurs but skilled workers who hired themselves out by the day, week, or year. Receiving from £40 to £50 annually, they could save a good deal of money so long as they remained single, but the married man just broke even; indeed if he had to rent a house and buy all of his food, £50 scarcely met expenses. Fortunately most of these artisans raised much of their own food and were thereby able to live in reasonable comfort and even acquire some property. Apparently almost half of them significantly improved their economic position.

The great majority of artisans in the rural areas, and probably a majority everywhere, were independent entrepreneurs who ordinarily kept a workshop in or near their houses. These were equivalent to farmers in that they were self-employed, but they usually ranked somewhat below the yeomen both in wealth and prestige. Their income and chance of increasing it depended upon their particular craft. The majority never rose above the middle rank, for the trades of cooper, cordwainer, blacksmith, tailor, weaver, or carpenter seldom provided a large return. On the other hand they also required little equipment and were in great demand, so that the apprentice could quite easily become a master. A few types of enterprise were by their nature more expensive to undertake and more profitable for the enterpriser. Distillers, ropemakers, goldsmiths, and the like were capitalists whose economic position compared favorably with that of prosperous farmers and many professional men.

Professional men as a whole also belonged to the middle class, earning considerably more than most farmers and artisans but not enough to raise them decisively into the economic elite. Two segments of the professional group were exceptional. Lawyers ordinarily received large incomes and formed part of the "better sort," while teachers often had so little property that they ranked economically even below skilled workers, though they may have had greater prestige. The other professionals, among whom ministers and doctors were the most numerous, typically earned £100 to £200, a sum which allowed some luxuries and enabled them to accumulate £500 worth of property. This property in turn added to their income and further raised their standard of living. They therefore could spare the cash to educate their children for the professions or for trade: indeed it seems possible that the clergy at least was to a large extent a self-recruiting group, partly because most Americans could not send their children to school whereas the ministers could and did. In the middle class too belonged the overseers, innkeepers, ships' captains, retailers, clerks, and most government officials.

The upper class was composed of large property owners. By European standards there was, of course, no upper class at all, since there was no hereditary aristocracy. There were in certain areas families who had retained wealth and position for several generations, and who were then and have been since called "aristocrats"; but the word, if it is to be used at all, must be defined to fit the American scene. Probably it is better simply to structure revolutionary society on its own terms. Entrance into the upper class followed at once upon selection to certain public offices, and most often upon acquiring a certain amount of property. Any definition is certainly arbitrary, but a reasonable one is the ownership of £2,000, which made one well-to-do, or of £5,000, which meant wealth. The southern planter who owned 500 acres and 20 slaves possessed at least the former sum, which was, incidentally, the amount required for membership in the South Carolina Senate. Probably 10 percent of the landowners, the same proportion of ministers and doctors, most lawyers, a few artisans, and not far from half of the merchants qualified as well-to-do or wealthy— the total being roughly 10 percent of the whites. These men had incomes which were almost by definition in excess of £500,[1] and they controlled about 45 percent of the country's wealth.[2] It is important to remember that this was not

---

[1] Not all of this £500 had to be in cash, of course. Most well-to-do farmers probably cleared far less than this, but supplied much of their own food, fuel, and shelter.

[2] Anyone who uses this figure for comparing the distribution of wealth then and now should be informed that the slaves are not here included as part of the population. If they are added, the figure becomes a little higher because the population is larger by nearly one-fourth, so that more individuals would be included among the top tenth of property holders. Their share of the wealth would become about 50 percent overall. The following table shows the approximate situation. Figures in parentheses are obtained when slaves are included.

Share of Wealth of the Richest 10%

	North	South
Frontier	33%	40% (40+)
Subsistence farm	35	40 (45)
Commercial farm	45–50	55 (65)
City	55–60	60+ (65)
General	45	50 (55)

a closed class. Another tenth of the men owned estates of £1,000 or so, and movement from one rank to another was frequent. Although the very wealthiest Virginia planters formed a fairly tight social group, it is probable that entrance into the lesser planter society was much easier. The urban elite even before the Revolution contained many men who began life with little property.

Such was the class structure of the United States viewed as a whole. There where, however, several quite different sub-societies based upon geographical and historical factors. Each colony had in 1763 certain peculiarities, and the contrast between North Carolina and Virginia, adjacent though they were, was as striking as that between the Old Dominion and New Hampshire. Moreover every colony contained three or four distinct social structures. Fortunately these sub-societies reappear everywhere so that the country can still be treated as a whole.

Most colonies still had a frontier area. Pioneer societies were of two types. In some cases land speculators obtained large tracts which they then rented, sold, or occasionally farmed. Ordinarily the speculator was not a resident, so that no upper class was present, but real property was more than usually concentrated in the hands of large proprietors, while the lower class of landless men was more numerous than on most frontiers. The typical frontier class structure, however, was "democratic": most men belonged to the middle class, property was equally distributed, and the poor man found it easy to become a farmer.

Subsistence—or more accurately subsistence-plus—farms existed wherever the farmers could raise or market little produce in excess of their immediate needs. Poor soil, inadequate transportation, lack of capital, or a shortage of labor, were inhibiting factors. Since agriculture was not particularly profitable under these circumstances, few wealthy men lived in such areas. The lower class also was small, for few men could afford servants or slaves, while the hired hand quickly obtained a farm of his own or left for better soils. The great majority of the men were small farmers who, together with a few artisans and professional men, formed a very large middle class. Property was equally distributed; the subsistence farm society, like that of the frontier, was democratic.

In areas where agriculture was profitable, commercial farming developed. The result might be only a general increase in the prosperity of small farmers, but typically some landowners became rich, controlled an increasing amount of the property, and bought or hired an expanding labor force. Class distinctions quickly appeared. The society (at least in the North) also became more diversified because the large farmers tended to specialize in staple crops and to buy whatever else they needed, while their higher incomes allowed them to purchase luxuries. More artisans were present, more traders, and more professional men. The southern "plantation" social structure did not ordinarily contain such a large non-farm element (unless some slaves are counted as artisans), but exceeded the northern commercial farm sections in the size of the upper and lower classes, the concentration of property, and the general wealth. While the commercial farm area was first undergoing development, men were able quickly and easily to increase their property and prestige. Once that process had been completed, opportunities for those without capital diminished and class lines tended to harden.

By contrast, urban societies everywhere offered opportunity to men of all ranks. The cities contained many wage earners and some slaves, so that the lower class was even larger than in commercial farm regions, except for those parts of the South in which slaves were especially numerous. With the same exception the towns contained the highest proportion of wealthy men, who had an unusually large share of the city's property. Despite the economic inequalities which characterized urban society, the middle class was seldom less than half of the whole population, the general standard of living was high, and economic opportunities in a great variety of occupations afforded the poor man a chance to acquire property.

Just as the unequal distribution of property proves the existence of economic classes, so also the different styles of living testify to the inequality of income. The revolutionary family which had to pay cash for everything needed at least £50 annually. The lower class and even some skilled workers received less than this. Had they depended entirely upon a cash income, they must have lived below the subsistence level, but fortunately several factors intervened to save almost all of these people from actual want. The majority— slaves and indentured servants—were supported by their masters. Others owned a little land on which they produced much of their food. Still others were single men without dependents who needed much less money and in fact could save a little. By the time they married they usually had acquired a farm or a skill which raised them into the middle class. Therefore the members of the lower class were guaranteed at least an adequate livelihood.

The middle class generally enjoyed a comfortable living. Small farmers did without much money but raised almost all of their food, made some of their clothing, and supplied other household needs, so that they usually showed a net cash profit. Professional men, substantial farmers and artisans, and other members of what was by colonial standards an upper middle class, generally exceeded the £100 or thereabouts which their style of living required. The upper class too was fortunate. Merchants, lawyers, and planters very seldom earned enough to live like European aristocrats, but in the new world £400 or so would enable anyone who produced his own food to live like a gentleman.

Crucially important to the early American was his ability to improve his economic and social position. Comparisons with other societies are dangerous when there are no comparable facts, but the evidence points decisively toward a much higher degree of mobility in revolutionary America than had been usual elsewhere. Several circumstances contributed to this result. One was of course the absence for most Americans of legal or social impediments. All whites were permitted to acquire property, and as they did so they progressed up the social scale, acceptance even at the highest levels coming almost at once. Another factor was the general economic expansion combined with a rapid growth in the population. There was always more room at the top. Important too were the vast quantities of unoccupied land, some of it excellent, available at a low price with several years to pay. This land contained untouched natural resources, notably lumber. Finally, the American could move easily from place to place. Had he been in some manner constrained within his home neighborhood, his prospects would have been considerably diminished, for economic opportunities in the older farm areas, while greater than in Europe, were much less than in the newer regions; but he was always able to move to the town or to the frontier.

This geographical mobility did not usually involve long-distance migration. The occupation of western Pennsylvania, Kentucky, and Tennessee naturally required a considerable journey, but during the years 1763–1788 most of the movement was local, the distance travelled short. The young man moved a few score miles at most, to a town or country lying roughly westward as transportation facilities dictated. The occupation of a frontier, as far as the present study reveals the situation, was carried out by those living adjacent to it. The westward course seldom was reversed: few men returned to the east. Probably the process was largely a rural phenomenon, for city folk did not have the farmer's skills, and ordinarily stayed in the towns. There may have been some movement of artisans to the country where they continued to practice their trades, but opportunities in the towns (at least in the North) were good enough so that a "safety valve" was seldom needed.

The man who started without property had the best chance of advancement if he went west. Indeed four out of five pioneers obtained land, usually within a few years after their arrival. Immigrants, even indentured servants, had nearly as good a chance for success as native-born whites; the failures occurred among the unskilled regardless of their origin. Those frontier areas subject to large-scale speculation sometimes offered less opportunity to the prospective landowners—much of the land in New York and northern Virginia was rented to tenants rather than sold—but ordinarily the man with some skill was almost certain of entering the middle class.

If he lived in an older community the certainty was gone but the probability of advancement was still fairly high. About one out of three landless laborers in such areas obtained land without moving out of the county. More than half of the artisans advanced economically and even indentured servants had some success. Obviously the fact that the good land had long since been occupied was the principal limiting factor, and had all of the people stayed put, those at the bottom might have been fated to remain there. Fortunately the constant movement out of the country created openings locally, and if one failed to seize the chance, there was always another one farther west.

But though someone of ability might look forward with confidence to entering the rural middle class, he could seldom achieve higher rank. If the situation in Virginia is at all typical, an established rural upper class admitted very few new members. Those who made good came not from among the small farmers but from the businessmen and lawyers. Admittedly conclusions based upon one colony ought not to be pushed too far, but it seems that in the South it was rare for any parvenu to achieve eminence among the landholders (by revolutionary times) unless he did so through buying land on a frontier which rapidly became commercial. Probably the same was true in the North.

Urban society was much more open than that of the commercial farm areas. Although the unskilled workers (including mariners) seldom acquired much property, the chance of becoming an independent artisan was excellent in those occupations which demanded little venture capital. Success in the larger enterprises and in commerce was more difficult. Nevertheless even the wealthy merchant class of colonial New York was composed partly of self-made men: whereas not over one in ten wealthy Virginians were *nouveaux riches*, about one in three members of the Chamber of Commerce were of humble origin. The proportion of self-made men was even higher after the war, but this probably was an abnormal situation due to the forcible displacement of Loyalist merchants by enterprising rebels.

Just as the revolutionary American could increase his wealth, he could also advance in prestige. The "social class" or "status" order which the colonists brought with them from Europe was based upon a hereditary system of ranks, symbolized or identified by the discriminatory use of titles. This hierarchical society (which even in England was not inflexible) gradually disappeared in America partly because no European aristocracy was present to perpetuate it, but largely because of the actual condition of social equality and the remarkable ease with which the colonial could improve his position. Therefore the old order was eventually replaced by one which developed out of the new economic circumstances. The indigenous class structure was based upon property rather than inherited status.[3] When a new prestige order was created, it corresponded closely with economic classes. It seems reasonable to suppose that, since titles were losing their symbolic significance, the Americans found a substitute in their style of life, by which they distinguished themselves visibly from their inferiors.

The outcome made social advancement relatively easy. Perhaps the principal method was simply by making money, for there were no social barriers which property could not surmount, and there existed a general admiration for the man who acquired an estate. A high regard for material possessions permitted anyone to achieve status approximately in proportion to his income. Another way of winning esteem was to obtain a high political office. The degree of democracy during the revolutionary era is disputed, but no one denies that preferment included Americans from more walks of life than was the case with contemporary European officialdom; while the Revolution itself unquestionably opened the doors to a greater number of artisans and farmers. The position of justice of the peace did not mean quite so much as in England but it was still an important and prestigeful office which could be reached, at least in the North, by men of small property. Education, though available principally to the upper class, occasionally elevated the man of merit, while during the war some

[3] See Sigmund Diamond, *The Creation of Society in the New World* (Chicago, 1963); Bernard Bailyn, "Politics and Social Structure in Virginia," in James Morton Smith, ed., *Seventeenth-Century America: Essays in Colonial History* (Chapel Hill, 1959), 90–115.

soldiers of lowly birth won high rank and universal regard.

This social mobility was of course limited just as was economic mobility. Titles still had some significance. The great majority of "esquires" were large property holders, while "gentlemen" owned about twice the average wealth. Still, only a minority of the upper class merited the "esquire," while in the North most of the "gentlemen" and one-third of the "esquires" were of humble birth, and "Mr." meant practically nothing at all anywhere. Despite the frequent public eulogies addressed to farmers, they had no monopoly of these symbols of prestige, for such titles were granted to merchants, professional men, and even to artisans.

Although Americans seemed to express an excessive regard for farmers and were publicly critical of lawyers and traders, they had a generally accurate view of their own society. They preferred to think of it as one of equality and proudly pointed to such features as the large middle class, the absence of beggars, the comfortable circumstances of most people, and the limitless opportunities for those who worked hard and saved their money, Still, few had any illusion that perfection had been achieved. The existence of slaves and poor whites, of rich merchants and planters, and of what seemed to many an increasing concentration of wealth, prevented any complacency and aroused anxious criticism of the inequalities which marred the vision of the Good Society. Our modern division of American society into three classes corresponds closely to their contemporary analysis, and they likewise recognized the economic basis of class. European travellers similarly saw that the American social structure, while far less aristocratic and more fluid than that of the Old World, had obvious economic and social inequalities.

Cultural distinctions were even more evident. Just as the prestige order paralleled the economic class structure, so did the culture reflect one's wealth.[4] The much higher incomes of the "better sort" made possible a standard of living which visibly distinguished them from the rest of the people. These differences existed not only in their food and drink, their use of silver, and their clothing, but in the architectural style of their homes, the paintings adorning the walls of their houses, and the music they enjoyed. Attendance at the theater was principally an upper-class activity. The possession of books varied with one's income. Most of the lower sort had none. Members of the middle class did own books, but usually they had only a few, which were almost entirely religious in nature. On the other hand almost all of the wealthy men—especially if they were professionals—had libraries which often included a great variety of works. The ordinary American was also deprived of the education which might have raised his income, his status, and his cultural level. Slaves almost never learned to write; servants rarely did so; and wage workers seldom exceeded a bare literacy. Even members of the middle class were seriously handicapped. Only in New England were free schools available, and private institutions were rare on the frontier or in subsistence farm areas. The tuition charged by private schools was low enough so that children of middle-class families could attend, but only if they lived at home. The cost of room and board prevented all but the larger property holders from sending their sons away. Therefore few farmers or artisans could hope for a higher education. The possibility did exist, however, especially in

[4] An excellent description of colonial culture from this point of view is contained in Max Savelle, *Seeds of Liberty* (New York, 1948).

the northeast and above all in New England, which thereby came closer than any other section to achieving the American ideal of equal opportunity.

Was revolutionary America progressing toward this goal or were class lines hardening? What changes occurred during those twenty-five years? Any answer must be tentative, for the time span is short and information scanty, while the Revolution was an abnormal circumstance which obscures the general trend.

The long-term tendency seems to have been toward greater inequality, with more marked class distinctions.[5] These differences were, however, not so much cultural as social and economic. The fundamental cause was the increasingly commercial character of the country as contrasted with the more prevalent subsistence economy of an earlier period. The frontier was receding, and areas once largely self-sufficient (such as the Virginia Piedmont) were occupied by prosperous commerical farmers, while towns appeared even in the interior. Since both the commercial farm and urban societies were characterized by greater class distinctions, the country as a whole contained larger lower and upper classes and proportionately fewer small property owners. The greater wealth benefitted everyone, but most of the profits went to the well-to-do. Probate records show that the concentration of wealth was increasing in Massachusetts, New Hampshire, and South Carolina, though not in New Jersey. The landless worker was no longer able so easily to improve his status when the best land became occupied, while the farmer found it harder to surmount the barriers erected by the large landholders. It is probable that the composition of the New York Chamber of Commerce prior to the Revolution, consisting as it did

[5] This conclusion is confirmed by Henretta's study of Boston, in *Wm. and Mary Quarterly*, XXII (1965), 75–92.

mainly of prominent of old families, represents a declining rate of mobility into the urban elite.

The effect of the Revolution was to reverse these trends, at least temporarily. The causes for this reversal lie far beyond the scope of the present work, but among them are probably the displacement of some wealthy Loyalists, the increased political power of farmers and artisans, and a certain social levelling. The consequences are to be seen particularly in the greater ease with which men could enter the urban elite, the rising standard of living especially among farmers, the declining significance of titles (the "esquire" for example being granted more often to small property owners and men of humble background generally), and the comparable democratization of the officer class. All of these were much more prevalent in the North—a point of some significance.

The American of the 1780's therefore had reason, as he viewed his society, for some cautious optimism. Classes remained, to be sure, and he might note with alarm the concentration of wealth and the growing number of poor, but the Revolution had made great changes, and westward the land was bright.

Needs and Resources

THE MOST VALUABLE and almost untouched source materials for the socio-economic history of early America are the probate records, especially the inventories of estates. Every colony kept these records and many of them have survived. The states of New Hampshire and New Jersey have published condensed versions which include the name of the individual, his place of residence, occupation when given, and the total value of his property. The New Hampshire series stops with the Revolution, after which probate records were kept by the counties instead of by the colonial government. The New Jersey publications continue after 1790. The Massachusetts records are deposited in the various county court houses. They are indexed, but the historian will want to refer directly to the original volumes which were kept, of course, chronologically as the cases arose. The situation is similar in Connecticut and Rhode Island. Many volumes of New York wills have been published in the *Collections* of the New York Historical Society, but these do not itemize inventories. The Virginia records are conveniently available on microfilm in the Virginia State Library, from which the reels may be borrowed. Each county kept its own records, an astonishing proportion of which have been preserved, and the result is a remarkable collection. The North Carolina material published by J. Bryan Grimes in his *North Carolina Inventories* (Raleigh, 1912) are too few for historical research of the present type which requires many cases for generalization. On the other hand the South Carolina probate records, preserved in the state archives at Columbia, are exceedingly valuable. They were kept by the central government throughout the period and appear to be complete, though disproportionately few westerners are represented.

The men who evaluated these estates did so conscientiously. When the property was sold it brought a sum very close to the estimated worth. However the estates tended to be slightly overvalued during the mid 1780's, when prices were lower than usual. In any case the error is of no importance for structuring society, since all estates were overrated by about the same proportion.

A much more considerable error results from the changing value of the currency and the different values assigned to the local money in terms of the pound sterling. In general the following table is accurate for "lawful money" from the end of the "French and Indian" war through the 1780's: [1]

	Value of the Spanish Dollar	*For Sterling, Subtract*
The English pound sterling	4s 6d	
New England and Virginia	6s	1/4
New York and North Carolina	8s	9/16
New Jersey, Pennsylvania, Delaware, and Maryland	7s 6d	3/5

Theoretically the South Carolina and Georgia pounds were pegged at 4s 8d, but in practice before the war the lawful money was worth 1/7 of sterling. After 1783 most figures there were given in sterling. Until the Revolution the monetary situation in both Rhode Island and New Hampshire was fluid. Theoretically the local Rhode Island cur-

[1] *N.Y. Gazetteer*, March 4, 1785 and other newspapers; Simon L. Adler, "Money and Money Units in the American Colonies," Rochester Hist. Soc., *Publications*, VIII (1929), 143–173.

rency was worth nine times lawful money in 1751, rising to 14:1 by 1755, 20:1 by 1758, and 23½:1 in 1763, lawful money being equal to sterling minus one-fourth as elsewhere in New England.[2] In New Hampshire depreciation proceeded at a similar pace, legally reaching 20:1 by 1757 and remaining there until 1764, after which date this inflated "old Tenor" (abbreviated as "O.T.") supposedly gave way to lawful money ("L.M."). In reality the depreciation reached 20:1 by 1750 or earlier, rose far above the legal ratio, and lasted until after 1766; moreover certain appraisers thought in terms of the old values long after the legal change had taken place.[3] The only safe procedure is for the researcher to keep in mind typical sterling or lawful money prices of certain common articles so that the currency used can be determined, and to state carefully, wherever possible, whether currency or sterling is meant. It is also essential to remember the differences between the colonies and states: in this period a salary of £40 per annum in Massachusetts, for example, was equal to one of £50 in Pennsylvania and more than that in New York.

Most of the inventories listed only personal property, which means that land, houses and other buildings, ships, and sometimes pew rights were omitted. The New England records are especially valuable because real estate was included. In a very general way, the ratio of the value of personal to real property was 1:2, but the proportion is worthless in any individual case, nor is it valid for estates of less than £50 or more than £1,000.

Another limitation of the inventories is that certain elements in the population are not adequately represented. In

---

[2] *R.I. Col. Rec.*, vi, 361.

[3] The rate of exchange with England also was unstable. For example, North Carolina's currency was legally about 1/3 below sterling but in fact the ratio was usually 5:9.

South Carolina the backcountry people seem rarely to have encountered the probate judge, probably because the records were kept in distant Charleston. Slave estates, naturally, were not recorded. Neither, apparently, were those of indentured servants, although some of them must have had a little personal property. Therefore when this source is used to structure society it must be remembered that the bottom 10 percent or more of the white population is missing.

With this exception, the inventories afford an excellent chance to examine economic classes in the whole country, the particular colony or state, or the sections within the state. The deceased's place of residence was not usually indicated in South Carolina but elsewhere it is possible to distinguish pioneers from established farmers, urban artisans from rural, and country traders from shopkeepers of the towns.

The property owned by different occupational groups can also be determined from these records. What the person did for a living is only occasionally given in the documents but usually can be inferred. Ministers were sometimes called "clerks." Artisans are sometimes not identified, but their occupation can frequently be discovered from the inventory. However it should be remembered that many farmers owned carpenter's tools or the implements of other trades. The farmers are best known by their property. The word "husbandman" always, and "yeoman" almost always, signified a farmer. Where no clear identification can be made, at least the non-farmers can usually be distinguished from the country dwellers. The non-farm men with small estates can safely be called laborers. Those of larger property probably were artisans or white-collar workers of various sorts such as professional men or government officials. This miscellaneous category will be too small to worry about unless there is particular reason for exactitude.

The degree to which property was concentrated can best be studied from these inventories. One way of doing this is to define an upper class arbitrarily and then determine what proportion of the property was held by that class. I have chosen instead to deal with the wealthiest 10 percent of each community. The true concentration is always slightly higher than is found by this method because indentured servants were omitted. It is essential to accumulate a large number of inventories, for otherwise a single large estate, fortuitously included or omitted, might vary the result to an excessive degree.

Many other important subjects can be studied through these inventories. The Massachusetts collection makes it possible to analyze the landholdings of many types of northern farmers, especially since some inventories distinguish and evaluate various sorts of land (mowing, pasture, salt marsh, etc.). The value of crops is sometimes given. The cost of various articles can also be discovered from inventories. The prices of artisans' tools, of farm equipment, of clothes, beds, furniture, books, slaves, guns, violins, oxen, houses, shingles, barns, ships, carriages, and innumerable other articles are included. The content of homes and the distribution of consumer goods can be determined. The nature and value of livestock, the tools of artisans, what merchants had in their shops, what professional equipment various sorts of "doctors" used, and the ownership of debts, are other examples of the useful information furnished by these records.

Probate records contain much material in addition to the inventories. Many men whose estates were not evaluated left wills which itemized their property. Executors often made detailed reports and guardians declared their expenses. The latter, for example, sometimes specified the cost of maintaining children, including clothes and schooling. Many men who seem to have owned much property actually were insolvent, and much about the failure as well as the success of Americans is preserved in the probate offices. The student who wishes to analyze in detail the economic or social history of a community will find these records essential and rewarding.

Tax lists are second in importance only to the inventories for a study of classes and the distribution of property. They are of even greater value in that all of the people are represented, including slaves and servants. Moreover in some areas where probate records do not exist or are inadequate, tax lists have been preserved. Finally, land was almost always included. On the other hand, not all articles were taxed, the incidence varying from place to place and time to time, and a disproportionate share of the burden was borne by polls, land, and in the South by slaves. Also the preservation of these records has been erratic.

The New England colonies and states levied taxes based upon the annual income from real property and the value of certain types of personal property including stock in trade, money at interest, and farm animals. There was also a poll tax. Assessment lists, from which the tax was determined, are the most valuable because they itemize these properties. A large number of them for the period about 1770 are preserved on microfilm in the Massachusetts Archives; they cannot be borrowed, however. Locally levied taxes were primarily on land and polls. There was sometimes a "faculty tax" levied on non-farm income. In Connecticut, for example, a lawyer might be assessed for £50, merchants for £25, doctors and innkeepers for £15, and artisans for £5 to £10, all being variable. The faculty tax was relatively low, for each poll was rated at £18, cultivated land at 8s to 10s per acre, and cattle at £1 to £4 each. Farmers and men with large families were therefore taxed disproportionately.[4]

A considerable number of the New England tax lists have been published in the local histories or historical collections. See citations in Chapter 1, and also William B. Stevens, *History of Stoneham* (Stoneham, Mass., 1891), 58–59; Jane Eliza Johnson, *Newtown's History and Historian Ezra Levan Johnson* (Newtown, Conn., 1917), 218–220; Henry P. Stiles, *The History of Ancient Wethersfield, Connecticut* (vol. 2, New York, 1904), 422–428. The Connecticut State Library contains the following: Milford, 1768, Groton, 1783, Simsbury, 1782, Killingworth, 1788, Lyme, 1786 and 1787, Redding, 1787, Guilford, 1790, Goshen, 1741 and later years. The Milford tax list for 1782 and Bethany's for the same year are in the New York Historical Society, catalogued incorrectly as Milford and Bethany, New York.

Outside of New England the tax basis varied, so that the laws must be consulted. New York records are scarce. The New Town list for 1787 and that of Salem for 1794 are in the New York Historical Society. The New York State Library in Albany has an excellent collection of Albany County tax lists for 1779 and a few others which are also valuable. I gratefully acknowledge permission to microfilm these. See also E. Marie Becker, "The 801 Westchester County Freeholders of 1763," New York Hist. Soc., *Quarterly*, xxxv (1951), 283–321. Some of the extensive Pennsylvania records are published in the *Pennsylvania Archives*, third series. Various New Jersey lists are cited in Chapter 1,

---

[4] See the interesting debate in the newspapers, especially *Conn. Gazette* [New London], Jan. 9, 1778, Sept. 7, 21, 28, Oct. 5, 1781, April 5, 12, 1782, and *Conn. Courant*, April 18, 1780, Feb. 12, 1787. Probate records show a concentration of property slightly higher than that indicated by tax lists. The difference is generally not above 10 percent.

and see also *The Genealogical Magazine of New Jersey*, XIV (1939), 32–37. The state library at Trenton has a considerable number, beginning in 1774, which have been microfilmed. Land was the principal article taxed. The Delaware assessment lists, preserved in the state archives at Dover, are of interest because they were based upon the supposed annual income of every taxpayer.

Some Maryland records are to be found at the state library in Annapolis, which has preserved quit rent rolls, but the most important collection is contained among the Sharf papers at the Maryland Historical Society. These 1783 lists sometimes evaluate the different sorts of land. The Virginia records are the most valuable of all, for they are nearly complete from 1782 on and have been conveniently assembled at the Virginia State Library. Unfortunately few exist before the Revolution. See, however, the Lancaster, Richmond, and "Southside" records analyzed in the test, especially Chapter v. Pittsylvania 1767 tax lists are in the *Va. Mag. Hist. Biog.*, XXIII (1915), 79–80, 303–304, 371–380; XXIV (1916), 180, 191, 271–274.

The North Carolina lists cover a longer period but most of the counties are not represented. The records include slaves before the Revolution, land, cattle, and horses as well as slaves after independence, and briefly, money at interest and stock in trade. All are available on microfilm (see Chapter II, note 7).

Such South Carolina tax records as have survived are in the state archives at Columbia. These include the quit rent rolls of 1768–1774, essential for studying the distribution of land; but unfortunately the location of the land is given only by counties, which stretched from east to west. This fact renders more valuable the scattered post-Revolutionary tax lists which included land and slaves. We have only a few, but fortunately all sections of the state are represented.

Ordinarily tax records did not state the occupation of the individuals. In New England this can sometimes be inferred, especially when a faculty tax was levied, and a few of the lists do specify occupations. The Pennsylvania lists also do so occasionally. Most of the tax records distinguish between landholders and the landless, and they make possible a description of the class structure because the most important types of property—land and slaves—were usually included. Undoubtedly a study of the many records preserved by town or county clerks would be most rewarding, but historians have not yet fully utilized even those records which are more readily available.

Land grants and other deeds conveying land are also helpful for the student who wants to trace the fortunes of individuals or the history of a community. The Virginia State Library at Richmond in particular has accumulated many volumes of this sort of material, all of which is on microfilm. Research into such sources is essential for studies in horizontal or vertical mobility. The student should also use marriage, birth, and death records, many of which have disappeared, but some of which have been published (especially in New England). Valuable for ascertaining mobility rates are genealogies, local histories, and the sources used by genealogists.

Diaries and account books are essential for understanding the people of the revolutionary era and furnish valuable data concerning income, property, and consumption habits. There are a remarkable number of these, few of which have been published. An exception worth noting is the diary of Matthew Patten of Bedford, New Hampshire. Since most eastern libraries have collections of these sources it may be invidious to mention particular ones, but the Joseph Downs Manuscript Library at Winterthur, Delaware, is outstanding not only for its materials relating to artisans but for account books and diaries generally. The holdings of the Maryland Historical Society and the Connecticut Historical Society are also unusually extensive.

Travel accounts, both by Americans and Europeans, are indispensable for conveying the atmosphere of the period, and they contain besides a vast amount of information. Most of them have been published. Among these the Duke de la Rochefoucault-Liancourt's *Travels*, though based on the 1790's, is the most valuable. Especially useful are Brissot de Warville's *New Travels*, Fithian's *Journal and Letters*, Kalm's *Travels*, Schoepf's *Travels*, Burnaby's *Travels*, Smyth's *A Tour*, and Barbé-Marbois' *Letters*. The *Travels* of de Chastellux are also helpful, but so much of Anburey's *Travels* is lifted from Smyth and other writers that it must be used with care.[5] De Crevecoeur's works are interesting but he writes from his artistic imagination and is unreliable despite his reputation.

Collections of letters are much less useful than one would suppose. They contain a great deal of political and business information, some of which is relevant to the present work, but the point of diminishing returns is quickly reached. Yet hours of reading are occasionally rewarded and undoubtedly the manifold letters which I have not used would fill in many details.

Newspapers are of great importance not only for the ideas contained in their articles but for advertisements and indeed almost their entire contents. All but a few have been used for this book, the footnotes to which attest some of the potentialities of this source. Some three dozen of the more important papers are available on microfilm as are many short-lived ones. The guidebook *Newspapers on*

[5] Whitfield J. Bell, Jr., "Thomas Anburey's 'Travels Through America': A Note on Eighteenth-Century Plagiarism," *The Papers of the Bibliographical Society of America*, XXXVII (1943), 23-36.

Microfilm is kept up to date by frequent revisions. In addition the American Antiquarian Society is proceeding rapidly with the mammoth job of duplicating on microcard its remarkable collection. All of the magazines have been microfilmed.

The revolutionary generation produced a number of important books. The most useful is probably *American Husbandry* by an unknown Englishman. Jedidiah Morse's *American Geography* is excellent, as is Thomas Jefferson's *Notes on Virginia*. The well-known "Early American Imprints" contains on microcard everything published in the United States during the period covered here. The laws should also be read. Among miscellaneous primary sources the royal commission's records on the losses of American Loyalists is of great value. Much of interest is contained in the first volume of Knight's *Documentary History of Education in the South*.

Secondary works are of surprisingly little help, although there are a few excellent monographs. The general accounts of the period contain little of value on the class structure, income, the distribution of property, mobility, or prestige factors, except in a general way. The class structure of Virginia has been examined in some detail. For the colonial background see Thomas J. Wertenbaker, *The Planters of Colonial Virginia* (Princeton, 1922); Bernard Bailyn, "Politics and Social Structure in Virginia"; and Sigmund Diamond, "From Organization to Society: Virginia in the Seventeenth Century," *American Journal of Sociology*, LXIII (1957–1958), 457–475. My two articles describe Virginia's society in the 1780's (see Chapter II, note 2). The first few chapters of Robert and Katherine Browns' recent book develop the thesis that Virginia's society was "democratic." The Browns give a number of individual examples but do not attempt a full statistical analysis. No northern colony or state

has received comparable treatment. The present work testi-
fies to the contribution made by Charles S. Grant's study of
Kent, Connecticut. The recent article on Boston's social
structure by James A. Henretta is very useful. It is based
upon the tax lists of 1687 and 1771. Carl Bridenbaugh's two
volumes on colonial cities are also helpful.

The economic status of the slaves has been treated in a
few limited works, but there is no general account. Indentured servants are described in Abbot Smith's *Colonists
in Bondage* and Warren Smith's *White Servitude in Colonial South Carolina*. Much remains to be done. Scattered
material on free labor is contained in Richard Morris' *Government and Labor in Early America*, Victor Clark's *History of Manufactures*, and Samuel McKee, Jr., *Labor in
Colonial New York*. See also the Bureau of Labor Statistics,
Bulletin, 499. Carl Bridenbaugh's *The Colonial Craftsman* is
the best work on the artisans. There is some additional material in Richard Walsh, *Charleston's Sons of Liberty*. No
account exists of any of the professions, but some of the
data for such a study is found in Shipton's biographies of
Harvard graduates and (to a lesser extent) Dexter's similar
volumes on Yale. Interest in economic history has led to
research on the merchants, though rarely from the present
point of view. Bernard Bailyn's *New England Merchants in
the Seventeenth Century* (Cambridge, 1955) is an exception. Richardson Wright's *Hawkers and Walkers* is excellent. Lewis Gray's *History of Agriculture in the Southern
United States* is outstanding. The colonial upper class is
described in Esther Singleton's *Social New York under the
Georges*, Frederick P. Bowes' *The Culture of Early Charleston*, and Leonard W. Labaree's *Conservatism in Early
American History* (New York, 1949). The only studies
of social mobility are Grant's book on Kent and two
articles: William A. Reavis, "The Maryland Gentry and So-

cial Mobility, 1637–1676," *Wm. and Mary Qtly.*, 3 series XIV (1954), 418–428, and Katherine Crary's "The Humble Immigrant and the American Dream: Some Case Histories, 1746–1776," *Miss. Vy. Hist. Rev.*, XLVI (1959–1960), 33–66.

Almost every subject relating to the social structure of early America needs research. The economic class structure of the entire country should be studied in detail. Our information concerning Virginia, though fuller than that for any other colony or state, remains inadequate, especially since the probate records have not been exploited. Elsewhere almost nothing has been done. The Massachusetts assessment lists for 1771 illustrate what can be accomplished: they include enough of the towns so that one can compare the different types of society, especially in regard to occupation and agricultural property. Work is particulary needed in the inventories of Pennsylvania and New Jersey, but more can be done in every section. The completion of a careful analysis county by county or where possible town by town may then open up some extremely interesting possibilities, such as the correlation of the different class structures with political behavior or religious affiliation.

Wealth and income data are also needed. The wages paid to laborers and journeymen are now fairly well established as are the incomes of doctors, lawyers, and ministers; but little is known concerning the earnings of independent artisans, the net profits of farmers, and the money made by merchants and shopkeepers. The essential information is not easily come by, but perhaps can be culled from the account books and diaries. The property owned by these occupational groups seems clear enough in broad outline, but a more thorough use of probate records can fill in much detail. Computers might be employed profitably to handle the thousands of items inventoried, which would then permit some significant comparisons between sections, occupational groups, and classes. It is interesting, for instance, that when a person had acquired £500 worth of property he became able to buy books. Was there a sharp dividing line in consumption standards and perhaps cultural achievements at that point? Does that line also separate those who owned silverware from those who use pewter or wood? Detailed analysis of inventories might prove most informative.

One of the most fascinating and least researched subjects is the opportunity, in early America, of advancing in wealth and social standing. Sociologists often measure the degree of vertical mobility in a society by ascertaining the proportion of men who improve upon their father's position, subtracting from that figure the proportion of those who retrogress to obtain a net mobility rate. This approach cannot be used for the revolutionary period except in certain areas where birth records have been preserved and where other essential sources such as land and tax records have survived. Even then the difficulties are great. However it may be practicable to trace the children of artisans, farmers, merchants, and the like recorded in the Massachusetts assessment lists. Vital records are available, probate records are full, genealogies are numerous, and the census of 1790 could be used. The migrants to New Hampshire and other New England states might also be traced whereas this is almost impossible in the South.

The technique used in the present work is simpler because it avoids genealogical difficulties. A number of men in some status, such as landless laborers, living in a particular area, are traced through whatever records exist, for a period of years. Those who cannot be found are eliminated (the proportion ought to be small). Ideally one should know enough family history to be certain that the John Jones who secured land in 1780 is the same John Jones who was landless in 1770, but such knowledge is usually impossible to obtain and the errors, if carefully minimized, should not change the generalizations. Almost any study undertaken anywhere will be a contribution. The student will also want to discover the factors which encouraged or hindered mobility and the process by which individuals improved their position.

Studies in the social origins of elite groups also offer many opportunities. These are not difficult to conduct because the men involved are relatively prominent. Where biographies, genealogies, and local histories do not suffice, wills, inventories, tax lists, land records, and the like usually furnish the information needed. The background not only of merchants and large landowners but of ministers, doctors, lawyers, and high-ranking officials can be examined. Eventually the results can be compared with those obtained in other places and for other times.

The use of titles as symbols of prestige also needs some clarification. The present material was drawn principally from New England, and although I believe that the generalizations are correct, more detailed research is necessary. Our knowledge of the background of military officers is also inadequate. Ample material exists in most of the state archives for such research.

The subject of social classes has had only preliminary treatment in this book. Whether much evidence can be found for the existence of class consciousness in early America may be doubted. But class lines—the social rank order—were evidently recognized and adhered to. In the South, the great planters seem to have associated with one another rather than with the general run of folk: to have danced, visited, played cards, raced horses, married, and sat in church with their equals. Merchants' diaries (such as that of Christopher Marshall) indicate the same habits. This class affiliation, if not identification, might be studied by an analysis of the membership of various societies—religious, intellectual, convivial—and through marriages. If distinct social groupings are discovered, then the relationship between them can be analyzed. One aspect of social mobility is the individual's ability to shift from one organization to another of greater prestige.

Finally the connection between the various types of social structures and the country's culture, or cultures, assuming that such a connection exists, has not yet been defined. The most obvious approach, and perhaps a fruitful one, is the use of inventories to determine (for example) the distribution of art objects and of musical instruments. Diaries ought to be very helpful also. Attention should be paid to the religious, educational, literary, and artistic attitudes and attainments of the several classes, of different occupational groups, and of sections.

In all of these researches the student should remember that early America was a society in flux. The time span covered by the present volume has proved too short to permit an assessment of changes, especially since the Revolutionary War interrupted the continuity of these developments. We need to know what changes were occurring in the class structure, whether property was becoming more concentrated, whether class lines were hardening, what was happening to the relative prestige of different groups and the status order generally, what the trends were in incomes and standards of living. All these and many other important questions can be answered from primary materials which in some cases have been published, and for the rest are lying in eastern libraries and archives, seldom used yet open to all—infinite resources to meet infinite needs.

Index

Virginia, 55; in Charleston, S.C., 59–60, 63–64; in South Carolina, 64; in southern subsistence farm areas, 61; standard of living of, 161–63; definition of, 161; leisure time of, 162; social origins of, in New York City, 190–91; among Boston merchants, 192; social origins of, in Philadelphia, 191; social origins of, in Boston, 193; use of term, 233; education of, 263; culture of, 254–65

Richmond, Pennsylvania, 194n

Richmond, Virginia, school in, 243

Richmond County, Virginia, mobility in, 178–80, 194

Rigby, James, Pennsylvania schoolmaster, 96

Ringgold, mercantile firm in Maryland, debts owned by, 137

Roberts, Reuben, farmer of Chester County, Pennsylvania, 182

Robeson, Pennsylvania, 25

Rochefoucault-Liancourt, Duke de la, cited, 26, 32n; quoted, 102, 228n, 229, 254, 256

Rockbridge County, Virginia, 51

Ronald, William, wealthy Virginia merchant, 184

ropemakers, property of, 81–82; in Boston, 191; general position of, 275

ropewalk, value of, in Marblehead, 78

Ross, David, wealthy Virginia merchant, 184–85

Ruffin, Edmund, wealthy Virginian, 185n

rum, cost of, 119

Rush, Benjamin, quoted, 94, 233–34

Russel, John, farmer of Chester County, Pa., 182

Rust, Colonel Henry, large landowner of Wolfeborough, N.H., 17

Rutherford County, North Carolina, 48

Rye, New Hampshire, 34n

St. Cecelia Society, South Carolina, 266

St. George's Dorchester parish, South Carolina, property of shopkeeper in, 137

St. George's hundred, Delaware, 32

St. Helena parish, South Carolina, library of minister in, 259

St. James's parish, South Carolina, 57

St. John's College, Annapolis, salaries of teachers, 95

St. Paul's parish, South Carolina, 57; doctor in, 100

Salem, Massachusetts, 35, 37–38; schoolmaster of, 144

Salem, New York, 24

Salem County, New Jersey, 33

Sandisfield, Massachusetts, 13

Saratoga district, New York, 15–16

Savannah, Georgia, minister in, 97

Schoepf, Johann, traveller, cited, 107–08; quoted, 165, 222

schoolboy, cost of supporting, 119

schoolteachers, in Lunenburg County, Va., 46; income of, 91–95, 141; property of, 95–96; economic rank, 113; competence of, 142; economic status of, 141–42; standard of living of, 142–44; in Chester County, Pa., 182; prestige of, 219; general position, 275